CONFLICT AND COUNTERPOINT
IN LESBIAN, GAY, AND
FEMINIST STUDIES

Conflict and Counterpoint in Lesbian, Gay, and Feminist Studies

Jacqueline Foertsch

palgrave
macmillan

CONFLICT AND COUNTERPOINT IN LESBIAN, GAY, AND FEMINIST STUDIES

First published in 2007 by
PALGRAVE MACMILLAN™
175 Fifth Avenue, New York, N.Y. 10010 and
Houndmills, Basingstoke, Hampshire, England RG21 6XS
Companies and representatives throughout the world.

PALGRAVE MACMILLAN is the global academic imprint of the Palgrave Macmillan division of St. Martin's Press, LLC and of Palgrave Macmillan Ltd. Macmillan® is a registered trademark in the United States, United Kingdom and other countries. Palgrave is a registered trademark in the European Union and other countries.

ISBN-13: 978–1–4039–7899–8
ISBN-10: 1–4039–7899–9

Library of Congress Cataloging-in-Publication Data

Foertsch, Jacqueline, 1964–
    Conflict and counterpoint in lesbian, gay, and feminist studies / Jacqueline Foertsch.
        p. cm.
    Includes bibliographical references and index.
    ISBN 1–4039–7899–9 (alk. paper)
        1. Gay and lesbian studies. 2. Women's studies. 3. Feminist theory. I. Title.

HQ75.15.F64 2007
306.76′6—dc22   2006051598

A catalogue record for this book is available from the British Library.

Design by Newgen Imaging Systems (P) Ltd., Chennai, India.

First edition: May 2007

10 9 8 7 6 5 4 3 2 1

Printed in the United States of America.

CONTENTS

ACKNOWLEDGMENTS

I wish to thank the valued colleagues who have given me great support during the several years of this book's production. These include English Department members from Auburn University, especially Paula Backscheider, who read parts of the manuscript, Alicia Carroll, and Penelope Ingram, and many at the University of North Texas, including participants in two scholarly writing groups, whose insightful work and whose interest in mine have meant much. Also inspiring has been my association with UNT's Study of Sexuality Program, especially the many marvelous presenters at the SOS lecture series, including Harry Benshoff, Kelly Donahue-Wallace, Sean Griffin (of Southern Methodist University), Jacqueline Lambiase, Marilyn Morris (program director), and Deborah Needleman Armintor, among many others. I am grateful as well for the thought-provoking exchanges I have had with William Leap and the Lavender Language collective, especially David Peterson, my excellent friend. Thanks also to Timothy J. Parrish, as always to Geoffrey Galt Harpham, and to dear friends, whose examples of creativity and collegiality are always with me: Kathryn Duncan, Christian Gregory, L. Kay Marsh, Darla Rushing, Margaret Smith, and Annette Trefzer.

I appreciate also the many readers who have reviewed parts of this work at various stages of its career, especially the editors and readers at *Critical Matrix*, Calvin Thomas who has provided many helpful comments, and Alexander Doty whose advice and encouragement have been invaluable. Many thanks to Amanda Johnson Moon, Emily Leithauser, and Kristy Lilas at Palgrave for their interest and guidance, and to Maran Elancheran and the staff at Newgen Imaging Systems for ably conducting this project through its final stages.

Finally thanks to beloved family—Mom and Dad, Christine and Michael, and my dearest Aurora and Solana. This book is dedicated to them, and to my friend and mentor, Frank Eddington Durham, whose talent and courage improve all who know him.

Introduction: Open Books, Private Lives

Questioning the "Authoritext"

Anyone who has ever instructed a group of students to "open the Kristeva and turn to page 24" has engaged a metonym that both enlarges and diminishes the theory-theorist-reader relationship: an individual (the theorist herself) has been transformed by the reader into something much wider-reaching and longer-lasting (the theories that will outlive her by, perhaps, centuries) in a gesture that both confirms and creates the durability of texts and the staying power (if "immortality" is too strong a term) of their authors. That seemingly innocuous "the" preceding the author's name lends it a mythic, monolithic quality, impressing and intimidating students, while making the author present somehow, right here among us, in ways that are bound to excite student response. I designate this linguistic phenomenon the "authoritext"—a play on both the concept of authoring a text and the authority claimed, challenged, and borrowed into—by visiting writers (all those selected for the syllabus) and inviting readers of texts. To credit a theorist with her ideas in this way—to not only acknowledge that she is primarily responsible for their being here but to also use language that enables these very ideas to, in turn, take responsibility for *her* being here—is to recognize the ways texts both bring their authors to us so convincingly that we feel we actually know them and substitute so effectively for their actual presence that our knowledge of the life behind the work is ultimately irrelevant.

In *Enemies Within*, I considered AIDS literature by gay male authors, the important relationship between bodies and texts in that genre, specifically the ways in which texts can preserve, embody, and even sexualize relations between men when these men are worlds or generations apart or when these relations have become fraught with risk in the flesh during a sexual epidemic. Additionally, a body, especially a gay male body, may code itself in covertly or obviously readable ways to, as Neil Bartlett explains, self-consciously produce and reproduce a "type," that is, to become text itself. Because this body, especially one with HIV/AIDS, may be weak, immobilized, infectious to sexual partners, and finally unable to maintain the struggle against sickness and death, texts embodying the gay male and/or HIV-positive experience can touch readers of all types safely but powerfully—once more, even when the body of that author or of his biographical subject no longer exists. Texts, then, while not cures for the limits of bodies, can alleviate the suffering these limits impose and preserve aspects of tragically truncated lives for survivors, and for future generations, who seek contact.

It can be argued that all texts revive and embody their producers in this way; as Foucault observed the "author function" to legitimize, define, and indeed realize the authored text, so there is the implicit assumption, especially when dealing with contemporary writings by living authors, that said authors vitally inhabit or at least "stand behind" the words they publish in palpable, significant ways. In short, when we open a theorist's text, we expect him to open himself to *us*—to make arguments coincident with his personal convictions, sexual lifestyle, political agenda, and lived experience. Yet the openness readers expect from texts raises complex questions. Especially because the theories considered here all deal fundamentally with sexuality and sexual practices (some of these sampled from the theorists' own lives) and because their authors hail overwhelmingly from female and gay male populations, to what extent is an encounter with these theories a "sexual" experience for the reader? To what extent does this opening of books suggest a spreading of legs, and to what extent is this gesture a violation or a seduction?[1] How to connect with these theories in one's own work, since critical response may rest on false assumptions about the author or be perceived as an attack upon this author's presumed past experience or current lifestyle?

The situation is further complicated when we consider the ways the fields of sex, gender, and sexuality studies challenge the concept of theory itself.[2] Intensely idiosyncratic and emotionally wide-ranging, many writings in this area belong only loosely to the category of the theoretical. As a genre, theory distinguishes itself from narrative, autobiography, and even confessional modes through its very *abstraction*—its often dense and disembodied terminology and also its production of analytic models reproducible in other contexts. Notably, this first mode of abstraction may exclude those interested in the subject but not fluent in academic jargon. Meanwhile, the second mode is decidedly *inclusive* (i.e., applicable) in ways that the more privatized genres mentioned above may not be: while these certainly offer the revelation of a personal self (the fish that feeds for a day, so to speak), the theoretic mode reaches beyond a personal or group identity, offering tools that can be turned productively to the reader's own, potentially quite diverse projects (the fishing lesson that feeds for a lifetime). The fields of feminist, gay, and lesbian studies have sought to explode the notion that the discussions we enter into bear significance "in theory" only, offering political and sexual strategies that readers can take to the streets and to the sheets. Yet the effort to concretize experience and to theorize (to "abstract") what is minutely particular to the sexual identity of the writer himself will often fail, not as writing but as theory: the work will likely still be of terrific *interest*, but of little practical *use*. When a theorist in lesbian, gay, and feminist studies speaks, is s/he acting "openly" (i.e., honestly *and* inclusively) to expand definitions and categories and to reach out to readers approaching these texts from radically different perspectives, or—for perhaps perfectly necessary reasons—does s/he feel the need to mark territory, exaggerate differences, and restrict certain areas of discussion to only those sharing a similar outlook? Where, finally, is the theorist in the theory s/he espouses and, more importantly, how should the reader seek to join or separate the two in response to this authoritext?

My effort to delineate the relationship among gay, lesbian, and feminist schools of thought will require my occupation, however temporarily, of positions not my own. Clearly, the argument could be made that the limitations of individual experience will prevent me from perceiving the connections and divisions operating among the groups, perhaps especially those shaping the discursive bond between the two groups (gay men and lesbians) that exclude myself. Again, recalling Foucault's ultimate critique of the regulatory aspect of "author function," its implication in "our era of industrial and bourgeois society, of individualism and private property" ("What Is an Author?" 119), this project will question the dividing lines enabled by authoritextuality, to consider "open books" freed from the sexed and sexual particularities of their authors: although my ability as a straight feminist to understand the lived experience of a lesbian or gay man is of course limited, my experience as a reader of theories describing these lives, philosophies, and politics has been rich and productive. In addition, discerning the genders and sexual orientations of each of the theorists to be considered here (provided such a task even interested me) would be difficult to accomplish, while the notion that only a gay man can produce "gay male theory" or that feminist criticism is the strict purview of women writers is widely disproved. Necessarily, therefore, my involvement here—my effort to speak to, speak for (paraphrase and recontextualize), and be spoken to by these diverse schools of thought—will be with the theories themselves and not the theorists behind them.

While the identities of these writers—unless they are the actual topics of their arguments—will be thus respectfully unassumed and de-emphasized, my own position as the straight-identified feminist who defines the terms of this discussion must be set in plain view. A vital task will be to theorize "my" (both my own personal and straight feminism's) position as a member of the hegemonic, homophobic mainstream, passing judgment on the arguments by and about sexual subjects whose experience I will never fully understand, while of course delineating as strong a gay-affirmative position as I can. While I will outline the range of heterosexualities (and even feminisms) counter-posed to various forms of homosexuality in culture or discourse, I will presume that even the most left-leaning, well-meaning feminist politics include a component of homophobia, perhaps recognizable only to those it victimizes. While I will present the work óf several feminists whose myopia on this issue is more pronounced than my own, I will also attempt to dissect my own homophobic impulses and presump-tions, analyzing the ways these limit my abilities as a theorist and activist.

Feminism's historic role as oppressor of the gay and especially les-bian perspective is in part balanced by the growing sense, produced once more by texts themselves, that traditional forms of academic feminism and women's studies are on the wane.[3] A bisexed focus (that is, inclusive of men's studies) has led to the development of the field of gender studies; "queer theory" includes not only gay, lesbian, bisexual, transgender, and transexual approaches but also sex-positive, antiheteronormative investigations of and by straight women and men as well as explorations of all nonnormative sexualities—while third-wave feminism often complicates its original focus on sexual politics with issues of race, ethnicity, social class, globalization, postcolo-nialism, the environment, and of course diverse sexual orientations and practices. In fact, the feminism considered here will often be that viewed from the gay and/or lesbian theoretical perspective; apart from asserting that an "outsider" (the straight feminist) may provide a perspective not available to insiders in gay and lesbian studies, I am equally interested in the (straight) feminism perceived and defined by those "outside" of it, analysts of gay and lesbian sexuality. While the reader is thus bound to be struck by the preponderance of gay and lesbian theories in the Works Cited list, the very in-the-airness of feminism, its multiple tenets and insights that by now go almost without saying (or citing), speak to its entrenchment and broad influence and in part explain this imbalance. Finally, it is the decidedly and inevitably "feminist" text being written here and the coincident authorial perspective behind it that will do the most to complement the homocentric tenor of the works selected for this study.

PHOBIAS AND PHILOSOPHIES
TRIANGULATING THE FIELD

This book divides its attention between what may be broadly defined as "the political" (in chapters 1 and 2) and "the philosophical" (in chapters 3, 4, and 5) in lesbian, gay, and feminist studies. Briefly, my discussions of the politics of this field focus on the *author*, and the related issues of authorial intent, the authority of experience, and reader response. In other words, the political in the writings analyzed in chapters 1 and 2 gets personal. Emphasizing the identities and agendas of the producers, consumers, and condemners of radical sexual politics and functioning largely to correct the phobic impulses in the reader or cultural adversary, these writings are polemical in stance and are structured according to a core conflict: feminist, sex-positive, gay-affirmative progressivism versus right-wing, misogynist/homophobic narrow-mindedness. These writings mark off turf and restrict access to same—often for entirely legitimate reasons.

In chapters 3, 4, and 5, my analyses of the philosophies of sex, gender, and sexuality studies turn to the question of *text*, specifically a poststructurally rendered textual indeterminacy that keeps gay, lesbian, and feminist interpretations of cultural artifacts in play against each other. Not only is a definitive reading of any text thus impossible to settle upon, but also, in many cases, simultaneous responses are impossible to maintain: the very articulation of a position by one school of thought cancels the validity of one or both of the other schools. Aware of the powerful alliances created among these groups in real-world political arenas, I gaze with fascination at their many moments of discord when the writings themselves are compared and analyzed; as I professed my own intent to shift the focus from authorial identity to textual effect, so I ultimately argue that political points of conflict should be moved beyond if possible, while the philosophical differences that simply define each group's epistemology must be allowed to stand yet considered with care.

If charges of gyno-, homo-, or hetero-phobia often fuel the turf wars and personal attacks defining the political in this field, I point in my philosophical discussions to the fluidity of culturally determined identities that places each of us in the role of oppressor under various circumstances. Douglas Crimp, for instance, has written about the "cross-identifications" enacted by gays, lesbians, and feminists in their lives and work. His example is B. Ruby Rich, an openly lesbian writer, who has praised the feminist content of *Silence of the Lambs*, and the role played in this film by lesbian icon Jodie Foster—even though many gay male critics have come out strongly against the film's overtly homophobic themes. For Crimp, Rich's defense of her response— " 'Guess I'm just a girl' "(qtd. in Crimp 311)—encamps her with the (straight) feminists at that moment and not with a member of the "gay" population who might otherwise take offense. As a lesbian and as a feminist, Rich is a dual citizen of two frequently opposed societies, and in fact each group represented on the lesbian/gay/feminist triangle can engage in subversive *and* phobic behaviors and discourses.

Feminists maintain a persecuted status—either as women or as liberal (and thus minoritized, feminized, or disempowered) men, and as gay-affirmative advocates fighting a difficult battle in a homophobic society. Yet frequently these well-meaning feminists function as little more than privileged members of the heterocentric mainstream, ignoring the diverging perspectives of gay and lesbian counterparts; this is in spite of or sometimes because of their perception of themselves as progay and therefore freed of the burdens of homophobia. Gay men's conflicted roles are also somewhat obvious; as men, they belong to the oppressor class, yet as gay they are daily victimized, perhaps even more so than lesbians, due to their greater political, cultural, and economic visibility. Lesbians, as women and as "gay" people, are doubly victimized, yet the example of Rich above demonstrates how lesbians (and feminists and gay men) can play the victim card (as Crimp says Rich does but also as Crimp himself does) against cultural conservatives and even against political allies, so as to create space for their own agendas, but always through the silencing of other speakers. In addition, we must acknowledge that *as* an accomplished, ascendant academic profession, succeeding on many fronts in the creation and expansion of a critical field, gay and lesbian theory has its phobic element as well—a heterophobia that, while certainly appropriately directed against the conservative mainstream, may be misdirected against feminist counterparts who resemble these cultural conservatives as little as do gay and lesbian theorists themselves (see Schlichter, esp. 549, 557).[4] All of us in this conversation mean well, yet all of us are to some degree guilty of a phobic response to each other that, while it may be politically efficacious, is theoretically counterproductive and should be, whenever possible, written around.

Meanwhile, it is equally counterproductive to posit untroubled alliances between historically diverse or contentious groups when the points of conflict are constitutive of their respective identities and thus richly informative as to the nature of these identities.

In chapter 1, I outline the debates polarizing lesbian, gay, and feminist critical approaches, considering the roles assigned to each in the paradigms of the other camps. I note the relative rarity of the truly dialogic (let alone trialogic) or "crossover" text: citing several studies that promise an authentic conversation between two or all three groups, I show how these efforts often fail to articulate the nature of the relationship in question, misread the qualities or motives of the conversation partner(s), or stage a straw-dialogue with an imagined counterpart only to address more directly one's home field of inquiry. If gay men continue to diminish the cultural role played by lesbians in alarmingly heterosexist fashion, lesbian theorists may misappropriate the issue of sexuality in text and society, relegating the somewhat outdated study of sexual difference to their benighted feminist counterparts. Meanwhile, feminist writings in part live up to the charges of sexphobia and homophobia, while their emphasis on inequality between the sexes seems a necessary response to some antifeminist sentiment found in recent gay male theory. Finally I turn at length to the influential example of Eve Kosofsky Sedgwick's *Between Men*, a text significantly divided between feminist and gay perspectives, whose divisions ultimately demonstrate the difficulty of simultaneously treating cultural artifacts from more than one perspective. By way of shaping this argument, I emphasize the straight/feminist aspect of this trialogue, that which I feel most qualified to explore: the influence of feminist theorists (such as Sedgwick, Daphne Patai, and Lisa Tillmann-Healy) in this debate and the role played by "heterosexuality" (from academic feminism to violent homophobia) in gay and lesbian theories.

Chapter 2 investigates the complicated semantic histories of three terms essential to this field—sex, gender, and sexuality—the ways in which these terms have been deployed idiosyncratically, inconsistently, and sometimes incorrectly to further political agendas but often creating confusion at basic discursive levels *and*, ironically, limiting the significance of the very sexualities and politics these theories set out to define. I consider the insights of gender theorists such as Barbara Johnson and Judith Halberstam (in *Female Masculinity*), both of whom define "gender" in terms of the feminine and especially masculine qualities of women in their critical sightlines; I then compare their use of the concept of gender to its much more pervasive sense: if Johnson and Halberstam in fact explore a spectral range of masculinities and femininities that constitute each individual's gendered makeup, how are we to interpret ubiquitous critical references to "the opposite gender" and gender construed simply in terms of "woman" and "man"? I point out that the tendency to read gender in terms of men and women results from our movement in recent years away from the formerly useful category of "sex"; now that several influential poststructural feminists have placed a moratorium on the term, "gender" is forced into an untenable double-duty that in fact reinstates heteronormative assumptions by attaching fluid gendered identity to hard-wired sex dichotomies. Alongside this strategic but ultimately questionable semantic slide between sex and gender, I consider the often inadvertent semantic slip between "sexuality" and "gender" and between "sexuality" and "sex," arguing that, thanks to the radical deligitimization "sex" has undergone at the hands of sophisticated sex theorists and historians, we may now reclaim the term and the conceptual category of sex to enable gender to describe the more fluid, multifaceted cultural phenomenon that it actually is.

Chapter 3 marks this study's transition from political to philosophical themes, from a stance in favor of improving lines of communication to one that looks more openly upon definitional lines that simply distinguish one school from another. Here I discern the relationship of *mutual exclusivity* that defines numerous contexts in feminist, gay, and lesbian studies; in multiple instances, a theory hailing from a particular perspective perforce suppresses or cancels the possibility of the others in the very course of its articulation. I solicit examples from several fields—literature, sociology, urban culture—to demonstrate this phenomenon: considering the characterological triangle of Winston, Julia, and O'Brien in George Orwell's *1984*, I note how a feminist critique of Julia's removal from the narrative necessitates a reading of the Winston/O'Brien bond as "unnatural." Gay theory's efforts to renaturalize, even intensify, this male-male relationship result automatically in the de-emphasis of Julia's role, a catch-22 that only resolves itself in alternating, not simultaneous, interpretations. My second example is a language analysis by the sociologist Martin P. Levine, who considers the use of male and female pronouns applied by gay men to each other. Here I argue (contra Levine) for the inverse relationship between feminine referencing and sexual attractiveness by gay standards. Finally, I turn to the issue of gay and lesbian forms of public self-expression, noting how straight society's tendency to be scandalized by erotic public display (more likely to be engaged in by gay men) causes preferred lesbian modes of urban space occupation (women's festivals, political rallies, etc.) to disappear into the background. Throughout, the inverse relationship is my defining term, as I observe the advancement of one field's argument, always at the expense of one or both of the others.

Chapter 4 investigates the divergent reading practices of feminist, gay, and lesbian theorists. Noting how difficult it is to determine a text's politics—due to the exigencies of literary irony, social context, changing literary styles, and the obscurities of an author's own political agenda—I analyze the way feminist, lesbian, and gay readers impose meaning onto narratives stubbornly refusing to tip their hands, drawing helpful boundaries but indulging in interpretive "stretches" sometimes too tenuous to hold. I consider the work of representative feminist, lesbian, and gay readers, responding to the terms they use to define their respective projects, then note the prominence of two novelists— Jane Austen and Henry James—in the arguments of many influential theorists. Surveying recent Austen and James criticism from feminist, gay, and lesbian perspectives, I ask what is so attractive about these novelists for proponents of each school and present various answers to this question.

Chapter 5 examines the current field of lesbian, gay, and feminist film studies, specifically the persistent dichotomy between psychoanalytic and cultural studies–based approaches, as this often divides feminist from lesbian and gay film criticism. I investigate the predominance of psychoanalysis in film theory, noting that even gay and lesbian critics perceiving the heterosexism at its heart must attempt to refute or even simply adhere to its proliferating strands of influence. I consider the way straight and lesbian feminist film theorists diverge on the question of "the desiring woman"—a phenomenon whose existence is obliterated by the psychoanalytic apparatus, yet whose functioning, subversive presence is essential to much lesbian theory. I consider gay male film theory's own interaction with the woman question—through its continuing fascination with the screen diva and its more recent response to the feminist psychoanalytic (i.e., hetero-centric) approach to film. I conclude with readings of two films (and - critical responses to these) relevant to all three camps—the classical-era *All About Eve* and the more recent and controversial *Silence of the Lambs.*

My Conclusion turns to three key comments from leaders in the field of lesbian, gay, and feminist studies, each of whom has isolated a particular sticking point with respect to politics (i.e., division between groups) or representation (i.e., an interpretive impasse). Examining each comment in detail, I observe that they all turn a productively critical eye toward a point of conflict or a dividing line—one that simultaneously joins together diverse schools of thought (even if these are only joined in contentious debate) and leads almost certainly to intensified rigor, clarity, and energy in the discursive field. Despite the trend against "drawing lines" in current postidentity theories, I argue here that the lines and points of demarcation, however provisionally inscribed, are essential to knowing (i.e., delineating), shaping, and improving the critical "trialogue" amongst lesbian, gay, and feminist theorists.

This study seeks from its opening moments to consider debates in lesbian, gay, and feminist studies as they are illuminated by the metaphor of the "three-way tie"—*Three-Way Ties* having once been considered as the title for this work. By this term I hope to suggest the scenario of the photo-finish among three competitors whose many strengths are so equally matched as to create exciting contests whenever they meet and as to make the determination of a "winner" in any particular contest as impossible as it is pointless. Likewise, the term is meant to suggest the many ties that bind these three densely interimplicated schools—in their successful moments of coalition formation, their shared philosophies, their occasions of sibling-style disagreement yet also their damaging phobic responses to each other. To enlarge upon the S&M-style dynamism suggested by these "ties that bind," the kinky, subversive image of the "three-way" should suggest here a contest of sexuality and power engaged in by the strangest of bedfellows with nevertheless exhilarating outcomes.

To my mind, the terms "conflict" and "counterpoint"—featured in this book's current title—provide for equally necessary, threatening, and productive gestures: the offenses, accusations, and defensive maneuvers constituting conflict among these groups call attention to the marked individuality of each and the need to acknowledge boundaries even as these are crossed, rearranged, or dismantled; eventually conflict and its resolution can be seen to lead factions to occupy separately defined positions in productive tension with each other, the counterpoints without which the picture is incomplete and the entire structure in danger of collapse. Often the triangular relationship considered here will be of the equilateral variety—the three schools of thought in contention and conversation with each other—though on several occasions an isosceles formation is suggested by the situation of a left/gay-affirmative feminism approaching (with hope and hesitation) the fields of gay and lesbian studies. This triangle enlongates in the discursive moments of repellence between the first term and its two counterparts, and it flattens out as the feminist element nears the political and conceptual neighborhoods of its critical corollaries but drives these apart in the process. Certainly the isosceles figure and its various gyrations are those conflicting imbalances this project seeks to question and correct as it writes toward a more stable and evenly shared three-way arrangement.

This study engages in truly *critical* fashion with writing that has thus far met, and will surely continue to meet, with wide acceptance. I, too, have gratitude and admiration for all of the works solicited for participation in this discussion; they enrich a vital field of contemporary thought and have opened up worlds of understanding for myself personally. Therefore, when I consider the ways in which a particular argument forgets, ignores, or excludes a particular viewpoint, effect, or meaning, this is much less in order to fault the text in question than to zero in on the fascinating struggle between talented, capable critic and recalcitrant cultural artifact. As we have understood for many decades, the text never fully surrenders to the interpretive effort; the shaping and slanting that occurs in the course of an analysis provides a helpful sense of the shape and slant of the critical field it issues from, and I am thus acutely interested to examine here the form and content of those textual residues—of what remains to divide and distinguish the remarkable textual approaches offered by lesbian, gay, and feminist studies. I thus hope that the readings constituting this project are received in the spirit with which they are offered—respectfully and appreciatively and with a willingness to be critically engaged in return.

SHORTHAND'S SHORTCOMINGS: A NOTE ON TERMS AND DEFINITIONS

In this study I will do my best to avoid the semantic confusion I began to critique above but acknowledge here that shifts in the needs of my argument may necessitate corresponding linguistic transitions. The term "gay women," for instance, may fit better than "lesbian" when I consider the alliance between "gay men and women," or various women's roles in the "gay/straight opposition." Elsewhere, "homosexual" may pair better with "homosocial," even though I ordinarily avoid that all-but-outdated reference. I will use the term "feminist" occasionally to refer to straight, progressive women academics and political activists, though primarily in reference to the woman-focused writings that define themselves as feminist in orientation and intent, with a clear understanding of how presumptuous and limiting such a designation is: certainly, many straight and gay men and almost all lesbian women in academic and political circles would read themselves as feminists, with texts produced by such writers equally classifiable as feminist studies. I thus make the equation between feminism and heterosexual womanhood only as a shorthand mode for designating this third point on the triangle, the nongay/nonlesbian critical perspective whose focus on power imbalances between the sexes has been definitive for decades.

With terms such as "group," "school," or "camp," I sometimes refer to aggregations of authors, though as often as possible simply to collections of likeminded texts. There will be some overlap between these usages, but again the textual output will be our point of reference: I will, for instance, refer to Terry Castle as a "lesbian theorist" or as a member of "the lesbian camp," because she is the author of an influential text named *The Apparitional Lesbian*, not because her sexual history or identity as lesbian is known to me in any detail or is especially relevant to this study. Elsewhere, I will refer to Eve Sedgwick as a "feminist" writer when I consider the feminist aspects of her work and as a "gay male theorist" when I consider her work in the field of gay studies. I will apply as narrowly as possible the expression "gender and sexuality studies," a term that implicitly, though, I argue, incorrectly divides the field between gender-oriented feminist and sexuality-oriented gay/lesbian concerns. Not only do I reject the idea that the fields divide their purviews as neatly as this, I also do not even consider feminism's primary focus in terms of "gender," as I will demonstrate in detail in chapter 2. Focused as they are on the bones of contention dividing all three schools, this book's first two chapters will in fact refer less often to the trialogic gay, lesbian, and feminist approaches I elucidate in the later chapters and more often to the tidal forces and defining oppositions that so often polarize the field: heteronormativity/gay-affirmativity, left/right, homophobia/misogyny, homophobia/heterophobia, gender/sex, gender/sexuality.

I know that limiting the terms of this discussion to three—gay, lesbian, and feminist—may be regarded by some as theoretically untenable and politically unacceptable. After the important work done in recent years—to dismantle these monolithic denominations, to exponentially subdivide the list of sexual identities open to theoretical consideration and societal recognition—why shore up fragments now? Where are the bisexual, transsexual, and transgendered components of this discussion? What about the category of "queer"? To take up this last question first, focused as it is *within* the left-wing, sex-positive, antiheteronormative field of sex, gender, and sexuality studies itself, this entire project resides under the rubric of "queer" as it is often defined—as that which opposes itself, no matter the orientation of the proponent herself or himself, to sexphobic, homophobic mainstream culture. Again, as this project departs from the wealth of valuable recent writing explicitly targeting this mainstream adversary, I work infrequently with the queer-straight distinction as it is typically discussed and question the implicit downgrading of "ordinary" gay, lesbian, and feminist approaches that "queer" may promote. Despite the nuanced sense of the term used by many in the field, for many others,[5] queer remains a term interchangeable with gay and/or lesbian. As needed, I will borrow into this usage when considering the shared concerns of gay and lesbian studies (and the "queer theory" generated within this field), when I seek to emphasize these two schools' opposition to feminism—for example, queer versus feminist perspectives—and when I require the oppositional force or semantic range (including forms of the verb "to queer," the adverb queerly, the comparative terms queerer or queerest) that "gay" simply does not provide.

And as interesting and valuable as is the work being done in the emerging subfields of diverse sexual practice and orientation, its emerging status accounts for its lack of representation here: again, this project's emphasis on texts themselves distinguishes between countless diverse individuals—their infinite range of sexual practices and identities—and the bulk of textual output that thus far hails from identifiably gay, lesbian, and feminist perspectives.[6] Thinking has tended toward these original three distinctions for many years, and these seem to be the distinctions most worthy of extended attention at this point in the textual history. The conflicts among these three particular groups are likewise the longest-lived and, for me, the most complex and interesting of all the conflicts we might isolate at this point. Certainly, the relationships among all the various sexual-identity groups require continued consideration, even as they are not within the scope of this study.

My efforts to separate these texts into their respective categories may strike some as even more problematic than my decision to limit the number of discussant groups to three. Certainly, many feminist texts have proven valuable to the lesbian cause, while many lesbian writings have found a receptive audience among gay male readers. Do I mean to argue here that these groups can and do speak only to each other, that their works have no crossover value for anyone outside of their specifically defined group? Again, while certainly the audiences for these texts are multiple and various, the texts themselves have most often been selected for the clearly defined, carefully circumscribed subject matter that they showcase. Too deep a concern for audiences would draw me into the territory of actual individual bodies, whose various truths will never be known to me, while the texts themselves refer to one (or the relationship between two) of these schools in ways that plainly lend them to the categorizing underway here. Finally, I emphasize that to theorize about these texts at all, to seek to isolate the patterns, conflicts, and breakdowns that constitute the relationships among them, *is* to attach them, however temporarily, to definitive statements that are bound to reduce and change them in some ways but, I hope, enlarge and enrich them in others.

CHAPTER 1

THE TRIALS OF TRIALOGUING IN LESBIAN, GAY, AND FEMINIST STUDIES

CROSSED LINES, CROSSED WIRES

The influential critical anthology *Fear of a Queer Planet* (Warner, ed.) belongs to a promising subgenre in the gender/sexuality studies canon—the "crossover" text looking to establish a dialogue between diverse factions in the field, in this case gay and lesbian theory turning its attention to the heterosexual mainstream. The book refers with its first word to a fear unique to self-identified straights, and attempts to mitigate such debilitating fears through the understanding generated by the writings within. Its chapters are grouped under two subheadings, "Get Over It" and "Get Used to It"—language even more pointedly selected to include this hetero other, as it no longer merely refers to but directly addresses the presumed phobic reader. Yet the writings gathered beneath these headings speak primarily *about* the straight opposition, instead of formulating direct addresses *to* it. Also, the question remains as to whether the homophobic population discussed in these works includes the straight, leftist academics most likely to encounter this text or only the larger conservative mainstream, which is almost certainly entirely out of earshot.

Of the many otherwise remarkable offerings housed in this collection, Cindy Patton's "Tremble, Hetero Swine" comes closest to the direct address indicated by the anthology's main titles. Meanwhile, this language is not hers but a quote from an anonymous gay letter-writer, blasting straights in a radical gay magazine. Patton calls this writer's violent plotting a "gay revenge fantasy," yet she ultimately insists that the diatribe against "hetero swine" is a parody of and response to only the radical right, its fears and hatred of gays and lesbians. An emphasis on the first term—*hetero* swine—would define all straights as a subset of the porcine population at large; Patton's shift in emphasis, however, to "hetero *swine*"—that is, the swinish element within the generally acceptable hetero population—changes the discussion from a fair and interesting argument between straights and gays to a lopsided and oft-witnessed staring contest between progressives and kooks. Finally Patton addresses not straights but "gay-affirmatives," introducing fluidity into the gay/straight opposition but leaving otherwise progressive straight readers wondering: is Patton's critique meant for "us," or do varieties of homophobia across the political spectrum need a more nuanced diagnostic method?

Such identity crises inhere in multiple attempts to explore a dialogue with subgroups in sex, gender, and sexuality studies: gay, lesbian, and straight feminist theorists have all made frustratingly loose references to "feminists" or "women" when the lesbian/straight distinction likely has significant ramifications for the argument in question, although all three groups are equally likely to reference the "gay" perspective when the men *and women* within this camp surely have diverging, sometimes conflicting points of view. I have already begun to indicate the equally vexing issues surrounding unshaded references to the "straight" opposition. These misidentifications, sometimes inadvertent and sometimes strategically deployed, can exacerbate tensions within the "feminist sisterhood," between gay and lesbian "brothers and sisters," or among all three of these divergent discourses. In many of these instances, the (perhaps inevitable) limitations of "speaking for" (ignoring, overriding, assimilating) the authorially absent group(s) emerge, making "speaking to" seem that much more difficult a proposition. As Kaja Silverman confesses at the beginning of her discussion exploring effeminacy in gay men,

> I have hesitated a long time before beginning this chapter. The question which provokes it . . . seems politically impossible to ask . . . not only because I am both heterosexual and a woman but because the question itself appears to solicit a cultural stereotype which many homosexual men have struggled to put behind them. My query, which I dare to pose . . . .. (*Male Subjectivity* 339)

Finally, the space and care required to qualify oneself as a viable crossover commentator, and the likelihood that these efforts will fail to convince a sizeable portion of the potential readership, cause all who attempt such a move to face the task with trepidation.

Because of my own subject position as a straight leftist-feminist indebted to the insights of gay and lesbian studies, I am especially interested to delineate the position of "the straight" or "the feminist" (again, these may be only minimally overlapping categories) in recent gender and sexuality theories. Throughout, I will employ the term "trialogue" to indicate a particular corner of the gay/straight debate: not the queer confrontation with the stereotypical (almost clichéd) raving right-winger but the conversation that might be had between gays, lesbians, and educated (perhaps even well-meaning, gay-affirmative) straights who work and live beside each other yet who likely still have important issues to resolve regarding their divergent outlooks. Investigating writings that attempt but fall short of or actually hinder such three-way exchanges, I mean not at all to "correct" some oversight in the arguments published thus far, or to fill in missing pieces that have been somehow overlooked. On the contrary, this discussion is meant to indicate the difficulty involved in any attempt to bridge the "gay/straight" discursive gap, due to the vicissitudes of language itself, not to mention the elements of homophobia, heterophobia, and misogyny that are unfortunately still very much a part of contemporary critical thought. While it is essential to persist in these conversational efforts for the ever higher levels of understanding attained thereby, the path toward true trialogue is paved with hazards largely unrecognized and underanalyzed thus far.

HOMOPHOBIC HETEROWOMEN

In *Body Talk* Jacquelyn N. Zita expands on issues raised by Patton, since her argument employs varying definitions of her terms. Thus, "heterosexual," at first synonymous with "homophobe" and "heteromasculine hegemony," may be as narrowly construed as Patton's "Hetero Swine" or may cast a much wider net. She targets the most intense of homophobic reactions—"beyond vomit," as she quotes a relative at one point—and pins these primarily on "the heteromale" whose violent response stems, as other theorists have argued, from self-hatred and self-doubts about his own heterosexuality. Zita states that "white heterosexual men are more homophobic than white heterosexual women" and reads straight women as pawns in the process of "hold[ing] the heterobody of both sexes in place" (39). In the following passage—"I will explore how this masculinity relates to the 'otherness' of queers, heterowomen, transgendered bodies, and racially marked (nonwhite) others" (39)—straight women are included (and thus somewhat protected from the charge of homophobia) quite cozily among other victimized groups.

Yet elsewhere in the essay, Zita refers to an unsexed "heterosexual hegemony," and to deny that even gay-affirmative straight women such as myself have benefited greatly and oppressed gay and lesbian fellow-citizens frequently through membership in the heterosexual majority is the height of homophobic hypocrisy. Certainly I am hoping, in one respect, that Zita has discerned in her travels a straight female population whose reactions toward lesbian and gay sexuality cannot be characterized as repulsion, so that she refers in this argument to a particular, homophobic segment of straight female society. Yet in the other, more relevant respect here, I still hope she is talking to gay-affirmative *me*, about *my* homophobia and ways I might work past this. However, since no contemporary feminist voice expressing a "beyond-vomit" attitude about gays and lesbians would be deemed credible, it is apparent that once more I am being drawn alongside (as a gay-affirmative supporter) instead of spoken to.

SISTERS, BROTHERS, AND "MOM"

If the role played by progressive straights in Patton's and Zita's arguments remains in question, other gay and lesbian theories create alliances with this leftist, specifically feminist, figure, although in curious ways: perhaps descended from the second-wave lesbian-feminist "sisterhood," so fixated on the intricacies of women's oppression that questions of sexuality were largely ignored, the feminist element in these arguments reliably advances an essentially conservative "antisex" or "antipromiscuity" position. Old-school radical feminists such as Marilyn Frye and Sheila Jeffreys invoke this sisterhood, referring to "all women" in their work, to construct an opposition to the sexual habits of gay men.[1] (But see Bristow 67.) Elsewhere, Tim Edwards seeks, through feminism, to alleviate gay men's "persistent promiscuity and anticommitment attitudes or a plain lack of emotional communication and explanation" (1). He investigates gay theory's overlap with and debt to feminism, yet his dialogue with this "sister school" is tellingly uneven: in discussions of intergenerational sex (where the "mother's" voice is strongly present) and "private love" (where Edwards suggests intimacy and commitment as at least serial alternatives to casual or anonymous sex), feminist theories are frequently cited. The feminist presence is much weaker, however, in his chapter on AIDS and altogether missing in a chapter on sadomasochism and pornography and another on public sex. Thus, certain topics in this text suggest feminism more strongly than others, and the dropping and reclaiming of the feminist figure throughout makes it into something of a maiden aunt, hustled behind a curtain when the conversation gets too rough. In the arguments of Jefferys, Frye, and Edwards, feminism is both a maternal, mediating (but also asexual or antisexual) presence, and a polarizing, tie-breaking force, pulled in to the service of either the gay or the lesbian position to effect a "two-against-one" show of strength.

PROM DATES AND ICK FACTORS

"Straightness" manifests itself elsewhere in the gay/lesbian dialogue, specifically in the elements of misogyny perceived by some lesbian and feminist theorists to undergird certain gay male theories. To counter this, these lesbian respondents may foreground a "feminist" identity, focusing their writing on the "problem" with men and rejoining a (heterosexualized) battle of the sexes that they have moved beyond in most other respects. For example, Sally Munt has argued that "Gay [Male] Studies and Women's Studies *don't* intersect, historically having shown an antipathy towards each other" (xii); her phrasing suggests once more the significant indeterminacy within the terms "gay" and "women." Munt in fact clarifies her argument to designate "gay" as an overarching rubric for "gay and lesbian," but I am interested for the moment in the specifically male portion of gay studies and its particular history of antipathy toward feminism. When gay male theorists, in agreement with Munt, challenge the tenets of feminism, the question emerges as to exactly who the opposition is: has the lesbian contingent been subsumed (purposefully or inadvertently) within the larger category of women in a simple sex-based opposition? Are lesbians loosely included in this group to diffuse a more pointed attack against a specifically homophobic (or a potentially "romantically attached") straight opposition? Or, by contrast, is opposition to a "homophobic" but otherwise generic "feminism" meant to disguise controversial internecine gay/lesbian skirmishes beneath a more acceptable antihomophobic (i.e., antistraight feminist) retort?

Ellis Hanson, for instance, voices a critique of "feminist" film theorists, though his specific complaint against "affirming and crunchy" readings of notably lesbian films reveals that he is in fact couching a controversial swipe against his lesbian sister-school within a generalized (and much more acceptable) attack upon the (presumably homophobic) feminist adversary. (Hanson's argument will be treated in detail in chapter 5.) Elsewhere, Craig Owens,[2] in the early collection *Men in Feminism*, looks for ways to dissolve "the myth of homosexual gynophobia" yet takes a polarizing tack in his response to writings by feminists Luce Irigaray, Linda Nochlin, and Elaine Showalter.[3] Finally, D.A. Miller's attack on Susan Sontag's *AIDS and Its Metaphors* ("Sontag's Urbanity") succeeds when directed against her admittedly homophobic comments made a decade earlier. Reading the text itself, Miller faults Sontag for discursive gestures hailed in other contexts—dissolving the equation between AIDS and gay men, describing gay men in terms of an ethnic group (see D'Emilio and Seidman), and challenging metaphors of violence as they may incite violence against AIDS patients.

This diffidence toward the feminist/feminine "embrace" is echoed in some gay theorists' rejection of any association with "the effeminate"; Lee Edelman ("Tearooms and Sympathy"), for instance, argues that "Male homosexuality . . . must be conceptualized in terms of femaleness" in part "because the governing heterosexual mythology interprets gay men as implicitly wanting to be or be like women . . ." (559).[4] If gay effeminacy is a "myth" for Edelman, Kaja Silverman regards it as an unfairly imposed "cultural stereotype," though she goes on to criticize David F. Greenberg, Mario Mieli, and C.A. Tripp for their antieffeminacy arguments, with Tripp described as "so phobic about femininity that he actually goes so far as to propose that 'transvestism and transsexuality seldom involve either homosexual or effeminate men' " (*Male Subjectivity* 344). Is the antieffeminacy position a necessary defense against a sissifying mainstream, a newly opened vein of misogynist sentiment, or a troubling entanglement of both? Equally disturbing is its unwillingness to recognize the presence of actual gay-and-effeminate (gay-*yet*-effeminate?) real-life men, considered in the coauthored arguments of Michael Moon and Eve Sedgwick and defended in Jamie Gough's questioning of "the masculinization of the gay man" (119).

Elsewhere Edelman seeks to extricate himself from his "prom night pairing" ("At Risk in the Sublime" 216) with Patricia Yeager, from seeming compliance with the heterosexualized dynamic of male- then female-authored essays structuring the anthology he is a part of. Yet must "dialogue" between male and female gender/sexuality theorists, no matter how contrived that dialogue may be, necessarily constitute a "date"? I am reminded of Eric Rofes's delineation of the "ick factor" defining some gay men's response to women's (especially lesbians') sexuality, which, says Rofes, "may be at the heart of many gay men's inability to take women seriously, support lesbian concerns, or develop meaningful relationships with women" (46). In his very questioning of the heterosexist potential of the pairing of himself and Yeager, Edelman introduces the potential sexism of his own argument, to some degree reinstating the dichotomy between "theory" and "gender" (male and female realms) he so effectively dismantles earlier in his essay.

Multiple queer theorists have pondered an almost natural opposition between lesbians and gay men. Vera Whisman, for example, contrasts the lesbian perception of sexual orientation as a conscious, political decision with gay men's understanding of their orientation as an inherent predisposition. While Whisman's data are ultimately unconvincing—with an overwhelming percentage of women in her "chosen" category not choosing to be lesbians but only choosing to engage in lesbian activity at some point, having always had lesbian feelings—her thesis is corroborated by Steven Seidman. In his impressive overview of gay and lesbian studies, he writes: "Lesbian feminists repudiated the view of lesbianism as a type of sexual desire or orientation. They interpreted lesbianism as a personal, social, and political commitment to bond with women" (Seidman 112). By contrast, "gay men represented themselves as an ethnic group oriented toward assimilation . . ." (117, see also Jagose 48). In separate writings, Marilyn Frye and Sheila Jeffreys champion "political lesbianism" and critique the gay male "biologist" model for its lack of agency and confrontational politics.

Meanwhile, Diana Fuss reverses the equation when she contends that

> [i]n general current lesbian theory is less willing to question or to part with the idea of a "lesbian essence" and an identity politics based on this shared essence. Gay male theorists, on the other hand, following the lead of Foucault, have been quick to endorse the social constructionist hypothesis and to develop more detailed analyses of the historical construction of sexualities. (*Essentially Speaking* 98)

Fuss chalks up the difference between a firmly adhered-to "lesbian essence" and a freer-wheeling "construction" of gay sexuality to gay men's and lesbians' respective levels of oppression: although victimized by homophobia in countless ways, gay men are still *men* and thus enjoy not only more privileges in an androcentric society but also more "air time" in medical, legal, political, and cultural discursive fields. Even the taxonomizing and pathologizing of the gay male "specimen" in earlier centuries, often to the exclusion of his lesbian counterpart, at least fed the ontologic validity of gay men, their "right" to exist at all, and eventually led to the wealth of much more historically and philosophically astute discourse on "the homosexual (man)" that has followed in our own century.

Karla Jay, writing about "friendship between lesbians and gay men," points out that the affirmation of stereotypically straight characteristics—male self-centeredness and female other-directedness—lies at the heart of the differences between gays and lesbians. She observes that "one common complaint against gay men is that while lesbians have spearheaded drives to raise money for AIDS and cared for men with AIDS, gay men in general have been relatively slow in supporting any issue that seems to involve women, or primarily lesbians, such as breast cancer or child custody" (12). While heterosexual culture is in so many unacknowledged respects a "lavender world" after all, we must note its deep-rooted influence on the queerest of male-female relationships and continue to examine and question this.

HOMOPHOBIC HETEROPHOBIA

Certainly straight feminist arguments are as guilty of collapsing identity categories to advance phobic ends as are the gay and lesbian theories also considered here. It is certainly the case that gay- or lesbian-based theories include the prospect (or specter) of the straight "other" much more frequently than the reverse situation (see Silverman above and Gubar as exceptions), but that has not prevented the rare straight-informed argument from being any less egregious a contributor to the problem. As with several of the theorists discussed thus far, Daphne Patai confuses lesbian and straight women in her cultural paradigm, casting blame (for baseless sexual harassment charges against straight men) on lesbian women when obviously heterosexual women would be more likely at fault in any such instance. Any reader sensing the speciousness of her (entirely undocumented) claims against such overly litigious women senses that her "defense" of beleaguered straight men is primarily an excuse to attack gay women, revealing her ironically titled *Heterophobia* as little more than an exercise in modern-day feminist homophobia.

Patai defends the evidently besieged institution of heterosexuality that she claims is being "dismantl[ed]" by insatiable "sex regulators" (xv) and labels as "notorious heterophobes" (136) Catharine MacKinnon and Andrea Dworkin, whose extreme views have drawn negative response from many gender and sexuality theorists. Yet while most criticize MacKinnon and Dworkin for being anti*sex*, Patai faults them for being anti*straight*; her dividing this issue not between men and women or between factions within feminism but (from out of nowhere) between straights and gays reinforces the antilesbianism endemic to her project.

Throughout, she takes a mean-spirited delight in the minority status of gays and lesbians, noting at one point that lesbians are "vastly outnumbered by heterosexual women" (130) and at another that heterosexual intercourse is wished for by the "vast majority of people" (134); her clinical and distancing terminology—"homosexuals," "some lesbians"—secures for herself the status of authority; later she all but labels lesbians the "lunatic feminist fringe" (14). Discussing a feminist anthology, Patai remarks that it was "edited by two lesbian feminists" who present the work of "heterosexual feminists routinely approach[ing] the potential conflict between their feminism and their heterosexuality in an apologetic mode" (133). She thus implies that these "two lesbians" used their editorial authority to either force their straight contributors to toe the antiheterosexuality line or chose only those contributors who already subscribed to that position. Ultimately Patai allies straight women with straight men—a most curious move for a feminist argument to make—as equally negatively affected by the lunatic lesbian fringe. In her view, straight women are unwitting pawns in the battle between gay women and straight men that has evidently raged throughout history. While she vigorously critiques the radical feminism of Jeffreys and Frye, in fact all three of these "feminist theorists" engage in the sort of board game maneuvering that strikes the typical reader in feminist or queer studies as distinctly unorthodox: where Frye and Jeffreys position straight and lesbian feminists as dual "victims" of gay male sexuality, Patai's lesbian academic "victimizes" straight women and men alike.

If Patai's patently homophobic polemic is easy to exclude as a viable crossover text, Lisa M. Tillmann-Healy's "narrative ethnography" of her interactions with a gay softball team represents the well-meaning straight-feminist approach to gay culture that comes much closer to the crossing-over gesture I seek here and yet remains limited by persisting heterocentrisms most urgently needing address from a queer critical perspective. Originally joined by her husband Doug, the team is approached by Tillmann-Healy as a fieldwork "site" for her dissertation. She is open at the outset, to the team and in her book, about her and her husband's sheltered roots, and their growing awareness and acceptance of gay male lifestyles is the focus of this story, much more than the gay men themselves. In this heavily dramatized re-creation of the author's growth and development (including "thick scenic description, reconstructed dialogue, dramatic tension, foreshadowing, and temporal shifts" [11]), Tillmann-Healy raises questions important to a fuller understanding of friendships between gay and straight people: what can gay-affirmative straights from the hinterlands do to raise consciousness in their phobic families and home communities? What is the cultural significance of "flirtations" between gay men and straight women? How do self-identified straights maintain their straight status when their gay friends (or friends of their gay friends) presume closetedness instead, and do such friendships perforce indicate a willingness (on behalf of *both* parties) to "experiment," at least psychologically, with alternative sexual behaviors? What finally are the connections between the closet and friendship in gay/straight relationships? Even Tillmann-Healy's title, *Between Gay and Straight*, plays with the hinge-like dilemmas attached to these questions, since "between" suggests simultaneously a shared space that unites its occupants *and* various cultural and psychosexual obstacles coming between the involved parties. Significantly, a straight person (a woman and perhaps a feminist) is posing questions about gay men in this text, indicating the need for a gay respondent to take up the same or similar queries, though perhaps also indicating critical indifference toward such questions from gay theorists thus far.

Even more necessary, however, is a queer-inflected critique of Tillmann-Healy's well-intentioned but still largely questionable subject position. Her training in the most recent methods of cultural anthropology has evidently instilled some critical awareness of the fraught position of the great white researcher toiling in the "field," yet the basic premises of her scientific method go unquestioned. The assumptions involved, for instance, in reading a likely disparate group of gay team members, who may have little or no contact with each other off the diamond, as a "community" to be "approached," studied and interpreted like a tribe of isolated "primitives" objectifies these men in objectionable ways. Tillmann-Healy enlarges the effect by referring frequently to her project as a "journey" undertaken by herself and her husband—toward greater gay-affirmativity, yes, but the metaphor further reduces these human subjects to a mere "site" for her research and a "destination" of total gay acceptance for her to eventually reach. Finally, of course, the "journey" suggests a dangerous trek through a forest of lions, tigers, bears, and copulating men, though the persona adopted by the researcher is less Dorothy than Eve, hand-in-hand with her Adam (Doug) and wide-eyed with wonder as they exit the garden of Midwestern heteronormativity. The image exudes the naivety whose working past is the primary subject of her study but whose residual effects are plainly evident in Tillmann-Healy's word choice and research methods. Most striking of all, perhaps, are the steps this author takes to position herself as "safely" married and straight, innocently flirtatious with various team-members to whom she becomes attracted throughout the course of her research: what might have been added to the value of Tillmann-Healy's fieldwork had she risked involving herself with a *women's* softball team instead?

(WOMEN) BETWEEN MEN

In the several preceding arguments, "the feminist" plays a shifting, manipulated, manipulative, overdramatized, or flat-out artificial role: she is moved off- and on-stage in the development of various gay and lesbian theories, falsely identified with Patai (who is finally no feminist), and overrelied upon by Tillmann-Healy to initiate her approach to "the gay community." By curious contrast, the feminist role in Eve Kosofsky Sedgwick's widely influential (and heavily feminist-inflected) *Between Men* is minimized, eventually subsumed into the book's second life. The work is renowned for its collapse of the cultural opposition between gay and straight men, but this collapse was in fact discernible primarily after this text itself crossed over—due to the shifts in Sedgwick's own theoretical concerns and critical audiences—from "feminist" to "gay" studies. While readers might assess this text as a successful integration of these two critical schools, closer observation reveals it to be in fact remarkably divided between ultimately irreconcilable gay and feminist concerns.

In the wake of her follow-up study, *The Epistemology of the Closet*, Sedgwick has become a leading light in gay male theory, whose definitions of "the open secret," "homosexual panic," and the "hetero/homo binary" are now standards in the queer lexicon. Most influential of all, however, is the trope of the "homosocial," often read by gay theorists either as the lavender shadings sustaining and threatening homophobic society or as the publicly acceptable foreplay to explicitly homosexual relationships. Yet consider the dual existence of the term in *Between Men* as representative of this work's larger diverging tendencies: early in the Introduction the homosocial half-constitutes the homosocial-homosexual continuum (4) yet also defines patently homophobic/misogynist alliances such as Reagan-Helms (3). The search for a clarifying opposition between homosexuality and its opposite—heterosexuality? homosociality?—becomes problematic. When she argues, for instance, that "homosexuality can be either supportive of or oppositional to homosocial bonding" (6), we may turn to the Reagan-Helms example to discern the "oppositional" element, but how does one define homosexuality's "support" of homosocial bonding: as a collaborator in its own marginalization at the hands of the "homosocial" mainstream, or as a shaping influence on this mainstream phenomenon that transforms it into its opposite—a closeted (or emerging) homosexual mindset?

Later, the homosocial is explicitly opposed to the homosexual (and the feminine), becoming a term interchangeable with heterosexual "male bonding." When she describes, for example, "the fate of women who are caught up in male homosocial exchange" (16), Sedgwick is writing feminist criticism for a feminist audience. This use of the term predominates as she lays her theoretical groundwork, and her discussions of Gayle Rubin, radical versus Marxist feminism, and the moneybag hanging between Scarlett O'Hara's breasts can be categorized as feminist treatments of culture and literature. Late in the introduction, however, Sedgwick states, "it will be essential to my argument to claim that the European canon as it exists is already [a male-homosocial] canon, and most so when it is most heterosexual" (17). Clearly there is no interest, no argumentative payoff, in making a statement such as this if the term retains its previous definition as something that is already entirely akin to heterosexuality. Her comment is only provocative if the term homosocial is now in the service of the homosexual opposition, whose appearance in the heterosexual male literary canon elicits controversy and crisis.

Throughout the text, we glean a sense of this term from others in its vicinity: "*transactive* homosociality" (emphasis added) signals heterosexual males power-playing over the inert body of a silenced woman; talk of a homosocial "object choice" or, interestingly, of "homophobia" alerts the reader that the term has shifted (sometimes within the course of a single discussion) toward its gay inflection. In a discussion of the rake Horner (in Wycherley's *The Country Wife*), who at least appears to "love" women when no other male characters do, a phrase such as "the heterosexual or the homosocial aim of desire" raises tenacious questions: does "heterosexual" mark a man as a lover of women or hater of them? Does "homosocial" mark him as a "lover" of (or for) women or a lover of men? Does the "or" in that phrase signify an alternative or appositive relationship between the terms "heterosexual" and "homosocial"? The fence-sitting this term accomplishes here, however, gives way to a frequent and alternating stepping-off into each camp's yard throughout the remainder of the work.

Sedgwick's smart focus on the *class* basis for women's oppression— women as objects of exchange between men in the Lévi-Straussian worldview—leads her whenever it recurs toward the feminist mode of argument. In these moments, the woman's body—fixed, silenced, controlled—is brought to the fore and the relations between the exchanging men (those that other twentieth-century readers of these texts might characterize as queer) are largely ignored. Describing, even in her chapter on Shakespeare's "fair youth" sonnets, a "desire to consolidate partnership with authoritative males in and through the bodies of females" (38), Sedgwick's emphasis on "the bodies" of women, on their roles as chattel or living corpses, draws our attention entirely away from the relations between men unfolding in the background of the scene. Were she to read such oppressive relations as fundamentally homosexual, she would be conducting an antigay campaign; of course she is doing no such thing, but is making a valuable *feminist* comment instead.

Meanwhile, her frequent turn to "the Gothic" shifts the argument to the gay register. Sedgwick warns that the Gothic genre itself provides "obsessional" temptation to "simply drop . . . the female middle term" (82). She then posits that homophobia is directed against gay men *and* straight men and employed mainly to maintain the "exchange-of-women framework" (86)—an observation that connects well with the feminist analysis found elsewhere in the study. Yet here it floats by itself in the sea of queer theory that otherwise constitutes the discussion: a detailed response to Alan Bray's *Homosexuality in Renaissance England*, an investigation of the homosexual ("decadent") elements of some Gothic texts and their possibly or overtly gay authors, a delineation of types of gayness according to class in nineteenth-century British society. While Sedgwick does little to contest the findings of an "emergent female authorship and readership" (91) of Gothic novels, the "decadent" homosexuality and "paranoid" homophobia she finds operating therein instruct and influence those ruled by homophobic constraints (i.e., all men) perhaps even more than the female readership. Although she avers more than once that homophobia directly oppresses women as well, something of an impasse persists: reading even the image of heterosexual rape as "homophobia, in the absence of homosexuality" (164), Sedgwick's term does less to include women as victims of homophobia than to shift attention from the raped woman to the homosexually panicked rapist.

In her readings of Dickens, Sedgwick locates a homophobia that is indeed directed against homosexual (positive, loving, desiring) relations between men. She isolates an "openness" and "tenderness" in the live-in relationship between Eugene and Mortimer in *Our Mutual Friend*, though critiques its lack of an overt sexual charge. A little "gayer" yet are the male relationships on display in *Edwin Drood*, which demonstrate a love between men as "the first and most overtly and insistently presented aspect of their relationship" (181). Her "Coda" on Whitman's reception by devoted British readers explores homosexual themes in depth, even though a "discussion of male homosexuality and homophobia as we know them," she insists, "is not the project of this book" (203). Nevertheless, Sedgwick never revisits the woman question again, and the text ends in a much different domain than that in which it began. The increasing "gayness" of these interwoven Gothic discussions, coming to full flower in the Coda, causes the text to "unzip" as it progresses, exposing more questions than answers in the process; while Sedgwick adroitly intertwines issues of sex and class throughout *Between Men*, feminist and gay concerns do not seem to integrate or even share the stage.

Adding a foreword in 1992 (two years after the publication of *Epistemology*) to a new edition of *Between Men* (originally published in 1985), Sedgwick does not so much acknowledge the bidirectional character of this early work as apologize for not making it even more gay-centered, sensing no doubt that her now solidified role on the critical stage consigns all forthcoming editions of this feminist treatise to the bookshelves of a gay male theorists such as herself: "There's a way in which the author of this book seems not quite to have been able to believe in the reality of the gay male communities toward whose readership the book so palpably yearns. The yearning makes the incredulity. It makes, too, however, the force of a bond . . ." (ix). Mirroring this shift, the back cover of the 1985 edition features blurbs of critical acclaim containing neutral and inclusive references to "gender studies," "social arrangements in our culture," and "men . . . and . . . women," while blurbs from the 1992 edition describe the work as a monumental achievement in "gay studies" and include praise for its "breathtaking insights" and "exemplary politics" from *Gay Community News*. Sedgwick's reprint thus begins and concludes further afield in queer studies than even her Whitman "Coda" might indicate, yet the text remains predominately feminist in content and a source of valuable insight into the feminist field. In a different universe, we might argue that the odd moments of queer-theorizing disrupt and weaken this feminist project, but here they have largely redefined it instead.

TRUE TRIALOGUING

Sedgwick's text, then, has crossed over from a primarily feminist to a primarily gay audience and yet fails to successfully integrate its feminist and gay content. We thus remain distanced from workable definitions of and an address to the straight or feminist other in gay and lesbian studies, which has been the object of my search throughout this discussion. I thus conclude by analyzing a vein of argument that best effects this dialogue in the literature thus far, exemplified in important writings by Michael Warner and Lauren Berlant and by Douglas Crimp. Ironically, it is Warner's text, *Fear of a Queer Planet*, that I critiqued at the outset of this chapter, due to its failure to achieve such dialogue, yet in other writings, he and Berlant (and elsewhere Crimp) achieve this direct address to the straight feminist counterpart by theorizing strains of homophobia so deeply ingrained in the straight mind that the most well-meaning of straights are implicated. These writers challenge the territoriality of straights in distinctly urban environments (specifically New York), where one might expect to find the most gay-affirmative, sexually liberated, intellectually progressive population of all. Berlant and Warner call our attention to the tendency to background gay and lesbian sexuality so automatically that examples of these in broad daylight—identifiably lesbian or gay neighborhoods—create scandal (especially during the conservative Giuliani administration), discomfort, or at the very least, surprise: the epistemological crisis represented by a fleeting but foundational rearrangement of the heterosexist worldview whenever such a "sighting" is made.

Crimp describes the territorializing of public space committed in the very presumption of a homogeneously heterosexual environment. He considers his hesitation to direct cabs to gay neighborhoods or to kiss a boyfriend goodbye on the subway; the specifically urban setting from which these anecdotes are drawn further justifies his complaint: the more populous the street corner or subway one finds oneself upon, the less likely that everyone in the crowd will share one's sexual orientation, and thus the more problematic the presumption of sameness on behalf of even well-meaning gay-affirmatives. Crimp notes how this territoriality creates the closet of gay existence: in spite of gays' and lesbians' best efforts to be out in every aspect of their lives, heterosexist misperceptions return them to straightness again and again, so that "the closet is not a function of homosexuality in our culture, but of compulsory and presumptive heterosexuality" (305). I appreciate Mark Wigley's related observation that "Space is itself closeted" (qtd. in Bell and Valentine 16), while Bell and Valentine add something of a counterstatement: "the straightness of our streets is an artefact, not a natural fact" (19). They invoke Butler's "subversive bodily acts" in their analysis of "subversive spatial acts" (19), as a strategy for continuing the radical remapping of the heterosexist cityscape.[5]

These several vital gestures toward this new dialogue are limited only by their brevity: in fact Warner and Berlant target the more typical cultural conservative by defining "public sex" so tamely (i.e., so "privately")—lap dancing, gay and lesbian bars, phone sex— that few gay-affirmative feminists would ever stand guilty of opposing it; Crimp moves almost immediately from his universally "disturbing" example of the subway kiss to narrower critiques of classic homophobes including "Jesse Helms or Cardinal O'Connor or Patrick Buchanan" (306). Bell and Valentine's analysis of gay cityscapes is the most sustained, and the intersection of lesbian and gay theory and urban studies shows itself here as an especially effective site for trialoguing amongst gay, lesbian, and feminist perspectives.

We must note the relative rarity of texts such as these, which even purport to develop a discussion between differing sexuality groups. The lion's share in this critical canon refrain from "speaking for" more than one of these interested parties, rightly sensing the dangerous possibility of diminishing or silencing the described and interpreted but absent other, and choosing instead to confine remarks and readings to territory intimately and incontestably one's own. I have pointed to the ways that lesbian and gay urban studies is already beginning to open productive trialogues, though other analytic contexts—the academic setting, HIV/AIDS care and prevention—would surely reward exploration. Ultimately I seek here to chip away at the "political impossibility" (Silverman *Male Subjectivity* 339) of the prospect of "speaking for" (or, much more importantly, "speaking to") other discussants in the gender/sexuality debate by calling for more carefully defined terms—"gay," "women," "feminist," and "straight"—and for more nuanced discussion of the phobias and misunderstandings creating conflict among us.

CHAPTER 2

WHAT'S IN A NAME: SEMANTIC SLIPS AND SLIDES IN LESBIAN, GAY, AND FEMINIST STUDIES' KEY TERMS

WHERE O(R) WEAR HAS GENDER GONE?

In her brief but important meditation on "catch[ing] herself in the act" of reading as a lesbian, Barbara Johnson discerns a lesbian dynamic played out between the Jodie Foster and Kelly McGillis characters in the film *The Accused*. For Johnson, the lesbian erotics of the film are powered by highly charged "looks across" (163) the women's many differences: "class, education, profession, and size" (163). In other words, what separates these women is what draws them together—at least for Johnson in her particular subject position as a lesbian filmgoer. These differences, the reader recognizes without Johnson having to be explicit, define and differentiate these characters' *gendered* identities. Johnson perceives the placement of McGillis's Kathryn Murphy in "a male role" in the film, most likely because of her size relative to the diminutive Foster and to her position of "power," which Johnson acknowledges as this character's most seductive quality. While not explored by Johnson, this gendered picture is complicated when we consider the other elements on her list—specifically education and social class—that would reverse the gender dynamic between the women: Murphy's refined manner of speech and dress (frequently, skirts and high heels) rustles up against the tough talk and denim jackets of Foster's Sarah Tobias, helping us to understand that these women's gendered identities with respect to each other, though divergent and thus mutually attractive, do not confine either character to static, "classic" masculinity or femininity.

Johnson's reading also recalls for us the relativity and fluidity of gendered identity in a given context: McGillis has a certain physical size and plays a specific role in the film; if for some reason an even larger actress had been cast in the part, if her character had been even more powerful, her masculine qualities would be even more pronounced. Also, if it is possible to cast McGillis in "the male role," it is because McGillis brings to the part certain masculine qualities—not specifically male anatomy—that may or may not transfer to other films featuring herself: take for instance, *Witness*, "opposite" Harrison Ford and *Top Gun* "opposite" Tom Cruise. I call into question the oppositional nature of the heterosexual lead couple in these other two films, since the masculinities of Harrison Ford and Tom Cruise are their own distinctive varieties that likely illuminate or suppress McGillis's masculine qualities at different points in each film. In considering, therefore, the masculinities of (in ascending order?) Jodie Foster, Tom Cruise, Kelly McGillis, and Harrison Ford, we are reminded that gendered identity appears to us on a spectral range of subject positions, each of us inhabiting our own specific mix of classically masculine and feminine qualities, the number of gendered identities thus being infinite.

How then to square this sense of what gender is with the role the term plays in the writing of, for instance, Sheila Jeffreys, who comments that "many, to have sex, need to have a gender and relate to someone of *the opposite gender*" (104, emphasis added), or Michael Warner, who makes references to "the other gender" (*Trouble* 193) and "opposition of the genders" (195) in his writing? To be sure, both Jeffreys and Warner critique in these arguments the heterosexual hegemony, calling into question gender as "alterity *tout court*" (Warner *Trouble* 193). Yet both counter this emphasis on gender as difference with inquiries into gendered "sameness," a countermove that leaves the number of gendered identities at two: either men and women or "difference" and "sameness." Mindful of "gender" as the infinite, shifting range of masculine/feminine shadings alluded to in Johnson's argument, how is gender in Jeffreys's and Warner's argument to be read in terms of "opposition"? Given these two theorists' interest in moving us away from our knee-jerk, heterocentrist assumptions of "difference," why do Jeffreys and Warner turn their own arguments to the issue of sameness, when this simply perpetuates the oppositionality (i.e., heterocentrism) they speak against? If within the terms of Jeffreys's and Warner's arguments, the Foster and McGillis characters are "the same" gender, then what has happened to the differences—the "looks across"—that charge their erotic screen connection, and how shall we conceive of these differences instead?

The answer, of course, is that Jeffreys and Warner discuss something very different than what Johnson does—but use the same word to describe it. In their arguments, they access the common parlance of recent decades that requires our thinking of men and women in terms of gender, that relegates the concept of sex to the theoretical dustbin (for reasons to be considered below), and that therefore leaves the layer of identity makeup derived from an endless spectrum of masculinities and femininities hovering between the "gendered opposition" between men and women and the field of sexual orientation that is *not* evenly aligned: as Johnson demonstrates, her analysis of lesbian sexuality requires her to broadly consider the masculinities and femininities that make up the lesbian "look" (both the gaze and appearance) of *The Accused*. In concert with the wealth of critical commentary on the subject in recent years, I suggest that emphasis on "opposition" and difference in the conceptualizing of gender and sexuality marks a persistent heterocentrism that must be challenged and minimized in every instance. I further suggest that anchoring the concept of gender to the opposition between men and women— presuming an attendant, monolithic masculinity and femininity for each, respectively—only worsens the problem. I propose that the term gender should be reserved for references to the vast spectrum of feminine-to-masculine ratios that characterize the individual makeup, and that the difficulty we might encounter in ceasing to refer to men and women in terms of "gender" indicates the difficulty we still have identifying and excising heterocentrist thought and vocabulary from language. Yet making this semantic move would enable the kind of consciousness-raising with regard to sexuality and sexual orientations that transformed thinking about sex and gender during feminism's second wave (and that invited the move from "sex" to "gender" in the first place).

Finally, in light of the marvelous work being done by contemporary sexuality theorists, to thoroughly denaturalize and de-reify the concept of sex, I contend that a return to the use of this term will not (could never) constitute a simple backslide into essentialist, retrograde thinking—that the term has a newly subversive, utterly delegitimized meaning in the critical field and can be safely and effectively deployed to describe the phenomenon of difference (between males and females, men and women), freeing up the more dynamic and complex notion of gender to describe the equally dynamic and complex range of gendered identities it actually describes. If the project of lesbian, gay, and feminist studies is to call into question the idea of (two) stable gender categories and a (single) natural sexual orientation that automatically results from the correct occupation of said categories, we must cut gender loose from its hardwired attachment to "men" and "women," whose fundamental opposition to and difference from each other always, automatically returns us to these correct occupations and natural orientations. As we do, we should consider the conditions under which references to sex can lighten the semantic load suffered by gender in recent decades, as well as think more carefully about political and philosophical ground lost when gender is confused with sex or sexuality or is otherwise misapplied.

Engendering a Semantic Trend

Considering language use in sexuality studies, Judith Butler ("Against Proper Objects") takes to task the editors of *The Lesbian and Gay Studies Reader* for misnaming the categories of gender as "male" and "female" instead of "man" and "woman."[1] Her critique indicates a problem with the application of an updated term (gender) to outdated conceptual categories (the male and female sexes) and questions the overuse—the flinging about, if you will—of the term gender to describe more (or less) than it actually does. While Butler's focus is on the editors' introduction to the *Reader*, this semantic tic emerges throughout its hundreds of pages, exhibited not only by the editors but also by several contributors to the volume. In her article for the collection, for instance, coeditor Michèle Aina Barale slides freely from "masculinity" and "femininity" to "males" in her discussion of gender in Ann Bannon's *Beebo Brinker* ("When Jack Blinks"). Use of the term "man" seems necessitated only by the fact that a lead character is named "Jack Mann," and Barale returns almost immediately to the terms of Butler's complaint: "He may be 'every man Jack,' but he is also Man, *der Mann*, representative of not only the entire category male, but, as male, representative of the category human" (606). Monique Wittig considers "the categories of sex (woman and man)" (104), while Adrienne Rich makes frequent use of "men" and "women," then refers to "the sexual imbalance of power of males and females" (232), with no shift in context necessitating the change. Marjorie Garber creates an appositive relationship between "male subjectivity" and "gendered subjectivity" (324), then layers on an equation between "gender identity" and "masculine identity, male subjectivity" (324–25).[2]

In the headnote to Rich's essay, the editors credit Rich with giving "impetus to the feminist political movement to reunite on the basis of shared gender" (227). For the reasons I indicated at the outset and will discuss in detail below, this phrasing constitutes another such slippage between the categories of sex and gender: the odds that even two women will share the same gendered makeup being nearly impossible, it is even less likely that large, disparate constituencies of the feminist movement could have anything in common other than their female *sex*. In this essay, I share Butler's concern with the problematic overuse (or underuse) and misapplication of the terms sex and gender, the exclusions and limitations that occur in the idiosyncratic or inconsistent deployments of "mere" semantics. However, I am as interested in the inadvertent switching of terms that characterize at least some of the examples in the *Reader* (the semantic "slip") as I am in the strategic misnamings and misuses of conceptual categories (the semantic "slide") that have been implemented to counter the very exclusions and limitations I refer to above but that, at this point in our evermore sophisticated ruminations on these subjects, may require readjustment. For despite the ways in which I agree with Butler that language should be carefully deployed to secure its maximum political benefit for all parties, I work here in direct opposition to the career she has made out of gendering the concepts of men and women for the express purpose of doing away with the category of sex.

What are the differences between thinking of gender in terms of subjecthood (the nouns, or modes of being, "man" and "woman") and of attributes (the adjectives, or ways of being, "masculine" and "feminine")? Who "has" gender when we read it one way or the other, and does it change from a burden all humans carry to a humanity we are all rewarded with when we make this shift? Which terms might offer greater political agency or deeper theoretical understanding? In what follows, I will consider the options presenting themselves to those of us considering the meaning of gender for the contemporary critical field, as well as the ways these options shift and expand with the reintroduction of the concept of sex. The third term on this semantic triangle, sexuality, is less misrepresented than multiply defined, though when conflated with the looked-down-upon "sex" or the misapplied "gender," the results bear upon the larger issues discussed here and will receive consideration below. Primarily, however, I will explore where gender has gone during the decade-plus since the advent of gay, lesbian, and queer studies has complicated and dimensionalized the original work of feminist scholars, and argue for reclamation of the (newly conceptualized) term sex, once gender is more correctly situated and referenced.

Certainly Butler and the many gender and sexuality theorists influenced by her respond in part to Simone de Beauvoir's early and ground-breaking annunciation that "one is not born a woman," as well as to the more recent insights of Gayle Rubin regarding the constructedness of women, gender, and heterosexuality. Beauvoir observed the societal coercions that transformed "one" into a "woman," while Rubin assigned theoretical terms to the process—the sex/gender system—(in "The Traffic in Women" [1975]) and later expanded this model to call into question the naturalization of categories of sexual orientation and practice (in "Thinking Sex" [1984]). Let us consider, however, an important shift in perspective between the time of Beauvoir's writing *The Second Sex* (1952) and Rubin's more recent writings in the 1970s and 1980s: more than fifty years ago, Beauvoir surveyed the status of women of the early postwar period, women who were forcibly returned to the domestic environment as their role in the war industry declined and who were more constrained than ever by the new suburban isolation, the new mania for perfected homekeeping and mothering, and a conservative political atmosphere that presented them with no departures from the classic feminine physical presentation. She was dismayed by the ways in which women had *succeeded* in conforming to the sexual codes of their day, the ways in which the system itself had *succeeded* in making women in accordance with prevailing social standards. She writes of enormous loss in an environment populated by women reaping gains—financially secured, permanent "leisure" through marriage; legitimization (as saints and scientists) through motherhood; and ready-made social networks—for bending to their era's ideological prescriptions. In marked contrast, Rubin's emphasis 20 and 30 years later, thanks to the ground broken by Beauvoir's seminal work, is on the ways in which women have *failed* as idealized women, denouncing the abuses suffered by women who stray outside gender and sexuality norms and celebrating these "failures" for having at last heeded Beauvoir's call. The new critical focus on failure has even revealed the inner workings of gendered subjectivity during eras, such as Beauvoir's, of marked gender-occupation "success": from the writings of Rubin and other contemporary theorists such as Butler, we learn that gender presses upon us by floating ever above us, by representing an impossible ideal that one would simply kill oneself (for women this is likely to be through starvation) in an effort to attain. Thus while *everyone* may be assigned a gendered ideal, *no one* except perhaps Barbie and Ken (and we never can be too certain about Ken, can we?) has ever hit these targets perfectly. It is not our constant success with "doing gender" (Butler's term) correctly but our constant failure that keeps us all in the thrall of heterosexist gender norms.

Certainly both failing and succeeding as a woman are fraught with hazards that feminist theorists continue to analyze to this day. But the critical field finds itself situated within a markedly shifted cultural context that allows women certain failures—that admits to its own imperfect ability to control for these—and reap the rewards of social visibility, marriage and friendship, and financial security (most often by their own effort) less available to women of Beauvoir's day. Despite the ways that both women and men are still penalized for failing to conform to norms—most especially through media representations—it is the case that both groups find new ways to depart from the old standards with each passing year, that each of us fails womanhood or manhood—with varying levels of psychic regret and societal exclusion—in her or his own way. I suggest that these various failures constitute the infinite range of feminine-masculine mixes that constitute our contemporary understanding of gender, and that balanced critical awareness of the way the system succeeds *and fails* to contain individual identities opens onto a set of questions that outpace former concepts of gender as monolithic (idealized womanhood) or even as dichotomous (women and men).

If the first indication of system breakdown was the critical emphasis on gender's breakdown itself,[3] and the second the "engendering" of men that more or less doubled the size of the analytic field, a third indication might be the layering of sexual orientation—are lesbians "women," and if so, under what circumstances?—onto the original "gender" issue. This third line of critical inquiry recalls that from Beauvoir's day to our own, "womanhood" persistently presumes universal heterosexuality, even as it relaxes its standards regarding idealized femininity. Thus, if "woman" is a mythic trap set for all female humans, do all females (straight and lesbian) fall into this trap or do none of them ever really fall, since "woman" is nothing but a myth? Do lesbians, when they are inevitably forced to submit to "womanhood," suffer special bodily and/or psychic damage that straight women are not subjected to, or are lesbians by virtue of their rejection of the heterosexual norm ontologically freed from this womanhood in some way? Is a lesbian nothing more and nothing less than a (straight) woman who has succeeded in seeing through the heterosexual contract, and how is the antihomophobic agenda helped or hindered by any of these formulations?

The homophobic social code has provided lesbians a contradictory message: as women they are subject to patriarchal control, yet as "failed" women they receive none of the social benefits accruing to "successful" ones. In response, there has developed a catch-22 critical perspective whose own contradictions have gone unacknowledged and untheorized. For instance, Monique Wittig, reading Beauvoir, argues that "the refusal to become (or to remain) heterosexual always meant to refuse to become a man or a woman, consciously or not" (105).

On the following page, however, she reclaims her identity as "a woman" to join the class of "women" in their struggle for rights (106). Elsewhere, Teresa de Lauretis, quoting Gayle Rubin, points out "that 'lesbians are *also* oppressed as queers and perverts' . . ., not only as women" ("Sexual Indifference" 148), indicating that "women" is one category of oppression (among many) that includes lesbians. Later, however, she quotes approvingly from the work of Kate Davy (151) and of Marilyn Frye (153), both of whom separate lesbians from "the cultural construction 'woman' "(151) so as to gain visibility. To the implied question in these arguments, "are lesbians women?" comes the implied answer—"sometimes"; simultaneously we understand that woman = gender (a category of oppression) only about half the time, causing us to wonder how it can be considered in terms of gender at all.

In *Gender Trouble* Butler records the contextual and semantic shift I refer to above as she delineates "a political genealogy of gender," which transforms gender from "a set of repeated acts within a highly rigid regulatory frame" (33) to "the gender discontinuities that run rampant within heterosexual, bisexual, and gay and lesbian contexts in which gender does not necessarily follow from sex, and desire, or sexuality generally, does not seem to follow from gender . . ." (135–36). I argue, however, that continuing to think of gender in terms of "men" and "women," as Butler does in her admonitions to the editors of the *Lesbian and Gay Studies Reader*, fixes gender in its pregenealogy habits of regulation and congealment, while thinking in terms of masculinity and femininity enables its deconstructive undermining as Butler envisions: the blunt division into two enormous categories has enabled regulatory regimes to control enormous, and enormously disparate, populations through forced submission to the limited, singular modes of "social appearance" (33) and sexual practice prescribed by each categorical heading—a panoptical arrangement to be sure. By contrast, the masculine/feminine mode of reading gender suggests the endless variety and the "discontinuities" of "running rampant" that characterize Butler's political genealogy; likewise does it suit perfectly her theory of gender as drag: while Butler is correct to point out that "I never did think that gender was like clothes, or that clothes make the woman" (*Bodies That Matter* 231), the terms "masculine" and "feminine," while doing nothing to perpetuate distorted notions of gender as self-selected or changed on a whim, *do* help us consider the ways in which gender might best be considered as tailor-made, specific to each sexed body in existence, due to the unlimited options offered across its spectrum.

Adopting the masculine/feminine terminology would even strengthen Butler's challenge to the "metaphysics of substance," through which she has insisted upon the constructedness of sex (a claim I largely support) as well as the erasure of the term from the critical lexicon (a move I critique throughout this discussion). We must observe that use of the terms "man" and "woman" call persistently to mind the basic anatomic distinctions—penises and vaginas—notoriously difficult to theorize around, while *masculine* and *feminine* qualities of sexed bodies—fat distribution, breast size, broadness of shoulder and hip—indeed contain a cultural significance inextricable from their physical facticity. Yet here a complicating reversal presents itself, as small-breasted straight women and slope-shouldered straight men may be seen to fall farther from the gendered ideal than full-breasted lesbians (however butch or femme these women may be) and physically toned gay men (again, regardless of any butch or effeminate manner about them).

The man/woman mode of reading gender applies especially well to feminist discussions of sex-based inequality. Insisting frequently, and with great effect, on a single division within the human population, feminist theory can indeed make powerful use of these terms. Yet shifting to the arena of sexuality theory and culture, where multiple and more intricate distinctions between sexed beings are necessary, a fine-tuning of this single division seems equally necessary: if masculine *women* and feminine *men* (who may or may not be lesbians and gay men) become discernible alongside feminine women and masculine men who meet more commonly accepted standards, where has gender gone in this transition? Do men and women not shift to the ground of these various identities, with an entire spectrum of masculinities and femininities now figuring as the attributes through which cultural definition and political survival must be negotiated? And once sexuality theory has shown to us that the real slippage and subversion is to be found at the level of the attribute, is it possible to return to the more basic distinctions of "man" and "woman" that feminist theory introduced, when in fact straight men and women failing to conform to masculine and feminine ideals suffer *more* (though in completely different ways) than gay women and men who conform beautifully to these ideals (e.g., lipstick femmes and "top" leathermen)?[4]

I have come this far in the article proper without reference to a single male theorist, straight or gay, yet a final advantage to the adjectival terminology seems to be the inclusion of more male discussants in the conversation. In fact, male sexuality theorists show little interest in the concept of gender defined as part of the "sex/gender system," or when the debate is polarized between the terms "man" and "woman." These writers tend toward androcentric concerns (men's movements, masculinity, gay male sexuality), and intersect with questions of gender when they analyze *masculine* and *feminine* (gay or straight) men. For instance, Jamie Gough reads a shift in styles of gay identity, from one primarily effeminate during the 1970s to one largely masculinized since the 1980s; contributors to Joseph A. Boone and Michael Cadden's *Engendering Men* theorize consistently at the level of the attribute—"manly" and "effeminate" men[5]—while John Champagne studies gay and lesbian bodies pictured in an advertisement for the Gay Games, focusing on "masculinity" in the course of his frequent remarks on "gender." R.W. Connell enacts a move coincident with my argument above: when discussing gender in general (his heterosexualized perspective defaults to the straight example), the terms "men" and "women" are used. In the special cases when homosexuality becomes an issue, Connell switches to "masculinity" and "femininity" as terms of reference (e.g., 9).[6]

With the masculine/feminine designations, *everyone* may (or must) claim a gender assignment, and the fluid flexibility of this assignment is better described by these terms than by "man" and "woman." Specifically, populations within the overarching rubrics are more liberatingly heterogeneous: both the masculine and feminine gendered groups may include men and women of straight, gay, bisexual, transsexual, or transgendered persuasions. Of course, in our homophobic society nonmale members of the masculine category and nonfemale members of the feminine category are still frequently subjected to brutal harassment. Yet reseeing gender in this way forces these strange bedfellows into an epistemic proximity that, at least at the level of language, causes the similarities and unities among these types to emerge.

WHEN SEX IS GENDER IS SEXUALITY . . .

We can position the concepts of sex, gender, and sexuality on a spectrum beginning at a point of relative fixity and ending at one of endless variety, undecidability, and subversive potential. If sex is set at the fixed (biological, ascertainable, and, for many, entirely discredited) end of this spectrum and sexuality at the undecidable end, then gender is positioned at midpoint, seeming to contain some of the fixed and floating attributes of sex and sexuality, respectively. It therefore seems to mediate between and connect sex and sexuality to each other in necessary and productive ways. Gender convenes with sex in a manner that may not resemble its interaction with sexuality; it may fool passersby with respect to biological sex, or—coding this sexed subjecthood clearly—give no indication as to orientation or preferred sexual practices. As the "face" we show the world instead of the anatomy we cover with clothing or instead of the activities we cover with bedclothes or the darkness of night, gender leads this package into the psychic and social world and serves as its chief negotiator. Because of the way it connects with and floats free of these other, more inscrutable elements, gender seems most manipulable (at least by multiple external forces) and most discussable, most subject to theorizing and retheorizing. This, I think, is why there has been such zealous misreading of Butler's "gender-as-drag" theories over the years (and why Butler in *Gender Trouble* is certainly in part responsible for these misreadings): gender does seem to be so very much a product of the way we do our hair, wear our clothes, and walk down the street; all of these seem within our power to effect and change, and many of us may fantasize about gender masquerade or wonder about (or worry about or delight in) what our leather jacket is saying about us. All of us are interested in the line where individual agency and psychosocial determinism meet, and gender seems to contain this borderland and promise some interesting narrative about its formation and movement.

Gender's fluid interaction with the endpoints on this spectrum also results in its conflation with sexuality and sex in contemporary writing. While the relationships among these concepts are complex and meaningful, *as* relationships they denote the separateness of each concept (which is then related to the other); the attempt to simply substitute or interchange the terms must be called into question.

I consider here the relationship between gender and sexuality; having explored gender's many meanings in the discussion above, I observe now that the term sexuality has as many permutations in the critical lexicon, indicating both (straight, gay, bisexual, or transexual) orientation and myriad sexual practices. We recall the oppositional relationship between gender and sexuality implied in the arguments of Wittig and de Lauretis above, whose double-edged approach to the category of women require us to regard gender and sexuality (as in sexual orientation) as mutually exclusive. Other critics fix with ease a relationship between gender and *hetero*sexuality: the myth that all gendered subjects are straight subjects is perpetuated by a heterosexist mainstream and critiqued by sexuality critics, even as this notion is reinforced in the course of their arguments. Rubin, for instance, makes the case plain: "Gender is not only an identification with one sex; it also entails that sexual desire be directed toward the other sex" ("The Traffic in Women" 180). Elsewhere, Boone and Cadden interchange the terms when they applaud the feminist fore-grounding of "*sexuality* as a crucial component in any thoroughgoing analysis of textuality, . . . underlining the necessity of taking responsibil-ity for our *gendered* subject positions, whether male or female" (2, emphases added). Valerie Traub challenges critical indifference toward the distinction between gendered and erotic relations yet presumes that the copresence of "masculinity" and "femininity" (her terms for gender) in an erotic relationship must indicate heterosexuality (*Desire and Anxiety* 94); Johnson's reading of *The Accused* has already demonstrated that this is not the case. These writers work from the assumption that gender (for good or ill) belongs to straights, that the "orientation" of gender is heterosexual. While Rubin, and to some extent Wittig and de Lauretis, forges this equation purposefully (the slide), Boone and Cadden seem to accidentally mix the terms (the slip), while Traub, who writes explicitly to challenge such slippage, testifies to the difficulty of stepping fully away from the heterosexist trappings of the current understanding of gender.

Rubin ("Thinking Sex") argues for moving beyond the straight/gay binary so that sexuality may be seen as not just an orientation but as a practice attachable to any orientation. She visits frequently a lengthy list of socially marginalized sex practitioners—not only gays and lesbians, but also sex workers, masturbators, fetishists, transvestites, transsexu-als, cross-generational lovers, and even unmarried and/or promiscu-ous straights—so as to indicate that gays and straights do not divide this list in any definite way and that gay and lesbian sexual practice is not simply interchangeable with the perverse. Elsewhere Butler out-lines the benefits to be derived from Rubin's emphasis on multiplicity ("Against Proper Objects" 11), and Eve Sedgwick presents her own creatively phrased list: "certain zones or sensations, certain physical types, a certain frequency, certain symbolic investments, certain rela-tions of age or power, a certain species, a certain number of partici-pants" (*Epistemology* 8). Such arguments develop incisively upon Foucault's seminal observations regarding the shift, at the turn of the last century, from sexuality as unregulated practice to sexuality as a consummately "fixable" lifestyle or personage, and in Foucault's handing of this distinction, we sense an important association between sexuality as orientation and the juridical power systems that have solidified it as such (*The History of Sexuality Vol. 1* 43). Certainly, such associations have been radically, productively inverted by queer activists and gay and lesbian theorists vigorously exploring the cultural ramifications of nonnormative sexualities, yet the original work done by power structures to cement the equation between "diversity" and "perversity" has had a lasting effect: even when the practices described (sex working, S&M, pornography) belong with equal frequency to the repertoires of straights, the assumption—by both the nonacademic mainstream and even many critical theorists—is that there is a gay or lesbian sensibility behind it—hence the adoption of the word "queer" to refer to unorthodox sexual practice in general, and hence the tendency of discussions of these topics to be authored by (or to reference) gay and/or lesbian participants. Even in mainstream media, the now-standard reference to "race, class, and gender" reverts to "same-*sex* marriage" (instead of also being updated to "same-gender marriage") because in the latter semantic context the subject of discussion is gay men and lesbians instead of the (presumably heterosexual) "women" referenced in the former phrase by "gender." While there are certainly exceptions to the rule, an implied equation between *sexuality* and *homosexuality* results from the sense that a primary contribution by gays and lesbians to the general discussion has been an open, comfortable, productive focus on sexual practice and orientation.

By contrast, the equation *sexuality* = *heterosexuality* is often employed in critiques of straight sexphobia and sex regulation, the social controls that monitor and limit all forms of sexual expression, and again the work of Butler proves emblematic. In fact, in *Gender Trouble*, Butler does not very often use the term "sexuality," preferring the term "desire," but when she does, it is within the context of Foucauldian analysis of power, the law, and the inescapable "phallic economy." She criticizes the notion of "a sexuality freed from heterosexual constructs" as "utopian" (29) and later adds, "sexuality is always constructed within the terms of discourse and power, where power is partially understood in terms of heterosexual and phallic cultural conventions" (30). Valerie Traub distinguishes "homo*eroticism*" from "hetero*sexuality*": "my use of the linguistic root 'sexuality' is meant to imply heterosexuality's institutional and political mandate, in which identity was situated in relation to one's sexual congress as a socially ascribed subject-position" (*Desire and Anxiety* 112).[7]

Finally, there is nothing very sexy in these references to straight sexuality, centered as they are on the repression or control of sexual desire, against which a freer, more erotic definition of nonnormative self-expression sets itself. In chapter 1, I observed that gay and lesbian theories sharing in a typically (straight) feminist agenda are often read as adopting the erotophobic position. Here again, "straightness" and "sexuality" are oxymoronic terms, although certainly this theoretical tendency in part provides a much-needed counterpoint to representations of straight sexuality reflected everywhere in contemporary culture. As sexuality (or eroticism) becomes the province of homosexuality (or, more broadly, queerness), the orientation of gender is read as heterosexual, for multiple reasons: for its having been a key concept for second-wave (straight) feminists; for its tendency, as I observe at the beginning of this section, to keep its clothes on and thus signify sexphobia or normative sexualities; and ironically for its firm link in much contemporary writing to "men," "women," and heterocentrist concepts such as difference and opposition. By contrast, I have argued throughout this chapter that gender belongs, dynamically and subversively, to each of us; if we think in the terms Butler advises, of the scenario in which "gender does not necessarily follow from sex, and . . . sexuality . . . does not seem to follow from gender" (135–36), the relegation of gender to the realm of traditional, regulatory sexuality is a conceptual misfire.

Sex, Which Is Not One

Like gender and sexuality, sex is a term with varying claims to critical legitimacy, depending on the sense in which it is used; the marked difference between having sex and having *a* sex is an important feature of this issue. In its more neutral incarnation, sex defines the terrain outlined in my references to sexual practice above, yet using this simpler, shorthand terms to discuss sexual activity often risks confusing it with its demonized twin—sex as a biological distinction between male and female "animals." This latter, now-discredited sense of the term functioned in the second-wave era as a politicizing counterpoint, as the physical bedrock on which was founded much gender construction, oppression, identification, and revolt; Rubin's determination of the "sex/gender system" is a case in point. Yet the seemingly straightforward, natural, innocence of biological sex—the only sex, after all, one can talk about in polite company—is exactly the problem; its insidious neutrality is read as enabling the most damaging, deeply held assumptions. Sex seems most interesting to modern thinkers when it is defined as or functions as something else, and this biologized, concretized entity is regarded as either self-evident and theoretically passé or as the galvanizing villain of the sexuality studies piece. Because of widespread critical inclination to avoid the taint of biological sex, the confusion of "sex" with "sexuality" seems an accidental, but almost inevitable, slip between two closely related ideas, while the slide I calibrate between "sex" and "gender" (more specifically, the slide of "sex" into "gender") constitutes the most pervasively influential yet theoretically questionable semantic tendency of any considered here.

The slippage between the terms sex and sexuality is hardly the invention of the theoretical examples containing it but is so common in ordinary usage that the important distinction in the specific context of gender and sexuality theory is rarely noted. Rubin throughout "Thinking Sex," for example, gives in to the temptation to use the shorter term to refer to the longer one, in an effort to make the prose more forceful and various. Presuming that her reader will take her point no matter what, however, likely presumes too much; in an essay designed specifically to define terms and lay groundwork, Rubin's slippage creates confusion. Let us take, for example, a necessarily lengthy passage:

> A radical theory of *sex* must identify, describe, explain, and denounce erotic injustice and *sexual* oppression. . . . It must build rich descriptions of *sexuality* as it exists in society and history. . . .
>
> One such axiom is *sexual* essentialism—the idea that *sex* is a natural force that exists prior to social life and shapes institutions. *Sexual* essentialism is embedded in the folk wisdoms of Western societies, which consider *sex* to be eternally unchanging, asocial, and transhistorical. Dominated for over a century by medicine, psychiatry, and psychology, the academic study of *sex* has reproduced essentialism. These fields classify *sex* as a property of individuals. It may reside in their hormones or their psyches. It may be construed as physiological or psychological. But within these ethnoscientific categories, *sexuality* has no history and no significant social determinants.   (9, emphases added)

Is "sexual" here the adjectival form of "sex" or "sexuality" or both? Does not sex as a "natural force" connote the activity of sexual practice or the sex drive, while sex as the essentialized "property of individuals" suggests basic anatomic distinctions? Does Rubin mean, at the end of this passage, to distinguish "sexuality"—that which has no history or social determinants—from her several preceding references to "sex," which seems to have been successfully classified by academic studies? Or, as the terms are interchanged throughout, is there no special distinction being offered? As Rubin is touching here upon the essentialist-poststructuralist debate, the several classificatory dilemmas she instigates become ours as well: does sex(uality) reside in the hormones or in the psyche? *Yes*: sex is considered to be significantly hormonally affected, and sexuality considered to be created in or by the psyche. Is sex(uality) to be construed as physiologic or as psychological?

Yes, again: sex is considered to be primarily physiologic, and sexuality deeply psychological.

Rubin waffles between these terms throughout, yet near the end (and I argue that this is entirely too late in the game) acknowledges that "In the English language, the word 'sex' has two very different meanings. It means gender and gender identity, as in 'the female sex' or 'the male sex' [*sic*]. But sex also refers to sexual activity, lust, intercourse, and arousal as in 'to have sex' " (32). But should not a theorist such as herself be moving carefully beyond the common-usage indifference toward these terms' separate meanings, and setting up more rigorous and consistent standards to guide her readers? (See also "Traffic" 167.) Interestingly, she determines this semantic slippage to reflect a "cultural assumption that sexuality is reducible to sexual intercourse and that it is a reflection of relations between women and men" (32) without acknowledging how her own work partakes of this slippage, reduction, and homophobic effect.

In more recent writing, Sheila Jeffreys deploys terminology in ways I question on several counts; relevant here is the confusion created by several references to sex and the multivalent notion of "having" (possessing? engaging in?) sex that go unclarified because the term sex itself is never fully defined. Considering "possession or non possession of a penis," Jeffreys's reference to "what is understood as sex under male supremacy" may be understood in terms of biological sex, coercive sex, even sex's archaic meaning as sex organ, the penis itself. Later "sex" indicates an "eroticized power difference" between men and women ("The Essential Lesbian" 104). Certainly, the notion of eroticized difference relates to the opposition between the "presence" of the male member and the "absence" of the woman's genitalia, while equally plausible (especially when the word "power" is emphasized) would be a reference to active and passive roles in bed. Jeffreys immediately concludes that "Therefore many, *to have sex*, need to have gender and relate to someone of the opposite gender [*sic*]" (104, emphasis added). Certainly the traditional reading of "having sex" as in "engaging in sexual activity" presents as more obvious, yet Jeffreys's cryptic "needing to have gender" suggests "having sex (organs)" the way one has a gendered identity. Admittedly, the terms are slippery to work with, necessitating, however, all the more care when theorizing in reference to them.

If Rubin and Jeffreys conflate sex with sexuality largely inadvertently, Sedgwick, Butler, and others erase the distinction between sex and gender with various yet equally strong political and theoretical purposes in mind. Biddy Martin contrasts the work of Sedgwick and

Butler, arguing that "for Sedgwick gender becomes sex, and ineluctably follows the principles of binary division" while "for Butler sex becomes gender, that is, is socially constructed, and the principle of binary division itself is contested, even at the level of the body" ("Sexualities without Genders" 110). Yet Martin's distinction does not hold: both Sedgwick and Butler rely on a binarized definition of gender (see Sedgwick *Epistemology* 28 and my discussion of Butler above), and for both Butler and Sedgwick, "sex becomes gender" so as to further political goals. Butler, as Martin indicates, suggests that "perhaps [sex] was always already gender" (Butler *Gender Trouble* 7), and Sedgwick states that she will set sex under the rubric of "gender" so as to avoid the very sex/sexuality confusion that I describe as affecting Rubin's and Jeffreys's work above (*Epistemology* 29). Thus both theorists move sex in the same direction (toward the indeterminacy of gender), although they differ in purpose: whereas Sedgwick's motivation is primarily semantic clarity, Butler is fundamentally dependent on this move, so as to complete her overarching project—to strike at the base of the heterosexual hegemonic system through calling into question the last (and some would argue most unquestionable) element of fixed being—the sexed body itself.[8] Sedgwick performs this semantic slide for several pages in the course of a much wider-ranging work, while Butler insists upon the same conflation for the duration of more than one book-length project.

Sedgwick points out that, in effect, Rubin's "sex/gender system" is a concept that has turned in upon itself: where once the slash between sex and gender represented a separation, opposing poles of activity and meaning that constituted the "system," it is now seen by many as a linking device or perhaps as mentally dispensed with all together in a putative "sexgender" system. Now that this diacritical wall has come down, one term has almost entirely overridden the other, in order, according to Sedgwick, to "minimize the attribution of people's various behaviors and identities to chromosomal sex and to maximize their attribution to socialized gender constructs" (*Epistemology* 28). Sedgwick acknowledges that this lopsided emphasis is not so much invited by the phrase itself, or for that matter by Rubin's original intent, as by a politically calculated move: "The purpose of that strategy has been to gain analytic and critical leverage on the female-disadvantaging social arrangements that prevail at a given time in a given society, by throwing into question their legitimative ideological grounding in biologically based narratives of the 'natural' "(28).[9] Sedgwick is certainly correct that ignoring the slash and dissolving the lexicopolitical relationship enabled by it has advantages for "females."

We know, however, that—in addition to females identifying as subjects of oppression in the contemporary critical field—we also have women, lesbians, gay men, and others whose sexual identities and practices force them to the social margin. Despite the location of this observation at the outset of Sedgwick's foundational title in gay studies, *The Epistemology of the Closet*, this dissolution of sex into gender belongs largely, as I have argued throughout, to the strategies of an older-school feminist approach.

If Sedgwick points plainly to feminists' collective decision to dissolve the category of sex into gender for the sake of political expediency, Butler's more complicated attempt to philosophize this move provides a wish list of provocative questions for which there are no answers.[10] Sedgwick in a single statement indicates the death of sex as progressive social contrivance, while Butler argues over the course of both *Gender Trouble* and *Bodies That Matter* that in fact this death is real—that sex, itself is the contrivance, "was always already gender, with the consequence that the distinction between sex and gender turns out to be no distinction at all" (*Gender Trouble* 7).

The problem is that the sum of Butler's treatises on this subject may yet be subsumed under Sedgwick's straightforward acknowledgment that concepts such as sex and gender, as concepts, are amenable to manipulation by a collective thought process, that even sophisticated attempts such as Butler's, to prove the absence of sex in the ontological universe, are not in the realm of philosophy but of politics. Two other problems, as I have indicated throughout, are the absenting of sex into a category (gender) already occupied by a completely different phenomenon—the masculinity/femininity ratio of each sexed body in existence—and the foreclosing of the concept of sex, which remains essential to gender and sexuality theorists at work in areas such as body politics and the history of sexuality.

As a case study crystallizing the problem I discern here, Judith Halberstam, in her valuable *Female Masculinity*, urges an understanding of gender as "deviant," "ambiguous," and "variable." We might say that her focus is on only half of the gender spectrum that I consider here—the masculine half—although yet again on only a quarter (or less) of that same spectrum, the specific instance of female masculinity, yet her argument extrapolates well to our thinking of gender in general. Throughout, Halberstam productively insists upon thinking gender in terms of the attribute— "masculinity" not "manhood"—just as I have sought to do in the course of this argument. Although her tendency in the early pages— and in the book's title itself—is to read this gendered identity in the aggregate—"female masculinity"—she indicates a broader, spectral approach, for instance in her promise to consider "butch lesbian" and "female-to-male transsexual" variations (3) in a later chapter. Yet we must observe how Halberstam's tendency toward traditional semantics—applying the term gender *also* to references to men and women, simply because there is no other term she feels comfortable using—turns her argument against itself, undoing some of the important insight presented elsewhere in the essay. Halberstam laments the persistence of "dimorphic gender" associations (20), yet I suggest that it is primarily *our own* persistence in applying the concept of "gender" to men and women that sustains this destructive dimorphism.

As she critiques the culture of "gender conformity" that "descends on girls at the age of puberty" (6), as she attaches her project specifically to the "recogn[ition] and ratif[ication] of differently gendered bodies and subjectivities" (7), as she critiques a symposium at a performing arts center (and the book that emerged from it) and Paul Smith's anthology *Boys: Masculinities in Contemporary Culture* for "excluding discussions of more wide-ranging masculinities" (15), Halberstam is forcing open not only our traditional understanding of gender as "natural" and "inevitable" but even our postmodern, poststructural understanding of gender as that which has transformed a sexual duality (males and females) into culturally constructed men and women but left that duality intact. Elsewhere in the essay, however, her resorting to "gender" as the term for sexed categories—evident in her references to "class, race, sexuality, and gender" (2), "gender categories" (25), "gender differentiation" (26), "gender preference" (27), and "reversed gender" (28)—threatens the gains she has made. These several references indicate that Halberstam herself is still trapped to a certain degree in (and with) a dimorphic conceptual frame that contradicts and diminishes her larger argument.

For example, as she critiques the collected essays that resulted from the arts symposium on masculinity, Halberstam applauds the collection's introduction by Eve Sedgwick, who calls for "gender diversity," even if the call is never heeded in the writings that follow (*Female Masculinity* 14). The problem Halberstam and Sedgwick point to, however, when they make reference to "gender" in this case, is the preponderance of articles by and about *men*, to the exclusion of *women* authors or subjects in the collection. Yet it is the case that Halberstam is not at all interested in "gender diversity" as she defines it elsewhere in the argument: her tight focus on *masculinity* throughout this discussion—even a "queeny" film character is defined in terms of "gay masculinity" instead of effeminacy (4)—is meant to confront readers with the specificity of her project, especially the always under-read phenomenon of female masculinity.[11] While Paul Smith and his anthology seem to deserve the corrective commentary Halberstam provides, I note that even Smith provides more "gender diversity" in his work through his focus on masculinit*ies*; likewise his willingness to open up the beleaguered category of sex—"Biological men—male sexed beings" (qtd. in Halberstam *Female Masculinity* 16)—possibly enables a freer exploration of gender's actual manifestations, in the sphere of masculine attributes.

Halberstam suggests a "concept of gender preference as opposed to compulsory gender binarism," a cultural system in which individuals would be allowed to live gender-neutrally, "until such a time when the child or young adult announces his or her or its gender" (27). Despite the qualifying third option provided here (the "its"), it is clear that, despite her critique of "people who insist on attributing gender in terms of male and female" (27) and of our inability to "let go of a binary gender system" (27), she herself still sees gender in terms of a binary option by virtue of her envisioning of gender as something that one could eventually "announce," as something limited to three manifestations. As opposed to the infinite spectrum of masculine-to-feminine ratios that I posit as more correctly representing gendered identity, the idea that one could simply announce one's gendered mix, that one would be able to or even care to, indicates that for Halberstam the value-free scenario is still the one in which an individual grows up and simply goes one way or the other. Again, her tendency to persist in dualizing gender comes, I am sure, not from her succumbing to mainstream prescriptions about natural gendered identities but from the semantic drag upon the term created by outdated readings of men and women in terms of gender.

CONCLUSION

Despite the movement away from theorizing sex as a concept of biological difference, as much important work continues to be done (and remains to be done) in the understanding of this term as in developing further our understanding of gender and sexuality. Analysts of the body and body politics in contemporary culture rely on the *physical* differences between idealized (and pathologized) male and female morphologies to make their case; while medical technology now enables the radical revision of every anatomic part to conform to preferred or idealized standards, it remains important to continue considering the state of these original, often besieged physicalities: if original, often less-than-perfect physical states have no significance (i.e., signify nothing), what justifies the feminist complaint against eating disorders, the mania for plastic surgery, clitoridectomy, sex reassignment surgery at birth, and other similar procedures? Representative is Susan Bordo (*The Male Body*, "Reading the Male Body"), who has surveyed "the male body," specifically the all-important male penis, which she is careful to distinguish from the culturally inscribed "phallus."

Biddy Martin, including in her work a concern for the preservation of women's reproductive rights, claims that, for Butler, "the very materiality of the body is formed in its entanglements" ("Sexualities without Genders" 110), yet this assessment moderates Butler's extreme position—as she herself might be inclined to ask, "*what* materiality of the body?" In fact, Butler's deep suspicion of the "metaphysics of substance" and the bent of her philosophic training that leads her away from even concrete examples mark her arguments as much *less* interested in the materiality of the body than those of Sedgwick, who has demonstrated an interest in the body in multiple works.[12] Finally, Martin observes, "If Sedgwick casts gender too insistently in terms of miring, Butler has been charged with failing at times to make the body enough of a drag on signification" ("Sexualities without Genders" 110). Yet Martin, for whom the difference between "physical" and "cultural" continues to signify, could level this charge against Butler as well.

Alongside theorists of the body, sex historians whose aim is to thoroughly delegitimize the concept do the invaluable work of enabling this newly defanged but still productive term back into circulation, even as their (counter) arguments rely on traditional definitions of the term to make the case. Thomas Laqueur, for instance, investigates early modern medical texts, specifically the opinion espoused therein that the woman's anatomy was simply an inverted model of the man's, to make his case for "sex as we know it . . . invented" in the eighteenth century (149). Laqueur's arguments do not fully persuade, focused as they are on changing perceptions—of an anatomic difference that *remains a difference*—from the early modern period (and before) to the present, yet his arguments, designed to discredit sex as a natural category, in fact, enlarge the significance of sexual difference in human history and make this reader, at any rate, want to learn more.

Anne Fausto-Sterling *does* question the dual nature of anatomy in her well-documented analyses of sex characteristics in the human population. Through her research, she has concluded that 1.7/100 live births (a remarkably high frequency) include some form of non-dimorphic sexual development (53) and argues against the "emergency" mentality in the medical profession that encourages immediate surgical alteration at birth—and often, for modification purposes, throughout childhood. Our preoccupation with the more typical modes of sex differentiation subjects non-dimorphic babies to harmful, unsuccessful, and traumatizing reconstructions, says Fausto-Sterling, who argues, with Butler and Laqueur, that "only our beliefs in gender—not science—can define our sex" (3). For me, Fausto-Sterling's most convincing observation is that "There is no either/or. Rather there are shades of difference" (3) in each body's complex sex assignment. This comment causes me to realize that, while anatomic differences continue to remain largely fixed in my mind, hormonal apportionments *do* seem to differ in every human being, with greater and lesser doses of testosterone and estrogen seeming to account in many cases for the specifically gender-based variations across the masculinity-femininity spectrum considered above. I am deeply indebted to this argument for broadening my understanding in this respect, although I note that the marked variability of hormonal (and even chromosomal and genetic and resulting anatomic) configurations from one body to the next *do not* release these configurations from the biological (see also Kessler).

Fausto-Sterling and Laqueur are thus at interesting cross-purposes: Laqueur successfully demonstrates the enculturated aspects of biological sex opposition, while Fausto-Sterling successfully questions this opposition and yet does not manage to transfer this newly configured spectrum from the biological into the cultural register. In fact, when she argues that "sex is, literally, constructed" (27), she is referring to the surgically altered situation of that 1.7 percent of the non-dimorphic human population, suggesting by inference an equation between sex reconstruction and this narrow minority and between the remainder of live births and their nonconstructed dimorphic features. To insist upon the universal constructedness of sex in this context (and related contexts of breast augmentation, liposuction, laser hair removal, etc.) would *promote* capitulation to the ideologic status quo instead of subversion of it; Fausto-Sterling clearly intends to subvert, yet her strong *critique* of the ideological basis of sex (re)construction plainly counters the Butlerian trend to read sex's constructedness in progressive, subversive terms. Finally, like Laqueur's, Fausto-Sterling's fascinating work does more to pique my interest in exploring further the meaning sex categories continue to have, than to do away with these categories altogether.

Taking a cue from these scintillating arguments, I suggest a reclaiming of the category of sex that emphasizes its called-into-question status through use of the term sex*ed*: a sexed individual, a sexed power imbalance, and the like. This usage suggests the assigned quality, the givenness of sex, at birth and throughout life (even to those with "typical" sex characteristics), by regulatory regimes vitally dependent on fixed, universally agreed-upon determinations of male and female. In addition, "sexed" distinguishes itself from the confusingly deployed "sexual" and possesses the (admittedly unwieldy) noun form—sex*ed-ness*—for those who continue to reject straightforward references to sex in their work. As we learned from Luce Irigaray long ago, however, sex is not "one" (straightforwardly referenced), nor even two, in any way: its several meanings in common usage, its several permutations (as Lacquer and Fausto-Sterling have shown) across historical periods and bodies themselves, its several manifestations—"anatomical, chromosomal, hormonal" (Butler *Gender Trouble* 6), discursive, cultural, and political—in each sexed body to have ever been born—all of these new understandings of sex should enable feminist and gay theorists to reclaim the term on a regular, productive basis.

Fausto-Sterling quotes approvingly from David Halperin, who argues that "sexuality is not a somatic fact, it is a cultural effect" (416, qtd. in Fausto-Sterling 21). The citation surprises me, as it comes from an essay that begins, mere lines earlier, with an observation explicitly countering Fausto-Sterling's project, that "Sex has no history. It is a natural fact, grounded in the functioning of the body, and, as such, it lies outside of history and culture. Sexuality, by contrast . . . is a cultural production" (416). In this wide-ranging essay, Halperin touches on every issue considered in my own discussion: "sex" as sexual acts and as biological sex, sexuality as sexual orientation (and its markedly shifting formations), and gender as I have defined it here. Interestingly, it is Halperin's introduction of the issue of gender—*molles* and *tribades* with their respective masculine and feminine qualities (421–22)—that causes the term-switching I have questioned throughout: after multiple references to "anatomical sexes (male versus female)" (420) and "the sex of sexual objects" (421), Halperin introduces this gender discussion then references "the opposite gender" (meaning "men and women") (423), even though his reading of Jack Abbott and the complex gender/sexual environment he inhabited in prison returns to a consideration of gender in terms of masculine and feminine men. In all the examples I have considered here, it is Abbott's alone that speaks to me about gender in terms of "women"—his and his company's term for the subordinate group (Halperin 425) of *men* who function as receptive partners in the prison's sexual system.

Elsewhere, Elizabeth Grosz, whose free use of this term (e.g., "the sex of the author," "the sex of the reader") constitutes a bracing departure from the rampant "gendering" characteristic of the field, asks "what effect is an understanding of the *sexually differential* forms of body going to have on our understanding of power, knowledge, and culture?" (*Space, Time, and Perversion* 37). In *Volatile Bodies*, Grosz's section on "Sexual Difference/Sexed Bodies" succeeds in "extricating the body from the mire of biologism" (188) in her incisive reading of Julia Kristeva and Mary Douglas on sexual difference. Yet her aggressive approach to the subject does not prevent her from acknowledging "male and female bodies in their irreducible specificities" (189); "I am reluctant," she avers, "to claim that sexual difference is purely a matter of the inscription and codification of somehow uncoded, absolutely raw material, as if these materials exert no resistance or recalcitrance to the processes of cultural inscription. This is to deny a materiality or a material specificity and determinateness to bodies" (190). I contend that it is Grosz's marked openness to bodily materiality that, Möbius strip-like, both enables and is enabled by her free access to the term and category of sexedness. Her references to "sexual difference" (191, 208, 209) and "each sex for the other" (207) propel and complete her argument, "the two sexes" (193, 210) even being the last phrase of her book. Not surprisingly, Grosz's intensely philosophized focus on the body—in this discussion, men's and women's bodily fluids and their levels of signification—also corresponds, I argue, to her word choice.

Both Halperin and Grosz reveal in their writing the influence of Foucault, whose own focus on docile bodies and the pleasures of the body in no way limits the significance of his inquiry for poststructuralists, feminists, or gay and lesbian theorists. Halperin moves to an analysis of Ancient pedophilic practices, unhindered by impossible-to-prove assertions, and Grosz concludes *Space, Time, and Perversion* with a multiessay discussion of lesbian subject positions; both, then, theorize sex helpfully and demonstrate an easy association between the traditional deployment of this term and incisive queer theorizing. Arguments such as these help us recognize the full range of approaches to "sex" that are currently in circulation, and thus the value derived from retaining this term as a separate epistemologic category. Finally, I am arguing that reinterpreting sex as gender or sexuality forecloses a theoretically productive and politically powerful semantic and epistemological terrain of analysis, as happens whenever we allow our word choice to slip accidentally or slide strategically in the service of a politicized agenda. Maintaining separate roles for these terms is as important as maintaining the many other distinctions we must deal with—between females and women, men and masculinity, heterosexuality and gender, homosexuality and sexuality—in the development of our own careful and consistent, and thus clarifying and instructive, work in the fields of lesbian, gay, and feminist studies.

CHAPTER 3

THE CRITICAL IMPASSE: INVERSE RELATIONS AMONG LESBIAN, GAY, AND FEMINIST APPROACHES

O'BRIEN OR JULIA?

In George Orwell's *1984* the romantic union of Winston and Julia is interrupted by the triangulating character O'Brien, who functions not as a competing suitor for Julia's attention but as a powerful intellectual distraction for Winston, a source of intense emotional release that eventually challenges and destroys the foregrounded heterosexual affair. Thus, the character whose love and loyalty are being fought over faces a choice not between largely interchangeable options (suitor A or B) but between radically different "lifestyles": will Winston remain with Julia despite the fact that their sexual relationship has become to him an obnoxious barrier to authentic political action, or will he forsake the comforts of this stable arrangement for the dark secrets O'Brien promises but alluringly refuses to articulate? Indeed, Julia at first represents a radical sexual "alternative" to his depressingly desexualized existence and yet, even in the early chapters, O'Brien draws Winston further out on the limb: Winston becomes obsessed with entering O'Brien's world, their climactic meeting arouses in him an intense emotional and physical response, and O'Brien's brutal betrayal of Winston consummates itself in an S&M-style torture sequence enacted behind the locked door of Room 101. Meanwhile, Winston's passions for Julia and for O'Brien do not exist simultaneously or even merely consecutively in the course of the narrative but instead contend for the foreground in a textual fight to the death: Julia is declared by Winston to be a political and intellectual disappointment, a revolutionary "from the waist downwards" (129) only, and removed from the narrative almost immediately after this, reappearing only in the denouement. Certainly it is O'Brien who has planted this seed of discontent in Winston's mind, providing the model against which she somehow fails to compare, while it is also O'Brien, unbeknownst to the couple at this point, who arranges the assault on their hideout and subsequent capture. Julia's resurfacing at the end of the story not only follows upon but also confirms Winston's realization that she is his "true" love, largely because O'Brien turned out to be such a "false" one.

Note the way in which the narrative itself forces the reader to see these relationships in mutually exclusive opposition, and in terms of the "natural" and "unnatural" tendencies in human relationships that have abetted the sexist and homophobic mindset through history: if mid-century audiences, as they almost surely did, deemed Winston's turn to O'Brien as a "natural" instance of male-to-male bonding, this was likely due in large part to their reading of Julia's intellectual inferiority as a "natural" female predisposition. Hence, the "historically accurate" reading of this novel would include minimal if any effort to queer the relationship between the two men *or* lament the loss of Julia to the novel's love plot or political theme. Meanwhile, it is the more modern feminist approach that questions Julia's "natural" deficiencies; in fact, she is a clever political subversive whom Winston mislabels as a mere sexual functionary. But this approach simultaneously "denaturalizes" the relationship between Winston and O'Brien—in fact Winston's "love" for O'Brien snuffs out the last chance for freedom in this oppressive universe—in a way anathema to any gay-affirmative position it may wish to simultaneously defend. A third approach, the gay reading that in part returns to the original "misogynist" response, might emphasize the "unnatural" (inevitably queer) relationship between the two men, but only as a means to centralize and validate (i.e., naturalize) this relationship after all. The Winston-Julia bond would appear more conservative (pleasing to the authorities who delight in identifying, capturing, and punishing the couple) and therefore constraining by contrast.[1] Because this novel presents as ideal clear and readable distinctions between freedom and slavery, truth and falsehood, selfhood and insanity (and simultaneously vilifies Big Brotherian efforts to muddy the lines between), neither reading can be comfortable with the bisexual approach: Winston is forced to follow either Julia's way or O'Brien's, and the future of Oceania rests on his decision. In a way he indeed chooses both—O'Brien at the narrative midpoint, Julia at the very end (and largely by default), leaving critical readers who follow in the wake of this remarkable text to work it out amongst themselves.

In each literary, theoretical, or cultural example to be considered here, the strength of the lesbian, gay, or feminist interpretative claim in question rests in large part upon the invalidation of the couterclaims, a situation due no longer to self-interested political maneuverings (as analyzed in chapters 1 and 2) but to the constituting elements of the claims themselves. Can (and should) a text, a theory, or a cultural artifact be gay *and* feminist, gay *and* lesbian, lesbian *and* feminist, at once? What determines the assertion of one position that so automatically threatens the health of another? Certainly, all of the texts to be discussed here lend themselves to readings inflected by more than one of these three approaches, yet none is capable of lending itself to more than one *at the same time*. Visiting each pairing on the critical triangle, the analysis that follows will consider the inverse relationship between each camp's response to various cultural phenomena, and consider in each instance the additional conflicts generated by persistent, seemingly omnipresent strains of homophobia. Finally, these homophobic effects both foster the divisions between the schools in question *and* react to certain elements of discord already present.

Pecs or Implants?

To continue delineating the gay-feminist debate, I turn to Ross Chambers's analysis of the romantic triangles dotting the narrative path of Alan Hollinghurst's *The Swimming-Pool Library*. Here, Chambers notes that the world occupied by young and aristocratic Will Beckwith, his lovers, mentors, and alter-egos, is an all-male world divided between homosocial power systems and homosexual threats to these, an oppositional pairing that triangulates through its very reference to and inclusion of "mediating women." Seeking to employ the dynamic elucidated by Sedgwick in *Between Men*, and admirably in search of a feminist reading of Hollinghurst's resistant text, Chambers argues that "relations between men [in the novel] are mediated by women who—as a consequence of that mediating role—are excluded not from the total cultural system . . . but from the workings of power" (212). Meanwhile, it must be noted that the "mediating women" described in Sedgwick's work are vital narrative presences, as opposed to the offstage female characters referred to by Hollinghurst. Chambers himself points out that, "Mentioned as mothers, sisters or wives, women are otherwise banished from this segregated novel" (210), and Chambers's argument must rely on a linking of women *with* gay men as dual threats to the homosocial (i.e., heterosexualized, hegemonic) forces of society: the first successfully excluded, the second successfully subversive. But readers of this novel will find very little if any opposition between homosocial and homosexual forces as soon as the issue of women is introduced, since both conspire to remove women from the picture, while the gay-centered narrative in fact successfully backgrounds heterosexist interruption for much of its progress. Even to accept Chambers's reading, that homosexual relationships step in and effectively subvert where impotent and excluded women fail, will strike some readers as unlikely grounds for congratulating Hollinghurst's feminist agenda. If anything, women in this scheme would be doubly disempowered, first by the banishing homosocial men, then by the rescuing homosexual ones.

As with my reading of Orwell above, the feminist and gay readings fail here to coexist. Chambers, likely inspired by the feminist elements of Sedgwick's text, labors to include a role for women and for a feminist approach to a primary text that simply will not admit this: to the degree that women are present in Chambers's reading, the reading itself simply misses Hollinghurst's mark. While with *1984*, the feminist position may ultimately outpace its gay counter-reading (especially for those who see nothing especially lavender about the goings-on between Winston and O'Brien), here only an androcentric approach can respond to what this novel truly has to offer. And if anything, the "love" triangle among the conflicting characters and readings is even more curiously (because more traditionally) constructed by Chambers—a chivalrous gay subculture coming to the rescue of disempowered damsels in Hollinghurst's homophobically ruled universe.

Later Chambers turns to the presence of the female pronoun in the novel, the "she" directed toward attractive gay men, and posits that "it is only inasmuch as they function as object of desire (and so substitute for the homosocially excluded women) that males qualify for the personal pronoun that reintroduces the feminine gender into the situation" (213). Here Chambers's effort to keep women in his reading results in the curious image of gay men desiring the most attractive of "homosocially excluded women." *Is* their resemblance to women what makes gay men most attractive to each other? In this novel's larger effort to question and subvert the order of a male-dominated, heterosexist society, would it be as desirable objects for a group of gay men that the reemergence of women would do the most political good? Through a clever reversal of his argument, Chambers determines—only sentences later—that, in fact, it is the most masculine of male specimens who are sought after by Will and his set, while finally he insists that "athleticism and the feminisation of the object of desire go hand in hand" (213) in this novel, using the incident of two gym-goers ogling a "she" with "big tits" as his example.

At this point, the curiosities in Chambers's discussion stem entirely from the linguistic idiosyncrasies of the novel itself. This reader, at any rate, admits to extreme confusion as to the nature of the "she" and the "tits" being checked out in the preceding scene: likely we are not dealing with a biological woman, but are we observing instead a transsexual with great implants? a superstud with terrific pecs? Hollinghurst's language seems purposely over-the-top and designed to confuse; and the semantics attending his characterological clique's rating system—the more masculine the physical specimen, the more feminine the form of address—ring not at all true with the multiple other literary, critical, and sociological depictions I have come across, let alone from first-hand experience with actual gay men. In fact, the reverse rule seems most often in play—the *less* physically attractive (or less likely a cruising prospect—as friend, partner of friend, roommate, etc.) a gay man, the *more* likely the feminine pronoun will be applied.

I am drawn to two exchanges overheard by the sociologist Martin P. Levine, whose focus is the "dish" episode itself, not the circulation of pronouns in the men's conversation. In both incidents, one man questions another about a third man across the room, using neutral or masculine forms of reference that may indicate initial sexual interest. In both cases, the respondent, in the know about the removed party in question, sharply devalues that party's social and sexual currency, likely dousing any spark of desire the original questioner may have had:

"See that tall blond near the jukebox?" Sean asked, elbowing Randy.

"Oh *her*! *She's* been around for years!," answered Randy.

"What's *her* story?"

"Big cock, loves to get fucked, waits tables."

* * *

"Do you know the dark-haired man, sitting alone in the back booth?" asked Carl.

. . . "Oh *her*! *She's* been around since day one," replied Seth.

"What's *her* story?"

"A hairdresser who likes to fuck twinkies."

"What!" Bill chimed in. You got it all wrong. I know *him*. We met on the Island years ago. *His* name is Chad, *he's* a commercial artist, has a loft on the Bowery, and likes to fuck muscle numbers."   (74, emphases added)

Note the way in which, in both cases, the interlocutor immediately adopts the feminine pronoun ("What's *her* story?") once the removed party has been dished by the better-informed speaker. Note also how masculinity is reconfirmed upon the removed party in the second scenario at the same time that his humanity ("His name's Chad") and sexual attractiveness ("loft in the Bowery . . . likes to fuck muscle num-bers") are also established by the even better informed third discussant. This dichotomy is reinforced by field evidence elsewhere in Levine's study, when two friends look forward excitedly to a "hot" party: "Hal told me to tell you that he is having a 'pre-party' at his house before the Saint. He wants you to bring 'MDA' and 'coke.' Larry's coming with his new beau, who I hear is 'to-die-for' " (69). Rather obviously, the event referred to in this speech is anticipated as a scene of sexual excite-ment, and masculine pronouns are in use. Finally, Levine's (largely inadvertent) findings on pronoun use reverse Chambers's and Hollinghurst's readings of same in ways relevant to this study: what is least desirable in gay culture is insistently feminized, suggesting, at least in one respect,[2] a fundamental repellence separating what is female from what is gay-masculine in cultural representation.

This line of argument terminates in the position taken by multiple recent gay theorists (see chapter 1), who define the effeminate gay man as "myth," no longer merely representing what is undesirable in gay culture but construed as so insulting a figure to some that it is determined to have never existed at all (except in the mind of the homo-phobic mainstream). For some, gayness is profoundly threatened—politically, culturally, ontologically—by the insinuation of the feminine into that subject position, and it is important to consider the role actu-ally played by mainstream homophobia as spoiler of this particular connection: if straight society were not so intent on sissifying every cul-tural element not in compliance with compulsory heterosexuality—many of these elements in fact no more effeminate than the most contented heterosexual sensibility—gay theorists would likely feel less need to eschew effeminate gayness in any form. Finally what appears as the result of simple misogyny in many of these theories is as much or more so a response (an inevitably misogynistic response) to a pre-ceding and more forceful homophobic impulse from straight society that threatens gay men's very being.

SISTERS OR LOVERS?

Adrienne Rich's foundational concept of the "lesbian continuum" indeed enables a theoretical framework that would connect the situations of (straight) feminists and lesbians in a manner unavailable for feminists and gay men considered above. Rich opens the essay in which she introduces this term by proposing to "sketch . . . some bridge, over the gap between *lesbian* and *feminist*" (227), and delineation of this line connecting previously conflicting groups is one of the essay's enduring contributions to the field. In Rich's deft analysis, the grounds on which *all* women should recognize the damage done by the heterosexual status quo, and use this recognition to effectively resist, seem spacious and fertile; all women *do* have heterosexualized femininity thrust upon them, through inclusion in or exclusion from its economic and social benefits, and Rich's depiction of this continuum line effectively speaks for a generation of lesbian separatists and radical feminists, seeking ways to think about women's universal condition. For me, Rich's strongest moment of defense of her model comes through her definition of the "female erotic," an "energy . . . diffuse . . . [and] omnipresent, . . . an empowering joy" (240), which attempts to think the connection between straight and lesbian feminists down to the sexual feelings that for many would disrupt this continuum at its deepest structural level. If women begin to perceive themselves as sharing even the same form of sexual energy, the last (and first) presumed barrier between them would come tumbling down.

It is worth noting that Rich advances this argument explicitly in defense of the lesbian component of the feminist movement, a group whose voices are yet to be fully accepted but were all but silenced at the time this piece was written. While the continuum is certainly a literal reaching across to the dominating opposition, it constitutes no sort of compromise over full lesbian membership in the movement. Note that Rich names her model the *lesbian* continuum instead of the "feminist" or "women's" continuum. Her effort counters the perennial attempt to heterosexualize all women by lesbianizing them, a theoretical move that resonates with much more recent sexuality theories describing the fraught (if not false) consciousness of the straight mind. Certainly, the argument that "we are all lesbians" must have seemed a much more difficult dose to swallow than the more placating, middle-range notion that "we are all feminists." Yet only such radical language seemed able at this point to raise homophobic feminist consciousness to the proper level of awareness.

Rich's continuum, and the woman-identified-woman writings of other feminists of her era, in part creates the rationale for Eve Kosofsky Sedgwick's later and still-influential *Between Men*. The neurosis-inducing break in the male homosocial/homosexual spectrum that is her focus is noticeable largely in light of the relatively seamless relations among women on the same spectrum. Sedgwick notes that "the diacritical opposition between the 'homosocial' and the 'homosexual' seems to be much less thorough and dichotomous for women, in our society, than for men" (2) and moves on to develop this idea through a paraphrase of Rich's argument. Even at the current moment, cultural observers acknowledge the phobic proscriptions against hugging, kissing, and physical contact constraining relations between men in the United States at least, and the overdefensive, macho posturings controlling masculine definition and intersex relations throughout much of the West. Women continue to use their socially acceptable freedoms to be publicly physical with each other as a trump card in the sex wars, and the "lesbian chic" practice of women walking arm and arm (observed in the streets of New York on multiple occasions) recalls not only the genteel traditions of a bygone, latently feminist, Whartonesque era, but also reminds the observer that women's very lack of defensive maneuverings around each other has been an empowering tradition since Wharton's time and long before.

With the continuum model, a *direct* relationship between feminist and lesbian groups comes into clearer focus: one's lesbianism realizes/enables/increases—in short, *is*—one's feminism and vice versa. Feminism is defined as the search for freedom from compulsory heterosexuality and lesbianism is found to have been at the end of this search from the very start. With this model, feminists and lesbians want and do not want the same things, and the sense of a shared tradition, and perhaps more importantly, a shared fate, can create powerful coalitions through which, for instance, straight women protest in favor of AIDS patients' rights or lesbians create a powerful presence at an abortion rally. Rich's model enables a direct relationship of a distinctly political stripe, but through its example the recognition of literary and cultural interpretive paradigms shared by both groups seems also to be in reach.

Significantly, however, Rich's concept of the lesbian continuum was moved beyond (i.e., in part rejected) almost immediately after its inception. Rich herself worries, in the course of this same essay, about the tendency to "blur . . . or sentimentalize . . . the actualities within which women have experienced sexuality" (232), and while the actual "lesbian continuum" discussion constitutes only a page or so in Rich's lengthy and wide-ranging essay, the Afterword attached in 1986 centers on the question of misinterpreting and misusing this model. In a letter from three supportive colleagues, report is made of a women's meeting during which the continuum became so misinterpreted that "lesbianism and female friendship became exactly the same thing" (247). In the original essay Rich discusses her decision to use the term "lesbian existence" instead of "lesbianism" as a means of broadening and making flexible the traditionally sex-limited picture of lesbians. Here, the letter writers revert to this more direct and necessarily narrow term to call attention to some trouble inherent in the model itself. In other words, perhaps what happened at the women's meeting was not so much the result of *mis*interpretation but a natural response to a theoretically untenable concept. The reprint of this essay in the *Gay and Lesbian Studies Reader* is almost immediately followed by a contribution from Biddy Martin, an essay written less than a decade later that persuasively questions the continuum model. The argument Martin makes is incisively reinforced by Hilary Allen (quoted by Martin), who worries that "whatever is sexual about Political Lesbianism appears to be systematically attenuated: genitality will yield to an unspecified eroticism, eroticism to sensuality, sensuality to 'primary emotional intensity' and emotional intensity to practical and political support" (qtd. in "Lesbian Identity" 280). Note that what I described as Rich's strongest argument for the continuum, the diffuse and empowering "joy" that characterizes all women's sexuality, has already taken the first attenuating step down Allen's scale—from gentiality to "unspecified eroticism," after which the terms seem poised upon a very slippery slope.

I am interested here in how acknowledgment of straight and lesbian women's rather obviously differing modes of genitality has indeed been structurally fatal to other levels at which Rich's model might be deployed. To reverse Allen's argument above, the political, social, and cultural grounds on which all women's lives are indeed "lesbian existence" has definitively "yielded to" lesbian's and straight women's sexual difference, a variant deemed so essential to both (though perhaps especially the former) groups' self-definition that there now exists a separation between them that resembles the phobic defensiveness characterizing (and annihilating) the male homosocial/homosexual spectrum described by Sedgwick. While straight men fearing to be queered certainly describes the traditional homophobic response, lesbian resistance to being straightened responds to a very different phenomenon (feminist "homophilia") that lesbians have in fact recognized as simply another attempt by straights to control or demolish the source of their fear. I argued in "In Theory of Not in Practice" that straight feminists' willingness to stand up and be (mis)counted as lesbians constitutes a more powerful act than mere "acceptance" or "toleration" of their lesbian counterpart, yet when homophobia is discovered at the core of this feminist embrace of lesbian identity and sexuality, the essential structural divide separating lesbian and feminist modes of being comes into view: this feminist embrace of lesbianism, inaugurated by Rich as a lesbian embrace of feminism, transforms this lesbianism into a version of heterosexuality and transforms its own feminism into a homophobic gesture.

In the later *Epistemology of the Closet*, Sedgwick notes that "Since the late 1970s . . . there have emerged a variety of challenges to th[e] understanding of how lesbian and gay male desires and identities might be mapped against each other" (37), an understanding fostered by models such as Rich's and challenges to it, which have tended to draw lesbian cultural theory into alliance with its gay male counterpart and against its original straight feminist ally. More recently Cheshire Calhoun cites the continuum as one of the reasons why "Lesbian theory and feminism . . . are at risk of falling into a[n] . . . unhappy marriage" (558). Through an intricate line of reasoning, Calhoun arrives at her own inverse relation: "The feminist political opposition to patriarchal power relations *disables* lesbians from effectively challenging heterosexual society. The lesbian political opposition to compulsory heterosexual gender performance *disables* feminists from effectively challenging patriarchal society" (572, emphases added). Here Calhoun finds not only that the two groups cannot do the same thing but also that they do not even seem able to do their own thing without incapacitating the efforts of the other. While Calhoun offers a complex solution to this dilemma, it interestingly prescribes the enactment of another mutually exclusive situation: "It thus does not behoove feminist politics to begin by championing the importance of sexual interaction, romantic love, marriage, and the (couple-based) family. But it does behoove lesbian politics to start in precisely these places" (581).

In light of all of this anticontinuum theorizing, was no part of Rich's model (and the relationship it hoped to enable) worth preserving because of the potential for homophobic mishandling found at its base? How do arguments such as Allen's and Calhoun's constitute a recognition of the fundamental disunity barring the "isness" of lesbian existence from the "isness" of straight feminism? To the degree that sexual identity does constitute a limiting, definitive boundary around the ways we can and cannot be, the inverse relationship between straight and lesbian identities (and all the political, cultural, and theoretical work that would follow from this) takes shape: women, this argument goes, *are* necessarily either straight or lesbian; the straight feminist's adoption of a lesbian subject position not only does not enlarge this position but also does not leave it intact in its own register.

Instead this is an adoption-through-diminishment of the counterpart's subject position. Straight feminism's "false" or "political" lesbian consciousness comes from (and takes from) actual lesbian existence in a manner characteristic of the Derridean supplement—"that which takes (the) place (of)"—in a move that is originally defined to be supportive and subordinate, that is, to supplement, not supplant. As in the case of the gay-feminist pairing in the previous discussion, here too a form of homophobia—intricately tailored to the workings of a relationship designed specifically to exclude this—successfully invades anyway, destroying a potentially mutually beneficial relationship and/or only weakening aspects of this same relationship inherently threatened by structural collapse.

THE RALLY OR THE RAMBLE?

The editors of the anthology *Queers in Space* acknowledge a "tension between the roles of eroticism and communality in the formation of queer space" but consider the "permanent dichotomy" between queer men and women—"for men, [queer space] . . . defined by erotically charged, phallocentric experience; for women by a communal, cooperative, often 'sex-negative' experience"—to be a "false notion" and a "false duality [that] has trammeled the study of queers in space" (9). Later, they critique Manuel Castells's "interpretations of the differences in lesbian and gay male placemaking," determining them to be "somewhat simplistic, if not essentialist" (452). David Bell and Gill Valentine, introducing their own collection, likewise dismiss Castells and others who argue for lesbians' and gay men's "distinct lifestyles," positing that such ideas have been "heavily criticized and largely rejected" (4). Elsewhere Lo and Healy write specifically to "dispel . . . Castells' notion of lesbians' disassociation with space and territory" (42) by discussing cross-town stereotypes held by lesbians themselves in Vancouver's West End and eastern neighborhoods.

In the Bell and Valentine anthology, Sally Munt contemplates her beloved former days as a lesbian *flâneur*, when she lived "on the edge" in Brighton, a fading city in southern England that "introduced me to the dyke stare, . . . gave me permission *to* stare. . . . Brighton constructed my lesbian identity, one that was given to me by the glance of others, exchanged by the looks I gave them, passing—or not passing—in the street" (115). Munt's cruising activities indeed complement those of gay men, described frequently as initiating sexual contacts in this way; so do the women holding hands on Seventh Avenue in Brooklyn's Park Slope neighborhood, persuasively described by Tamar Rothenberg as one of the largest lesbian neighborhoods in the United States. The very concentration of lesbian residences and residents in an urban area already works against the sense of scattered invisibility created in other readings, and Rothenberg provides strong evidence for this palpable presence, citing the Lesbian Herstory Archives and the SAL (Social Activities for Lesbians) group as neighborhood institutions and interviewing multiple Park Slope residents who describe a lesbian atmosphere in the residential and commercial districts.

More persuasive yet is Sarah Elwood's discussion of lesbian living arrangements in the residential areas of Minneapolis and St. Paul. Even (or especially) in semisuburban residential settings of single family homes, the lesbian presence can transform a neighborhood as radically as gay men's ability to develop whole districts in urban centers—*because* of the less anonymous, more settled and organized living situation these women have chosen for themselves and in some cases their children. Elwood considers the instance of a lesbian couple walking down the street holding hands in such a setting (24), and I am struck by the potential for enlightenment and the danger of retaliatory violence such a gesture represents. Thus lesbians seeking to live their lives in these "scattered," quiet pockets of residential community may be surprised that the privacy they sought there was in fact more easily obtained on a busy, anonymous city street *or* may have moved to such an environment for the explicit purpose of claiming home space in an intently politicized way.

For all the evidence marshaled on the issue of lesbian visibility, however, each of the examples above is countered by numerous counterexamples of continuing *un*equal, or at least markedly divergent, forms of gay and lesbian visibility—sometimes within the course of these same arguments. Bell and Valentine, for instance, feel that Adler and Brenner's description of lesbians as "*quasi-underground*" successfully counters Castells's theory, adding that "lesbian spaces are there if you know what you are looking for. . . . '[L]esbian ghettos' . . . are ghettos by name and not by nature. There are no lesbian bars, stores, or businesses in these neighbourhoods, neither are there countercultural institutions such as alternative bookstores and cooperative bookstores. The lesbians in these towns leave *no trace of their sexuality on the landscape*" (6, emphases added). Lo and Healy add that, as opposed to the findings of Castells, lesbian space "is revealed by more recent work as *subterranean and disguised*" (31, emphases added). Must we not, however, understand that these new terms do less to revise Castells's argument than simply reword (and thus reinforce) it?

Castells's original claims indeed smack of an essentialism appropriately countered by these writings; meanwhile, dispelling the (outsider's) view of static, eternal gay and lesbian "types" responding "naturally" to their divergent sex-based instincts should not blind us to the fact (even the positive, productive fact) that important differences between gay and lesbian urban lifestyles remain to be recognized and interpreted.

Elsewhere in their Introduction, despite their efforts to the contrary, the *Queers in Space* editors admit that "[a]lthough we searched diligently to find a broad range of contributors, *Queers in Space* still reflects the dichotomy of women forging communality in space and men having sex in it" (10). Rothenberg describes the protest march against antigay violence in a Park Slope diner as a founding moment of that lesbian neighborhood, while shopping and/or home-based social networking are the focus elsewhere in her essay, as well as in essays by Elwood, Lo and Healy, and Johnston and Valentine. Conversely, book-length discussions edited by William L. Leap and by David Higgs (both with all-male contributor slates) and authored by Michael P. Brown discuss gay public sex specifically as this relates to *men*, whose culture—represented by gay bars and bookstores, health clubs and baths, public parks and toilets, highway rest stops, and beach resort areas in world cities throughout history—is treated in analytic detail, to the near-total or total exclusion of the lesbian counterpart.[3] Munt's discussion of the cruising lesbian *flâneur* and S&M-themed writing by Pat Califia and Sue Golding represent singular exceptions to this otherwise overwhelming discursive tendency. Yet Munt's article contains a single brief paragraph devoted to her own role as a public sex participant (or at least initiator of sexual contact), with the remainder of the writing focused on various novelists and cultural critics who have adopted the *flâneur* as a protagonist in their work. Elsewhere, Rothenberg's Park Slope is determined after all to have "a distinct lack of lesbian places" (172), with more than one interviewee "mention[ing] the lack of any lesbian cafés, bookstores, bars, or other centres that could function as a community unifier" (172).

In another vein, Marc Stein, in his history of gay and lesbian culture in Philadelphia, creates the sense of parallel careers, balancing treatment of men's and women's history through almost constant references to "lesbians and gay men."[4] Yet his introduction contains many disclaimers—that "lesbians more often confronted public invisibility whereas gay men more often confronted negative visibility" (11); that "there were significant differences between the sexes . . . and between types of space" (10); and that "the vast majority of [textual

representations encountered in his research] . . . focused on male
sexualities" (10). Stein intends to "resist fully reproducing this focus
by devoting significant attention to the references to female sexualities
that did appear" (10), but his laudable effort to correct an imbalance
obscures an important problem—lesbian invisibility in Philadelphia
and the misogyny that accounts for this—and possible solutions of a
less textual, perhaps more oral-narrative or creative nature.[5] As with
several examples considered above, positing an urban lesbian visibility
commensurate with the gay male counterpart has important political
impact, but when these assessments do not yet accord with lesbians'
lived reality, we risk losing sight of this issue in all of its urgency and
complexity.

I am interested in these several attempts to minimize imbalance in
the histories and sociologies of these groups, so as to redress wrongs
or perhaps assuage guilt feelings while downplaying fairly significant
differences in space-occupation styles. Those adopting this technique
seem intent to present a "united front" to both straight and gay
readerships, shielding the evidence of persistent inequality or gay
misogyny from a homophobic audience ready to exploit such weakness, and reassuring gay and lesbian readers with a stance of solidarity.
Yet these differences can lead to necessary epistemological inquiries,
regarding defining distinctions between these two related but separate
cultural groups, while the effort to ignore these tends to pathologize
both groups or, by the arguments of some gay sexuality theorists, to
diminish the specificity of lesbian lifestyle expression.

In several of the readings considered here, lesbians are seen to
reside in urban neighborhoods in great numbers and to be transiently
identifiable in their tours through the living and shopping districts.
Yet a permanent, recognizable presence—for the benefit of passing
fellow-travelers curious about the lesbian atmosphere of such places
and of homophobic straights who would be better off encountering
such visibility more often—is decidedly missing.[6] One finds such
visibility, of course, in the rainbow-flagged commercial establishments
that line the streets of gay (male) neighborhoods and mark off territory in progressive, even revolutionary ways; despite its bourgeois
shadings, gay men's occupation of commercial public space is often
considered to be more radical, because it is not only much riskier, but
also much more potentially transformative of the larger social scene.[7]
Thus another distinction between gay male and lesbian lifestyles to
analyze, in addition to the cultural/sexual and private/public
dichotomies that by no means simply distinguish the two groups, is
residential/commercial: what are the issues of private space, public sex,

and queer visibility attaching to lesbians' more "residential" style of urban habitation versus gay men's more "commercial" (ad)ventures?

Notable in regard to this question is not Elwood's (ultimately hypothetical) example of women holding hands in a Twin Cities residential neighborhood but of an actual lesbian couple she interviewed who "flew a rainbow flag in their front yard and put up lesbian-related posters in their windows" (17). Such a gesture seems designed to single-handedly rezone a single family dwelling into a commercial establishment that hangs "ads" in its windows and posts ostentatious lawn signage to "sell" itself to a likely resistant customer base (i.e., the neighbors). Hardly the typical homeowner's decorating technique, especially the posters seem to promote a commodity within (lesbianism itself) and invite passersby to "consume" this commodity through willing or grudging acceptance (i.e., "We're here. Get used to it"). That this couple felt the need to be in-your-face about their sexuality in this way returns to a meaningful question: is it not enough to simply go about one's business as an interactive lesbian couple in a residential neighborhood to send a clear message as to one's sexual orientation and one's commitment to the suburban lifestyle? Is there a transforming (even revolutionizing) effect attached to the (problematically capitalist) commercial gay strip that these residential women sought to borrow from in the course of their sexual statement-making? What are gay men's and lesbians' shared and differing relations to the issues of commodification and gentrification in city neighborhoods, and how might these attachments limit or advance their commitment to otherwise leftist city politics?

I am struck by Michael Warner's aggressive defense of gay men's "reeking" consumptionism, calling in his remarks for an "imaginative" and "dialectical" view of capitalism (qtd. in Binnie 182) that would allow radical left gay men to indulge their bourgeois tastes with a comfortable conscience. The double-bind (if not outright hypocrisy) of this position is difficult to miss; even Jon Binnie, who cites Warner, completes his argument by critiquing London's gay Soho district for excluding "people who cannot afford the price of food and drink or are unwilling to pay the pink premium" (198) and quotes a more cautionary, overtly marxist statement from David Forrest (199, see also Sibalis 35). If, as it is widely acknowledged, gay men's higher income gives them greater power than lesbians to establish and patronize gay-centered businesses and renovate rundown housing that can not only rejuvenate an urban district but also price lower-income residents out of a market, then these classist entanglements must be confronted alongside the many revolutionary aspects of such neighborhood transformations, which I began to discuss above. Binnie warns that "[i]n times of economic recession, representations of gay men as uniformly affluent consumers must of course be treated with some care" (186), yet for better or worse the equation between "affluence" and "representation" itself—as this equation affects (and/or excludes) less affluent gays and many lesbians—seems more solidified with each "revitalized" city block and with each critical analysis constituting this field in gender and sexuality studies.[8]

While the writing surveyed here indicates lesbians' lesser investment (thus far) in recognizable commercial zones catering to a lesbian clientele, lesbians as well as gay men have been attached to the question of gentrification in various of these arguments. Maxine Wolfe has sought to problematize this connection by arguing that lesbian "space" is often shaped by the vicissitudes of *time*—"often [lesbian bars] are 'women's nights' at other bars" (318)—making them occasional, temporary, and ephemeral, while men's spaces are by contrast more established, locatable, and permanent. Elsewhere she is credited with

> classif[ying] gentrification as a process wholly detrimental to lesbian life. Lesbian bars tend to be in low-rent districts, and their owners and clientele are dependent on maintenance of such low rents; if a neighborhood is under gentrification pressures, landlords often need little excuse to raise rents, not least in hopes of attracting a more "desirable" clientele. (Rothenberg 178)

In this view, it might be gentrification at the hands of a gay male population that unwittingly or wittingly runs a lesbian establishment out of business. While not blaming gay men for the problem, Rothenberg notes that "gentrification" was responsible for causing the closure of Park Slope's only women's bookstore, LaPapaya, after a few years' business (175). Elsewhere, Michael P. Brown refers to a Christchurch lesbian bar "sited between two massage parlours" that "lasted little more than a year. According to some, its demise was explained because there were not enough lesbians to make the venue profitable; according to others, the inhospitable patriarchal location made the venue unattractive to any self-respecting feminist-lesbian" (81). Contrasting Vancouver's gentrified (primarily gay) West-end to its "funky" (primarily lesbian) eastern districts, Lo and Healy in part corroborate Wolfe when they argue that "[w]ithin this flamboyant materialism, the West-end lesbian is much less successful at proclaiming her visibility to herself and other lesbians" (39). What is it that constitutes the at-odds relationship between materialism and lesbian visibility in the cityscape under consideration here? Is visibility threatened primarily when the

West-end lesbian resident/visitor finds herself priced out of that market, or do even "comfortable" lesbian lifestyles find something resistant and suffocating in the "flamboyant materialism" that must be largely attributed to gay male cultural production?

Despite lesbians' general removal from the issue of economic gentrification, their frequently documented tendency to occupy low-rent housing in "diverse," "ethnically mixed," "working class" neighbor-hoods[9] keeps this question open a moment longer. Rothenberg notes that even the previously affordable Park Slope neighborhood has become too pricey for some lesbian inhabitants, who "move into bordering neighbourhoods, extending the area of *gentrification*" (178, emphasis added). If higher rents forced lesbians out of Park Slope in the first place, evidently the "gentrification" of surrounding areas created by their move has little to do with their income levels. What Rothenberg indicates elsewhere but does not connect to her comment here is that the Park Slope lesbian "class" is a pretty "classy" bunch, despite their lack of monetary means—college educated, middle-class, and attentive to the upkeep of their homes and neighborhoods. Does this profile lead to the sort of neighborhood beautification that forces out those less interested or less able to maintain homes in similar fashion? With her reference to "extending gentrification," Rothenberg implies it does, although Lo and Healy do not indicate the same phenomenon in Vancouver's eastern neighborhoods—which remains " 'funky' and interesting" (38), elsewhere " 'dirty' and 'crime-ridden'"(39)—despite the lesbian presence observed there. To the degree that lesbians' gravita-tion toward "ethnic" inner city neighborhoods has a whitening, gentri-fying effect that forces lower-income residents of color from their homes, lesbians' own involvement with the troubling aspects of gentrifi-cation must be addressed in the critical discussion.

On several occasions when distinctions between lesbian and gay urban occupation styles are not denied but instead recognized and analyzed by sexuality theorists, the potential conflict that may emerge from two populations seeking to differently inhabit the same patch of (ultimately limited) urban turf is a stated or implied theme of great importance.[10] Although he means to do otherwise, Gordon Brett Ingram, for instance, actually inverts the hierarchy of gay men's and lesbian's claim to outdoor space. He attempts to open the landscape for both gay and lesbian occupation when he argues that

[queer] use of public space is not limited to sex acts but is more often a space for complex group interactions, which can include women's softball and political demonstrations as well as anonymous orgies in

a park. Public outdoor space becomes strategic because it is difficult to
engage in such activities indoors and to find room for larger groups of
people. (" 'Open' Space" 104)

Note, however, the way the women-centered claims to space seem
much stronger here: while certainly it is nearly impossible (and, in the
case of the latter example, largely pointless) to hold a softball game or
a political demonstration indoors, rare would have to be the orgy
that got so large or explosive that it would not fit into some sort of
indoor setting, even if that were a warehouse downtown. In this
example, it is lesbians' traditional activities that seem to more naturally
and necessarily belong in the park or street, while men's sexualized
use of the outdoors has been acknowledged by many to be purposely
gratuitous.[11]

Finally, Sue-Ellen Case has argued (at a roundtable discussion)
against the assumption that gay men's outdoor sexual activity is
inherently more radical or subversive, using gay women's wider
political involvement as the preferred counterexample:

> If you simply have a one-issue politics and it's organized around
> sexuality or sexual practices, you lose any critique of other kinds of
> things, like the military or capitalism, then you have no broader critique
> on which sexual politics are based and you can go fuck in the bushes,
> but it doesn't mean that you end up having a very radical agenda other
> than that. . . . [W]hen sexual critiques are separated from other kinds of
> critiques, then one opens the door to more conservative agendas.
> ("The Final Frontier" 329–30)

Case thus challenges the assumption that gay men's use of public
space makes the more radical statement (335); her comment reminds
us that the discrepancy between gay and lesbian income levels may not
be the only factor explaining their different forms of cultural engagement. In other words, it is misguided to assume that lesbians *would
automatically* take part in the same kind of public sex practices if only
they could afford them, if only it were not so dangerous for a woman
in the park at night, and if only other such hypothetical situations
were real instead, when in fact lesbians may have in mind radically
different ideas about how to queer the public environment.[12]

COMING OUT OR STAYING IN?

While visibility carried terrific risks in the pre-Stonewall era and
certainly does to a degree today, "invisibility"—the closet, repression,
or denial—was and is equally anathema to the establishment of gay

rights and is therefore not considered a viable alternative to this risk. Some contemporary theorists may continue to advocate surreptitiousness, subversion, and guaranteed rights to privacy as preferred alternatives to dangerous public exposure, but others weigh the pros and cons of a *visible* queer existence, and again this is a sex-inflected discussion.[13] For certainly gay women's traditional occasions for outdoor self-expression (the softball game, the music festival, the reproductive rights rally) are read as both more appropriately "visible" (socially acceptable) *and* potentially *invisible*—so sexually indeterminate as to be indistinguishable from the similarly styled heterocentric activities occurring around them. Conversely, gay men's more sexualized public pursuits must be understood as intensely visible—so in-your-face as to be impossible to ignore when brought to light[14] but so thoroughly disruptive of social norms as to be rarely if ever in fact brought to light. As John Rechy has put it succinctly, "The only time it's political is when you get arrested for it" (338).[15] In this model, traditional lesbian activities occupy a middle ground between the extremes of gay men's acts: invisible, these acts are politically void; exposed to the public light, they may eventually inure the public to less intense forms of gay or lesbian visibility but in the short term will act as a lightning rod for negative public attention.

These issues are complicated by the fact that public "gay space" is as importantly defined for the communities inhabiting it as for the homophobic "general public" who would claim exclusive rights to urban (and for that matter, suburban and rural) turf—sometimes through violent repression and sometimes through refusal of recognition—and whose very homophobia in fact shapes the character of the conflict here, creating the dilemma facing gays and lesbians in this instance: shall gay "visibility" be constituted by examples of graphic sexual, organized political, or politically correct communal forms of expression? Shall the sexual elements of gay life be shielded (at least behind bushes or the cover of darkness but perhaps or preferably within bars, sex clubs, and private homes) from the public spotlight, with only protests, parades, and other daytime demonstrations allowed as the main features of a public gay identity? Or shall it be argued that the only effective political statement regarding the gay right to public space and self-expression is made *through* the publication of outlaw sexual displays? Under the watch of a homophobic and easily scandalized mainstream, for whom whatever gays or lesbians do together in public (play softball, hold hands) will be construed as a sexual and a political act, the answer to these questions cannot be "all of the above." Operating under the pseudoeconomic law that "bad" sex drives out "good," a mainstream community's exposure (through media or police reports, if not through direct witnessing) to scenes of overtly queer, overtly sexual activity in public will cause any comparatively less scandalous attempt at gay or lesbian visibility (the Pride march, the softball league) to bear the stigmatizing mark of these more radical activities or, worse, to fade back into total invisibility. (See also Walters 17.) We see, therefore, that the issue is divided between diverging gay and lesbian modes of public space occupation and by a homophobically myopic "public" itself, enlarging these divisions by forcing this diverse community to choose one form or the other.

CONCLUSION

Throughout this chapter, I have been less interested to define intellectual or physical impasses between actual straight feminists, lesbians, or gay men than to examine the aporiac structure of representations of these. Returning to our original examples, Orwell's *1984* and Hollinghurst's *Swimming-Pool Library*, we recall that the "actual" figures in question were mere story characters; perforce, the inverse relationships I discerned occurred solely at the level of (primary and secondary) text. In later examples, human actors were in view, but the analysis turned not, for example, toward conflicts dividing straight and lesbian feminists but toward the crisis surrounding Rich's attempt to theorize these with the lesbian continuum—not toward actual tensions (or harmonious modes of coexistence) between gay and lesbian urban dwellers but toward the ways in which the literature describing these groups' living patterns divide, and threaten each other's approach to, vital issues.

In each example considered, homophobic elements (be these straight feminists themselves or the nonacademic mainstream) were seen to complicate and intensify the debate already under way: in the first discussion, the mainstream tendency to sissify all things homosexual comes from without but triggers a somewhat misogynist response by those branded with the effeminate label. In the second discussion, the feminist tendency to water down lesbianism to strengthen its own position cancels out the feminist attempt to build coalitions that do not lead automatically to assimilation. In the last discussion, lesbians' and gay men's divergent modes of public self-expression are forced into conflict—in part because of a broad range of homophobic reaction to their visibility—from the ultra-right's stringent attack on a gay presence anywhere in the national landscape to the reservations of otherwise progressive straights, who question the prospect of city (let alone suburban or rural) streets given over to public sex consumption.

While every attempt must be made to remove the barriers created by homophobia from the examples of cultural representation, and of course of lived experience, considered here, I contend that necessary and productive critical impasses amongst these three groups would persist in even a utopian, posthomophobia environment, so inherent are they to the divergent ways in which each school of thought simply defines itself and approaches the broader culture. Each makes a particular, vital contribution to the discussion; the marked lack of theoretical overlap, as well as the threat posed to counterarguments in the very articulation of each school's position, was the focus of this chapter and will be in the remainder of the book. Sampling variously from multiple aspects of culture here (language, literature, cultural theory, urban environments), in the final two chapters, I will treat lesbian-, gay-, and feminist-theory's divergent methods of reading fiction and viewing film. The focus will remain on each school's inclination to read a literary or cinematic text in a manner that precludes interpretation by a fellow-school, as well as the resistance to harmonized interpretations generated by the texts themselves. My intent is not to solve, but to only describe and analyze, the dilemmas posed on these interpretive occasions, searching out the approaches and themes that define each school and pose it in dynamic tension with its others.

CHAPTER 4

WHAT WE READ: LESBIAN, GAY, AND FEMINIST APPROACHES TO FICTION

AUTHORIAL IDENTITY AND INTENT

Scene from a novel: a man confronts a woman—someone he has pursued with passion throughout the story but who has turned her reputation for sexual aggressiveness to her own advantage in every instance. He is of ordinary qualities while she is talented and beautiful, and the disparity incites the male character toward evermore hostile urges to capture and conquer her. In a climactic scene he uses his knowledge of her sexual proclivities to trap and disable her. She is assaulted, raped, and dies in a hospital a few days later. Despite her dire injuries, including severe head trauma, her beauty and intelligence remain intact, and she dies with a knowing smile on her face.

What evidence, within the account related here, would lead a feminist reader to embrace or vilify this novel? Clearly, a man has killed a woman, a crime we condemn in real life, yet the representational nature of the act complicates the matter: do we read a misogynist depiction of the classic "ballbreaker" or "tease," whose downfall at the hands of her mistreated suitor is meant to deeply satisfy? Or has the same scenario been played out with almost sadistic intensity but from a *feminist* perspective, to outrage and transform complacent readers? Reading this work as an exercise in misogyny, the feminist critic might interpret the woman's enigmatic deathbed smile as a purposely placed irritant, a sort of thing that refuses to die, that hints at some secret she takes to the grave, and is thus meant to heighten our pleasure when it is at last extinguished in death. Even more offensively, the smile may signify the woman's blissful memory of the brutal experience; she now figures as the classic rape victim (especially one with a history of sexual forthrightness) who "asked for it" and dies fulfilled, content at last as the subjugated figure she has always secretly dreamed of being. Finally, this "misogynist" reading—that is, this feminist's negative reading—would isolate authorial attempts to manipulate reader sentiment against the female character, to depict an aggressiveness and arrogance we are forced to hate, and to set up novelistic parameters that constrain even women readers within a misogynist male mindset.[1]

Strikingly, the feminist's converse, positive reading might include many of these same observations but assign the opposite value to them—cheering the rape victim's unsinkable pluck, agonizing over her eventual demise, and appreciating the novel (and its author) for providing the instructive, cathartic experience. From this favorable standpoint, a misogynist outrage has been depicted in graphic, arresting detail, designed to cause female *and male* readers to recoil at its horrors and develop a strengthened resolve to prevent such abuse in their lives and the lives of others. The woman's liberated sexuality would be read as a dynamic life force, wrongly construed as threatening by the pursuing male, and the slip-up that led to her capture as a humanizing tragic flaw. Her final wordless smile, fetishized since the artistic renderings of Da Vinci, might actually draw complaints from some feminist readers, while others would appreciate the subtle hint of women's enduring power. Such subtly, however, would register weakly in the larger context of the woman's death, without which the novel's political impact would be markedly reduced, the crisis depicted less urgently intolerable.

The critical impasse suggested in these contradictory readings necessitates a return to questions modern readers set aside when they embarked upon the poststructural interpretative era that coincides otherwise so well with their politicized approach to text analysis— namely questions related to authorial identity and intent. These notions, having been challenged by author-debunking theorists such as Foucault and Barthes and by the post–New Critical drift away from insisting upon (or even caring about) intentionality in literature, reassert themselves as valid areas of inquiry as we wonder *who* exactly is behind this narrative (male or female? conservative or progressive?) and what exactly s/he had in mind.[2] A male author's name attached to the above scenario would likely lead the feminist critic toward the negative reading, while a woman's name may cause us to look favorably upon this same scene's ultimate political intent.

Substituting "straight" and "gay" for "man" and "woman" in this scenario, we raise similar issues: how does the reader know when a homophobic hate crime is depicted for the purpose of denigrating gays as opposed to raising the ire of gay-affirmative readers? When is the "pathetic" gay or lesbian "victim" an offensive, disabling stereotype and when the necessary figure of pathos that may instill in the most phobic reader greater awareness of his implication in the problem? When does that deathbed Mona Lisa smile signal a tragically addled sensibility succumbing to the system that seeks to destroy it, and when is it the indelible sign of subversion, a gesture admittedly subtle and insignificant yet perhaps the only one possible in this still stringently homophobic world? When is gay bashing simply bashing for its own sake, and when is it penned in goriest detail to bring about the end of gay bashing in the extraliterary world?

Certainly, we know that in our lives as citizens and activists, nothing incites us to concerted, productive action as does a heinous violation of a person's or group's human rights because of race, income level, sex, or sexual orientation. Dare we confront the activist stripe within us that delights not in the crimes themselves but in the intensities of our hyperarticulated, physically charged-up responses to these? In the galvanizing presence of an enemy and his victim, we experience the individual or collective rush that comes with knowing what must be done and, if we are activists in the true sense of the word, with doing something about it. In the literary register, when a heroine escapes her antagonist, flipping the bird behind her as she goes, we may feel admiration, delight, or relief, but not those viscerally empowering sensations of pity and fear that motivate us to new mindsets and progressive action. Whence comes our need to speak, act, or create change when confronted with the happy feminist, gay, or lesbian hero? Whence would come so much of our scholarly output without scenes of violence, literary or otherwise, to rail against?[3] Certainly, in one respect, sex and politics of author matter not at all: whether such scenes are penned by a misogynist/homophobic male or a radical queer or feminist, the progressive interpretation speaks against violence. Additionally, a strong response—either negative or positive—is likely to increase readership for the controversial text in question, regardless of whether it is the celebrity status and bank account of an authorial enemy or ally that grow in response to this. Meanwhile, before the lesbian, gay, or feminist critic can formulate a response, s/he must discern a basic feeling about the work—condemnatory or congratulatory—as the entire tenor of the argument will be affected by this primary "take." Authorial intent thus re-presents itself as a nagging question, and the interpretation will be slanted in one direction or another depending upon the critic's understanding of this intention.

The dilemma is deepened by the fact that there is no automatic connection between authorial sex (or sexual orientation) and political tilt. Certainly, the older a novel tends to be, the more likely even authors belonging to oppressed groups will toe an antifeminist line or fail to acknowledge gay or lesbian undertones in their work; while the more recent a novel is, the more likely a mainstream (i.e., straight white male) author will espouse a feminist or gay-tolerant view, whether he truly holds with one or not. The difficulty created by these uncertainties is significant when we realize that, at the level of representation itself, misogynist and feminist gestures, as well as homophilic and homophobic ones, are *identical*—that historical context; changing narrative styles; irony, ambiguity, and subtext; and reader response can make a novel's political intent impossible to declare with certainty.[4] The complexities of lived experience, often reduced to moral black-and-whiteness on occasions of violent crime perpetrated by one human against another, remain complex and undecidable in the literary register; since it is understood, before the story even begins, that none of this is really happening, it is also agreed that moral codes governing real life will be allowed to shift and expand in the literary realm. Thus the very complexities and contrivances for which we turn to literature in the first place create the discursive situation that prevents us from trusting even basic perceptions of what we read, of whether we like a novel or simply love to hate it. In the case of either scene, either author, either interpretation, the lesbian, gay, or feminist critic risks the accusation of "reading into" a resistant textual moment to wrest a subversive comment from it. A countercritic could follow with an immediate refutation, since in fact the progressive reading rests like a house of cards upon an arrangement of language stubbornly unwilling to tip its hand, while the counter-reading is equally open to challenge.

To nuance what is an admittedly extreme example in the scene constructed at the outset, I suggest four modes of text expression drawn upon by feminist and queer theorists of literature and culture, two overtly political tones and two more subtle moods, where in fact much modern feminist, lesbian, and gay criticism takes place. In the examples discussed above, the hypothetical critic was forced to choose between extreme political views: virulent hostility against women or gays *or* unabashed support for one of these groups, albeit through radical means. In the discussion that follows, I will be less interested in the unabashed, all-out feminist, lesbian, or gay text than in those that have presented critics a much greater challenge—and for some, a much more interesting opportunity—by hinting at radical politics or sexuality but then burying these at the level of subtext. Feminist, gay, and lesbian critics have become adept at observing these radical sub-texts even (or especially?) in the hysterias that define virulently misog-ynist or homophobic works; in less extreme cases—in works that seem to have nothing to do with feminist or gay-affirmative subject matter—the critic discerns a telling subtext but still must decide whether to label this phenomenon subversive or inadvertent: that is, to give the author him or herself credit for laying the revolutionary groundwork or to speak in terms of a text that breaks free of its oppressive authorship to produce its own striking effects, unearthed by the critic him or herself. We are certain, for instance, to credit Charlotte Perkins Gilman or Oscar Wilde with couching a liberatory message or deviant sensibility within nonthreatening literary forms, but what about Jane Austen? What about Henry James? Shall they be credited with their novels' subversive qualities or faulted for not admitting to and pushing center-stage these core truths? In this dis-cussion, I will be as interested in debates amongst lesbian, gay, and feminist critics themselves as in the contest that takes place between the gender/sexuality critic and the enigmatic text.

RESISTING READERS, RESISTING TEXTS

In her landmark feminist literary analysis, Judith Fetterly indeed relies on authorial intent—found in William Faulkner's comments about his own characters—to demonstrate the feminist slant of "A Rose for Emily." For me, her case rests less on Faulkner's review of his work than on her distinction between the story's title (clearly a product of Faulkner's own devising) and the town's judgmental narrative per-spective. Because it is the author (in the title) who refers to the story's main character as simply "Emily" and because it is the town/narrator who insists upon the romanticizing, confining "*Miss* Emily," I indeed feel the author's efforts to rescue his protagonist from the town's clutches by insisting first and last on her humanization. Beyond this persuasive observation, however, Fetterly's (support for Faulkner's) critique of the town's behavior is a more difficult sell. The irony she reads in the town's waiting "decently" until Miss Emily is in the ground before moving eagerly to dismantle her decaying house is meant to condemn the town's actions. As I will note in greater detail below, however, irony is less often "a truth universally acknowledged" than a privately discerned tone of voice that does not translate easily into the silent medium of published criticism; for myself, the dwelling's terrific stench (courtesy, again, of the author himself) emanating from Miss Emily's enclosed life and suppressed criminal activity (her jilting lover has lain rotting on the bridal bed for decades) provides more than adequate rationale for the town's prurient nosiness, and the gusts of fresh air promised by the its forceful intrusions make these entirely forgivable.

For Fetterly, what stinks in this small southern town is patriarchy itself, the blind reinforcement of class and sex roles that keeps the men in positions of power and yet also keeps them in denial as to what "ladies" such as Miss Emily are ultimately capable of. However, Fetterly's effort to locate this bad smell in the townsmen works against the story's own inclination to settle this odor and related grotesqueries upon none other than Emily herself. After all, it is her rude refusal to receive the town's representative, her oppressive relationship to her Negro servant, her bloated body, her face with its fatty ridges, her eyes "like two small pieces of coal pressed into a lump of dough," and her nymphomaniacal crimes that the feminist reader must confront. Fetterly's sophisticated summation—"Homer Barron's rotted corpse . . . reflects back to [the townsmen] the perverseness of their own prurient interests in Emily" (36)—leaves room for question: while Homer's corpse may indeed be doing this reflecting, are the men who break down this door actually noting this image of themselves? Has the narrator, himself a viewer through the lens of patriarchy, figured it out? Is it only we readers (including Faulkner and the savvier members of his original audience) who see the townsmen reflected in Homer's stinking corpse, or do we perhaps only catch our own prurient curiosities reflected there? In other words, where exactly is the feminism in this text? At what point does it begin, how organic is it to the story itself, on how many levels does it operate? Where does it depend on a relationship with narrative or dramatic irony, and does that dependence strengthen or weaken its presence in the story? While Fetterly demonstrates effectively that the political persuasions of literary *criticism* (and the "phallic critics" and "resisting readers" who generated this) are relatively easy to discern, her work also inadvertently reveals that the layerings and multiplicities of literary language make such black-and-white determinations in primary texts all but impossible to prove.

While she is confident of Faulkner's progressive stance, Fetterly wrestles more intently with Nathaniel Hawthorne's "The Birthmark," a text that refuses to lean decisively in one direction or another. Again, her core thesis stands up well: "It is testimony . . . to the pervasive sexism of our culture that most readers would describe 'The Birthmark' as a story of failure rather than as the success story it really is—the demonstration of how to murder your wife and get away with it" (22). Yet does the text condemn (or merely describe? or smirkingly promote?) the successful murder that takes place at story's end? Fetterly begins her assessment with reference to "Hawthorne's ambivalence" (22), cuing her audience that this reading will take a circuitous path. While she observes that "Hawthorne is writing a story about the sickness of men, not a story about the flawed and imperfect nature of women" (27), she later notes that women characters functioning as mirrors "are projections, not people" and that "Hawthorne's tale is a classic example of the woman as mirror" (29). The pendulum swings again when Fetterly notes, "Hawthorne's attitude toward men and their fantasies is more critical than either Irving's or Anderson's" (30), while finally her acknowledgment of this author's refusal to be categorized leaves her reader more confused than ever: "While 'The Birthmark' is by no means explicitly feminist . . ., still it is impossible to read this story without being aware that *Georgiana is completely in Aylmer's power*" (31, emphasis added). Yet under what flag are we to place the italicized portion of the preceding quote: Hawthorne's misogyny, his feminism, or Fetterly's feminist response to Hawthorne's misogyny? One must be inside Fetterly's head at this point to understand whether we should feel energized or demoralized by Georgiana's victim status, and many may decide unilaterally to read such victimization as cause to dismiss the notion of Hawthorne as feminist.

Finally, Fetterly refers to Hawthorne's "implicit feminism" (31)— a term suggesting perfectly the half-baked quality of the progressive politics she attempts to tease out of this novel. She finds concrete support for his (and her own) position in a "dramatic" quote from the story: " 'It must not be concealed, however, that the impression wrought by this fairy sign manual varied exceedingly, according to the difference of temperament in the beholders' " (31). Implicit feminism indeed! Any reader listening in at this moment for a bold manifesto of women's rights will come away disappointed. Hardly a condemnation of the murderous Aylmer, this overly subtle, convoluted defense of Georgiana's appeal to various "beholders" indicates exactly the sort of feminism Fetterly has been required to outline throughout her reading—something furtive, weakly conceptualized, and gasping for life. She hears a heartening "touch of the satisfaction of revenge" (33) in Georgiana's last words, but in fact the doomed woman's forgiving

reference to "My poor Aylmer" and his "lofty," "noble" efforts convey
no such satisfaction. Likely Fetterly is listening intently for strains of
irony in Georgiana's dying words but is instead forced to supply them
herself: "Since dying is the only option, better to make the most of it"
(33). While readers find much to value in Fetterly's argument, they
may also sense how difficult it is finally to distinguish feminism from
its murderous opposite in literary representation.

EROTOPHOBIA VERSUS OVERSEXEDNESS

Fetterly is less forgiving of authors (Hemingway, Sherwood
Anderson, and Washington Irving) and critics elsewhere in her text,
yet even her toughest critiques are somewhat diminished for contemporary readers, due to the pronounced heterocentrism of her
approach, which cannot help but capitulate to the masculinist mindset
it is her primary intent to challenge. Her every reference to "sexuality" is actually a reference to heterosexuality, narrowed further (and
sapped of erotic charge) by being simply another word for fertility.
Reading "The Birthmark," Georgiana's "sexuality" is automatically
linked to what is "unclean" (i.e., menstrual) about her (25), while
later Aylmer is jealous of her "sexuality" and counters with his own
"desire to create human life" (27). Reading *A Farewell to Arms*,
Catherine's fertility and pregnancy are concepts interchangeable with
her sexuality (50), while emphasis is given to the impressive powers of
her womb (64–65). At this moment, Fetterly's heterocentrism bears
an uncanny resemblance to Hemingway's own; she quotes from a
character who leers at Catherine and tells Frederick, "She will make
you a fine boy" (Fetterly 50). In chapter 1, I explored the erotophobic tendencies of some feminist writing, as well as gay and lesbian perceptions of erotophobic feminist politics; here, Fetterly's "maternalist"
perspective reinforces this traditional perception, even as it has been
called into question by feminist literary critics writing more recently.

Ten years later, Elizabeth A. Flynn and Patrocinio P. Schweickhart,
the editors of *Gender and Reading* opposed Fetterly's acts of "resistance" to the gesture of "leaning into" an adversarial text, as described by
Jean Kennard in her essay "Theory for Lesbian Readers" contained in
that collection. While I find ultimately that Kennard's position is as
oppositional as Fetterly's, in fact Kennard and the editors discerning the
distinction between straight and lesbian approaches to reading move
toward the concept of appropriation, which Fetterly made no use of in
her work but which is frequently accessed by sex, gender, and sexuality
critics today. Where Fetterly looked at misogynist male texts and felt

herself either absented or "immasculated" (coerced into adopting the masculine viewpoint), a contemporary theorist such as Terry Castle, writing nearly twenty years after Fetterly, may observe blatant lesbophobia in an equally conservative text and extract a positive lesbian interpretation from it anyway. While the technique allows modern critics broader access to resisting texts, authorial identity and intent remain vital questions, since appropriation is a stance appropriate only to adversarial—either phobically antigay or inadvertently gay-affirmative—writings (whichever those may be determined to be). Despite the nearly two decades separating them, Fetterly's and Castle's texts compare well, as two groundbreaking attempts to delineate viable ways to subvert critical tradition and to find one's underrepresented or misrepresented self among literary masterworks. Yet if Castle's feels like the more adroit analysis by modern standards, it is as subject to the charge of oversexing her approach to literature—more specifically, seeing lesbian sexuality where it may not actually be—as Fetterly was to erotophobia.

For Castle, the "apparitional lesbian" is an antilesbian device—a ghost-figure in stories of women's love and friendship (e.g., works by DeFoe, Diderot)—that manifests as a disembodied "memory" or "visitor" who shares a desexualized kiss with a female protagonist, then disappears forever. Castle points out that such ghosting "drain[s the lesbian figure] of any sensual or moral authority" (*The Apparitional Lesbian* 6), that it is a form of "humiliat[ion] and excoriat[ion]" (7) in James's *Bostonians* and a "murderous allegorizing" (7) in the Western literary tradition. Meanwhile, this same figure has materialized, so to speak, in overtly lesbian novels such as Radclyffe Hall's *Well of Loneliness*, where a " 'legion' of spirits" (7) produces an orgasmic moment for the protagonist at novel's end. How (and why) a modernist lesbian author would appropriate Baudelaire's "sickly 'phantoms' wandering eternally in a ghastly living hell" (6) so as to construct a "palpable" and "haunting" cultural icon is explained by Castle as a "paradoxical affirmation of lesbian existence": "Within the very imagery of negativity lies the possibility of recovery" (7). But does this savvy thesis entirely control for the reader's lingering concern that the "ghost" in an authentically lesbian work such as Hall's is a most problematic choice of image?[5] How in fact does one reembody or literalize (instead of merely metaphorize, hint, or suggest) lesbian eroticism when a flitting, fleeting apparition is all we are given to work with? How do we know that the revolutionary advances made in works by early authors such as Hall are not significantly limited by faint-hearted (yet entirely understandable) capitulation to powerful social forces that had insisted for centuries upon the lesbian/ghost equation?[6]

While for the most part Castle persuasively renders the ghost figure's double life, questions remain, especially perhaps for nonlesbian readers: when straight audiences are blamed for not recognizing the "mortal and magnificent" lesbian Garbo on screen, even while Castle describes Garbo as "absent[ing] her [lesbian] self" (2) from *Queen Christina*; when the ghosted lesbian figure can only be contrasted to her more culturally visible "twin brother" by pejoratively attributing this greater visibility to the "male homosexual's . . . ingratiating" cultural pose (2); when Castle indignantly defends her right to "commit an offense against good manners by daring to speak of lesbianism without mentioning male homosexuality" (12), then on the following page criticizes Eve Sedgwick for daring to speak about male homosexuality without including the lesbian perspective[7]—these several attempts to "have it both ways" on behalf of the lesbian subject may cause readers to question the validity of the just as slippery apparitional. Can a figure so detrimental to lesbian subjectivity be equally, simultaneously beneficial, or is it upon the critic to ultimately draw a line in the sand, emphasizing rather than de-emphasizing the monumental differences between homophobia and gay affirmativity?

This concern deepens as we turn to Castle's reading of Sylvia Townsend Warner's presumably groundbreaking *Summer Will Show*. As opposed to male-authored, voyeuristic depictions of sex between women, or writings by lesbian authors (e.g., Cather, Yourcenar) with no discernible lesbian theme, Warner's *Summer* is, for Castle, classified "paradigmatically" as lesbian fiction for being not only lesbian-authored but also for depicting a "sexual relationship between women" (74).[8] Yet the sex in Warner's novel is, finally, as apparitional—or we might say elliptical—as it is in Hall's earlier work: in a pivotal scene Warner's heroine issues a "triumphant cry," then "hours later" her lover sucks on an oyster, providing the punch line to an in-joke we are pleased to recognize through Castle's deft analysis, but shall the thinness of this moment as the novel's sum total of overt sexual content not be acknowledged? Even the humor—the joke itself—must be seen to defuse erotic tension as humor almost always does. Castle treats this text to a lengthy, scene-by-scene commentary, reinforcing its status as key in her revisionary canon. While her reading demonstrates the relationship between the novel's heroines, the bond depicted is more romantic than sexual, indicating that while this novel may represent a step up from Hall's more agonized treatment of the theme, it falls short of a total revolution.

Castle notes that lesbian audiences tend to seek out, appropriate, and embrace lesbian figurations, "whether a given work of literature depicted love between women in a negative or positive light" (64). Meanwhile, there may be an important distinction between a lesbian audience (Castle included) that declines to distinguish between positive and negative lesbian images (or for that matter between intended and inadvertent lesbian images) and an audience that sees lesbianism (or, here, frank lesbian eroticism) even where it simply does not exist. Although Castle was right to begin her work by critiquing straight audiences for failing to see lesbianism when it glares down at them from the silver screen, equally troubling is the opposite impulse—to identify lesbian sexuality when this identification is exaggerated or premature. Such arguments can mislead the reader to believe certain milestones have been reached at certain historical junctures when in fact they have not. Returning once more to our comparison with Fetterly, we observe both of these critics engaged in the difficult work of extracting a self-affirming reading from a less than fully forthcoming text. If Fetterly's discernment of a feminist effect (and, more interestingly, a feminist intent) in short fiction by canonical male authors ultimately wavers, Castle's approach is even more complex: she posits the transformation of a trope from phobic to affirming, yet the persistently disembodied or absented quality of the sexual relationship between characters in even an overtly lesbian novel indicates the tenacity of this trope's damaging aspects and puts Castle in the unusual position of having to queer a work (i.e., treat it to some degree as a hostile witness) that is already paradigmatically lesbian.

NEGATING GAY READING, FINDING FOUCAULT

If Fetterly and Castle demonstrate the ways in which both feminist and lesbian literary analysis must use their work to resist and reembody their culturally inscribed absence, gay literary criticism has found the means by which to eroticize and embrace this very absenting, giving its project broad scope and great power. While in a specifically politicized context (e.g., the Wilde trials), absence and silence indicate a betrayal or crisis of injustice (see Koestenbaum), in countless other respects, the negativity of gay representation by the canonical mainstream has been perfectly converted to its opposite signification: in her seminal work in this area, Eve Sedgwick considers plot or character structured by themes of paranoia, the open secret, and the unspeakable (*Epistemology* and *Tendencies*). Joseph Litvak has characterized the "*ecriture gaie*" (*Caught in the Act* 273) of James's style as a "vagueness" that suffuses multiple Jamesian characters and situations, while Hugh Stevens describes an "erotic silence" (7) in James;[9] D.A. Miller (*Jane Austen*) constructs a persuasive analogy between gay sensibility and Jane Austen's "Style," which he refers to alternately as the narrative voice of "No One." Influenced by Leo Bersani's important essay "Is the Rectum a Grave?" multiple other gay cultural theorists have sought out a sexually subversive "anal" thematic in literature and film, countering the (hetero)sexist fixation with the penis and phallus and thus inverting the hierarchy between the presence of the phallus and the absence of the anal "hole." These several citations indicate the degree to which gay male theory has defined (i.e., made present) the absence of gay subjectivity.

This enterprise is strengthened by the gay critical interchange with theorists such as Freud—a reluctant or inadvertent forefather to much contemporary feminist, lesbian, and gay theorizing—and especially Foucault, whose gay subthemes function subversively even in his already-radical philosophies and whose work has had special significance for gay literary criticism. Foucault seems to have been closing in on a theoretical self-outing as he moved through the stages of his career; his early works bear little (if at all) on the themes of pleasure and sexuality he is most famous for, while his final works speak so plainly yet so round-aboutly (Litvak might say "vaguely") of his own preoccupations with nonnormative sexualities that what was never said in his work had been practically spoken anyway. Because Foucault eschewed the self-confessional mode and dealt often with generalized references to "sexuality" instead of specifically homosexual examples, is it our understanding of Foucault's gay orientation that has queered his writings, the early as well as the late, by association? His seminal readings of eighteenth-century all-male environments such as prisons and boys' schools have tended to "immasculate" the asylum, the clinic, and the confessional as well. Related is the question of whether this de facto androcentricsm derives from something subversively queer or discouragingly traditional (i.e., misogynist) in Foucault or in our approach to his work, whether something is lost or gained in our automatic conflation of sexuality with homosexuality, of the Foucauldian "subject" with "him." (See also Foxhall and Richlin.)

At any rate, Foucault has provided the gay critical approach a lexicon of productively suggestive terms—including pleasure, power, technology, and discipline—that enables gay critics to produce their own "*ecriture gaie*," vaguely or subtly indicating a gay perspective without having to name a project explicitly so. This tactic allows these writers to widen the significance of their work for audiences not necessarily in search of a gay textual approach and also to mobilize a flirtatious, suggestive subtext recognized by a narrower readership-in-the-know, which teasingly keeps us guessing as to these critics' larger motives. Thus, D.A. Miller can present a critical study entitled *The Novel and the Police*, offering to a mainstream academic audience a broadly cultural approach to canonical Victorian novels, yet send a more specific signal to his sexuality-studies audience, aware of both the homophobic state-sponsored repression and the S&M scene-making suggested by the image of the cop. Also Joseph Litvak can make use of suggestive concepts such as theatricality, scene-making, embarrassment, surveillance, and "the dynamics of power and pleasure" (*Caught in the Act* 210) with only the rare reference to any specifically gay inquiry under way. Once a theorist has set up shop in this particular neighborhood, his every reference takes on a double-life: readers begin to wonder about the sexual peculiarities of Jane Austen, Wilke Collins (Miller *Novel*), Edith Wharton (Litvak *Caught in the Act*), being sophisticated (Litvak *Strange Gourmets*), vacationing in Venice (Moon), and the entire 19th century. (See also Edelman *Homographesis* 6–7.) Again, it is Foucault who provides the original model of this open-secret style of critical analysis; our understanding of his ultimately gay-inflected insights queers the work of these younger writers, while these writers' constant return to Foucauldian philosophies reinforces the now-permanent connections between Foucault and gay subjecthood.

Early in his text, Miller reveals his intent to "mov[e] the question of policing out of the streets, as it were, into the closet—I mean, into the private and domestic sphere on which the very identity of the liberal subject depends" (*Novel* ix). While Miller will indeed speak about a broadly defined "liberal subject," he will also simultaneously (or, at times, alternately) discuss this subject in his (or her) more narrowly closeted state—paranoid about the keeping of a sexual secret and positive that the authorities will discover it. Throughout, we are implicitly invited to consider the relationship between the closet and "the carceral"—both traditionally conceived in terms of containment and hiding, yet transformed by a Foucauldian outlook into fora of interrogation, exposure, and confession. Post-Foucault, the closet and the carceral no longer hide but are themselves "hidden," carried internally, silently by each subject, self-policing in the absence of authority as in the case of Trollope's *Barchester Towers* where "the police literally and even metaphorically have no place to hold" (111). In chapters on Trollope and Collins, Miller's focus on various characters' gender "panics" further suggests a specifically gay subtext and further delineates this self-policing mechanism.

The inner/outer paradox effected by the Foucauldian carceral (and closet) reappears in Miller's continuing meditation on the "open secret," yet another hallmark concept in gay studies. The trope enables him to include himself—as keeper of an open secret—as an object of analysis, in other words, to employ the mode of self-policing he has been describing throughout and to indulge in the pleasures of confession and exposure, theorized by Foucault as well. He flirts with the question of his orientation and with divulging details from his private life, including such bodily particularities as a backache, a "personality disorder," and a broken heart (191). These details are rehashed in, of all places, the text's index, where Miller's self-citation (the academic's own mode of public confession?) is noticeably more detailed than the minimalist entries that otherwise comprise the catalogue. His own entry's inclination to divulge details albeit in secret, where almost no one will think of looking for them, enacts confession as guilty pleasure, just as Foucault observed that it was; as a surprise insertion at the very end (the sexual innuendo was likely intentional), the entry embodies a text (his own as well as those of nineteenth-century male authors) in ways that challenge gender norms and revise standards of masculine (traditional) reading practice. Finally, Miller's project crosses a spectrum from traditional literary analysis to a style of theorizing queered and personalized in theme and form, drawing from a similar spectrum in the philosophies of Foucault to maintain textual unity. Seeming to address separate readers on separate themes, Miller in fact takes the same reader across this spectrum with him, transforming him into a consumer of gay theory whether or not that was this reader's desire, as Foucault himself has transformed and been transformed on the same shifting plane since his arrival on the critical scene.

Just as implicitly indebted to Foucault is Joseph Litvak's reading (in *Caught in the Act*) of Henry James, which also derives its depth from the playing out of an unspoken game engaged in by critic and reader—outing James (both author and works), while all the while discussing something else. (See also Cooper 69.) Thanks to Foucault, other gay-oriented philosophers, and Litvak's own analytic work, an element of queerness tinges at least half (though sometimes both) of the multiple dichotomous terms determined by Litvak to have polarized the Jamesian canon: theater/poetry (or novel), transgression/discipline, vagueness/direct address (or questioning), embarrassment/self-staging, sadism/exhibitionism, power/pleasure, actor/director (or heckler), vulgarity/sophistication, hysteria (or histrionics)/artistic control. What Terry Castle has termed the "opacities of biography" create difficulties for critics such as Litvak, who read in James's life story tantalizing hints as to his sexual tendencies but little hard evidence. Turning instead to the works themselves, Litvak discerns a web of suggestive associations strengthened by James's own connection, however tenuous, with his fellow-playwright Wilde (whose own biography contains many fewer opacities) and especially by the queering powers of Foucault's terminology and insight. As with Miller's work, Litvak's broad exploration of James and the theater rewards multiple readerships—those interested in a "straight" analysis of these themes and those knowledgeable of and/or curious about Litvak's sexual subtext.

IRONIC REVERSALS, INTERPRETIVE STRETCHES

With respect to the marked suggestiveness of Foucault's lexicon, and to the milieu of innuendo, double entendre, and sexual wordplay characteristic of contemporary sexuality studies, the issue of authorial irony looms as a major focus. Where in these inviting, elusive literary works, if at all, do we locate authorial distance from the narrative voice, which calls into question the perfection of the protagonists and their happy endings (specifically their felicitous marital arrangements)? Is there an unmistakable narrative tone of voice that all who approach these texts can hear, or is this a private joke enjoyed by individual readers in their idiosyncratic retoolings of narrators and authors never having been credited with such subtlety before? In multiple instances encountered here, it is the discernment of authorial or narrative irony that makes the critic's case. Because a pervasive ironic tone can function as a resounding "not!" across the surface of an ostensibly conservative character, plot element, or thesis moment, it is terrifically helpful to locate such a reversal when seeking to rescue a text or author from the charges of misogyny, homophobia, or boring traditionalism. However, because irony functions *so* fortuitously, *deus ex machina*-style, to unsay what is politically retrograde in a chosen text, and because irony can often be so subtle, or pervasive, as to be entirely lost on certain members of a critic's audience, argument according to authorial irony may generate more questions than answers.

Above, I referred to Fetterly's listening for the irony in Hawthorne and Faulkner as this shaped each author's feminist intent; below, I will show her employing this argument again, to argue for James's critique of the misogynist Basil Ransom in *The Bostonians*. Elsewhere in her study, she reads Jackson J. Benson, who listens apologetically for the irony Hemingway uses to distance readers from his womanizing protagonist Frederick Henry, and raises the very question I pose against her own deployment of the term: "But if irony is so unrecognizable, one is justified in questioning whether or not it is intended" (57). I take the "unintended" alternative to indicate its status as figment of a redeeming critic's imagination; in this case, Fetterly's feminist perspective allows none of it, although plenty of other feminist readers, questioning the progressive credentials of Hawthorne, Faulkner, and James may regard the irony Fetterly hears in these authors with equal incredulity. In any case, for Fetterly, irony constitutes what is anticanonical, nontraditional, and subversive (i.e., what is identifiably feminist) in these male-authored texts. Specifically, it enables male authors to examine with critical distance the qualities in male characters so casually promoted in other less thoughtful contexts, or the masculine habits of misogyny that enlist reader sympathies against powerful female characters.

In keeping with her overarching theme of the apparitional in lesbian literature, Castle equates the irony in Garbo's performance as Queen Christina with an empowering self-removal of the lesbian actress from her character's heterosexual scenes. We have the situation, Castle notes, of a lesbian actress portraying a "notoriously lesbian queen," engaged nevertheless in a romantic encounter with her male lead. The irony Castle identifies in the performance undoes the heterosexual embrace; if the embrace is indeed "there," taking place on the screen, Garbo herself has slipped from its grasp, employing an ironic disposition to negate every meaning suggested by the Hollywood-specific moment. While a more explicitly male gay critical perspective might associate irony with the campy, demonstrative humor that clearly indicates a queer literary or cinematic moment, what is thus "ironic" for Castle in Garbo's performance is what is self-absented from a scene, what shields a private self from the violating misunderstandings of outsiders. The question that remains, however, regards the ultimate caliber of Garbo's "performance": as she is universally acclaimed as a masterful actor, was it not entirely within her range to pretend passion even for a male costar? Does claiming to "see through" this pretense indicate a weakness in the performance itself? Or is it a weakness in Castle's reading, whose glimpse of Garbo's inner self coming ironically through is primarily a construction of its own wishful intentions? Or, finally, is it a weakness in the homophobic misperceptions that will always keep 90 percent of Garbo's admiring audience in utter darkness as to the truth of who she was? In any of these cases, it seems obvious that one only sees the irony of Garbo's performance once one knows about her lesbian orientation. Whether this knowledge functions as a veil being removed (enabling us to realize the irony that was always there) or as blinders being applied (imposing onto the scene a critical distance that matches the newly realized distance between the woman she was and the characters she was forced to play) is an irresolvable issue.

Elsewhere, the first line of Miller's full-length study of Austen (*Jane Austen*) is an epigraph of Barthesian "irony"; Litvak listens to a closing moment from Austen's *Pride and Prejudice*—regarding "the 'admiring multitude' whom the marriage of Elizabeth and Darcy is destined to 'teach . . . what connubial felicity really was' "—and argues that "one hears . . . a certain sarcasm in this very phrasing" that signals Austen's own distaste for the exigencies of the marriage plot (*Strange Gourmets* 23–24). Does the sarcasm, however, emanate from the quote itself, or is it primarily a ringing in the ear acutely tuned for such linguistic slants?[10] The narrative has erected the love these two share as admirable; among the many bad marriages filling the margins of every Austen novel, the central union is meant to function as an instructive contrast. Austen's wit and irony are hallmarks of her style, and Litvak's interpretation is supported thus, yet the question is whether that distancing, defensive, cynical tone adopted by narrator and heroine(s) at the outset of her stories in fact survives the heart-melting encounters gone through by said heroines and by wedding-obsessed narratives by stories' ends. (See also Miller *Jane Austen* 40–56.)

More persuasively, Litvak attends Henry James's "theater of embarrassment" and concludes that in fact James was often in on the joke readers thought they were having on him. He argues that such "rhetorical knots might be explained in terms of an older, more honorific sense of Jamesian 'irony,' according to which the author, precisely making scenes or not, as he chooses, would turn out to have embarrassed *us*, his would-be debunkers, by masterminding all of the 'embarrassments' in which we imagine we have caught *him*" (*Caught in the Act* 213). The issue Litvak so astutely addresses in his readings of Austen and James, representative of the concerns of several theorists to be considered here, is, in short, whether or not the author is being straight with us (or, coincident with his concept of theatricality, putting on an act). In the case of both Austen and James, the gay, lesbian, or feminist reader presumes and is delighted that the author is *not* playing it straight, that an ironic tone is audible throughout, which dependably signals a calling-into-question of the fortified heterosexuality and/or altar-bound pursuits of a protagonist or narrative voice. And yet the arguments of these critics—especially those aimed at "mainstream" *and* gender/sexuality studies audiences—must maintain a level of plausibility to meet with acceptance; even interpretations pitched only toward the likeminded must avoid unfounded assertions, lest the effort to radicalize Austen, James, or their literary output fail due to a defensive, desperate quality in the work.

Terry Castle's controlled assessment of Austen's intense relationship with her sister Cassandra, published in the *London Review of Books* ("Sister, Sister"), created an oversized controversy, due certainly to its appearance in a mainstream (nonacademic) venue. The brou-ha was fomented by an incendiary headline across the cover of the issue in question—"Was Jane Austen Gay?"—and in her rebuttal Castle incisively critiqued the "morally bankrupt antihomosexual sentiment" ("Response") that characterized the hysterical response to her even broaching the question. While letters attacking Castle's argument implicitly accused it of a certain desperate quality, the detractors' own overwrought anxiety about disproving Austen's lesbianism by any means necessary undermines their counterstatements. In the original article, Castle's evidence ranges from solidly persuasive to transparently thin. Austen's letters indeed reveal an impatience with men's attentions and a close relationship between Austen and her sister, demonstrated by the intimate triviality of their correspondence. Meanwhile, Castle's argument often moves less by suggestion than by overstatement and association; she seems to exaggerate both the "flirtatious" tone of Jane's letters to her sister and, following a list of famous men Austen fantasizes about marrying, Austen's assessment of men as "ultimately insignificant." Castle posits "passion," "pleasure-addiction," and "seduction" between the sisters but shows little in the letters to demonstrate these, and she presses her case by likening the style of this writing to that of Gertrude Stein and Virginia Woolf. Castle's incursion into the mainstream press performed the important work of exposing traditional readers (old-style academics among these) to radical ideas but was attacked for the in-part speculative maneuvers upon which her argument was based.

Meanwhile, within the "mainstream" (younger, more progressive) academic environment, the interpretive stretch as executed by feminist and perhaps especially by gay and lesbian approaches to canonical texts will often enjoy great success. A receptive audience for such arguments, an audience that understands that surface-level feminist or gay perspectives will almost never be found in the pages of popular literature authored decades or centuries ago, is much readier to entertain these critics' entertaining speculations about an author's, character's, or narrative's feminist intent or sexual bent when verifiable answers to such questions are impossible to determine. Especially readers in search of the gay or lesbian perspective, for whom the concept of the contorted "stretch" contains an eroticized charge, the further-flung the observations, the more pleasing they are, and the more likely that less radical although still subversive readings will eventually find acceptance with wider audiences.

Like Castle, Eve Sedgwick in *Tendencies* rails against the erotophobic backlash following delivery of her paper "Jane Austen and the Masturbating Girl," though her indignant surprise that anyone still finds masturbation a disconcerting topic for cultural analysis doth protest a bit too much: if anything, lesbianism is by now a far less controversial subject than masturbation continues to be. Even as Sedgwick acutely delineates "onanism" as perhaps the last underexplored frontier in the sexuality studies field, as a theme of literary analysis, particularly in Austen's works, it may lead to even stretchier interpretations than those involving gay and lesbian characters.

In fact, the discernment of this trope, especially in a canonical text such as *Sense and Sensibility* is well suited to Sedgwick's critical agenda. From the first pages of her early *Between Men*, she has demonstrated her intent to aggressively sexualize literary relations and to act upon the presumption that her audience likewise recognizes these encounters as explicitly sexual. Thus, while the *romantic* love triangle has been a staple of fiction for centuries, Sedgwick in *Between Men* immediately terms this construct the *erotic* love triangle, suggesting either that for her the terms are interchangeable or that she will insist upon a new terminology from the outset, without feeling compelled to justify the transition. Certainly the eroticizing of romance enables a frank assessment of the feelings literary characters have for each other, and of their goals involving sexual unions that advance the plot. But the coinage also has the effect of shifting the entire Western literary tradition under the always more narrowly defined rubric of "erotica," and suggests that the reader must have been dozing during all the scenes of nudity, foreplay, intercourse, and orgasm populating her favorite novels. Is there anything, after all, so explicitly erotic in the novels that Sedgwick surveys in *Between Men*, aside from this critic's own desire that sex in literature were treated in more direct fashion? Finally, Sedgwick's attempt to call a spade a spade has led to a misnaming of another sort; what was too soft and fluffy in the concept of the romantic has been almost comically recast as something graphically hardcore in these low-key, canonical texts.

In Sedgwick's reading of *Sense and Sensibility*, Marianne is the classically masturbating girl because she cries in spastic outpourings as she pens a love note to the jilting Willoughby and because, before getting to that point in her relationship, she runs energetically through the countryside or flits in agitated fashion around her living room. In short she is sexually nervous, anxious, or frustrated, Sedgwick might say, and looking for a physical outlet; a reader of a more traditional persuasion might notice that Marianne appears to be in love. Aside from a few fortuitous references in the novel to Marianne's inability to "keep her seat" and Elinor's not wanting to "touch on" some "point," Sedgwick converts romance into eroticism (in this case positing Marianne as masturbator and Elinor as lesbian) largely by suggestive associations with other, much more explicit texts. These interpretive stretches work as effectively as they do because of the profoundly suggestive nature *of* sexual terminology. One need only place beside these scenes of Marianne a French physician's notes of a chronically masturbating girl to create the eroticized atmosphere the novel itself is much less inclined to yield. Because a little girl is masturbating somewhere in the vicinity of this argument, Marianne must also be a masturbator, and because Elinor's pupils dilate like sphincters, she must harbor lesbian feelings toward Marianne (*Tendencies* 124).

Sedgwick passes out copies of these graphic clinical notes when teaching this novel to graduate students, indicating her desire that these infectious texts stretch their influence onto her students as they have already stretched their influence upon herself. Situated within this viscous, clingy, endlessly attenuating web of sexual suggestiveness, the reader now has little problem reinterpreting Austen's G-rated oeuvre as explicitly triple-X, an essential first move, perhaps especially for reluctant heteronormative readers, in the queering of the Western canon. Sedgwick admits, once having been exposed to these graphic accounts, that she is no longer able to read *Sense and Sensibility* without their coming to mind as well, and the terminology she employs regarding their "pressure on the gaze" (*Tendencies* 127) connotes a blend of something erotically seduced and unpleasantly coerced. Has *Sense and Sensibility* been found or has it been ruined for Sedgwick by these powerful associations? Is one's own sense of the preposterousness of her assertions only weak defense against the ways this novel has now been turned into something decidedly pornographic, much to one's annoyance with the argument for having done so? Or does the stringent backlash against writing by Sedgwick (and Castle, and other critics using the interpretive stretch to make startling claims) result from readers' outraged realization that these critics are right?

By now, it may be obvious that the novels of Jane Austen and Henry James hold special interest for many writing in the fields of lesbian, gay, and feminist studies; both have enjoyed an avalanche of critical attention in the last five years. Linked genealogically, and only half-jokingly, by Kipling a century ago,[11] Austen and James share stylistic and biographical idiosyncrasies intriguing to theorists of feminist, gay, and lesbian perspectives. Both are master-novelists known for their distinctive narrative voices, incisive observations of social custom, and ambiguous political and sexual allegiances. Both remained single and indicated through private writings a diffidence about or a discomfort with the opposite sex; for both, critics speculate upon a queer orientation, with circumstantial evidence leaning strongly in that direction for James and less so for Austen. If anything, therefore, James promises a richer interpretive mine for gay and lesbian readers, while tapping into Austen's progressive political potential has been an ongoing feminist project. Meanwhile, it has been deemed important to likewise speculate on the feminist qualities of James's work and—through questioning closely related to the feminist inquiry—examine Austen's novels for what challenge they may provide to the heterocentric marriage plot. The remainder of this chapter will consider in-depth the discussion occurring amongst the lesbian, gay, and feminist subfields regarding the canons of Austen and James.

DIVIDING AUSTEN

The obverse of the playful, eroticizing literary "stretch" is a persistent textual (f)rigidity that characterizes multiple writings by both Austen and James. While certainly "stiffness" has sexual connotations, in this case I refer to texts that simply resist the critical manipulations of sophisticated theorists by retreating stubbornly to heterosexist or other politically retrograde positions. Thus despite the efforts of the best theorists in practice today, many of Austen's and James's characters *do* choose heterosexual partners, *do* marry with smiling faces, *do* enjoy the privileges of sex (if male), race, and class in manners oppressive to other characters; as D.A. Miller has succinctly acknowledged, "no amount of irony keeps Austen's narratives from developing . . . fully" the "oppressive logic of the conjugal imperative" ("Austen's Attitude" 1), while Lisa L. Moore argues that even the lesbian representations in *Emma* can be read "as not only an object of power but one of its agents as well" (110). Recent sexuality studies–based approaches to these texts therefore work to account for their obvious heterosexualities while pushing their often subtle strains of queerness and radical politics to the fore. The levels of obscurity descended to by some writing recently—Kate Croy's "sidedness" (the term remains obscure) imbricating her in the homosexual paradigm of *Wings of the Dove*

(Sedgwick *Tendencies*), James himself queered via lengthy inquiries into whether or not Edith Wharton was embarrassed to have once embarrassed him (Litvak *Caught in the Act*)—indicate the degree of textual recalcitrance these readers must deal with; even when the argument succeeds (as it often ultimately does), its recipient is tempted to wonder whether the destination worth so long a trip.

In the last two decades, Austen has received critical attention from feminist, gay, and lesbian readers who share multiple analytic concerns. Representing an especially high-stakes prize for these readers, her writings epitomize traditional ideological forces and her authorial image primness and propriety, both of which cry out to be plunged into the jello pit of contemporary gender/sexuality theorizing. Those who ultimately discern a conservative mindset at work in Austen's novels and those who insist upon the subversive social challenge emerging beneath their traditional plotlines make enormous efforts to critique or celebrate Austen's work, often using—perhaps not surprisingly by now—the same textual examples and politicized arguments. For instance, we might ask, does arguing that Austen's heroines are "desperate to marry" constitute a feminist/queer critique (of Austen's benighted, romanticizing heterocentrism) or feminist/queer commendation (of Austen's *refusal* to romanticize the typical marriage plot, emphasizing nineteenth-century women's generally "desperate" circumstances instead)? The answer to such a question depends in part upon the school of thought from which it issues.

To be specific, consider the feminist spin one might put to the issue of Elinor and Marianne Dashwood's desperation and the way this collides with the efforts to queer these women's situations presented by Sedgwick above. If the traditional feminist reading emphasizes the girls' increasingly dire social and financial circumstances, the economic hardship represented by their having to share a bed after moving from Norland Park to Barton Cottage, the jilting by Willoughby as a crisis that engulfs not only Marianne's heart and health but also the well-being of her entire family, and the older Elinor's special need to find herself a suitable provider before becoming the burdensome old maid she practically already is, we can see how all of these urgent situations are transformed into positive outcomes by Sedgwick's emphasis on the perverse erotic lives of the sisters. If, for instance, Marianne is perfectly satisfied by her frequent and gratifying masturbatory exercises, why should the reader (or Marianne herself) worry whether she finds herself a husband or not? Indeed the emotional spasms brought upon by the jilting episode seem to be just what the doctor ordered (even though she takes quite sick shortly after one such outburst), so her sexual health seems best ensured by continuing to enter doomed relationships with men. Elinor's lesbian attraction for her younger sister alleviates the potentially troubling reduced sleeping/living circumstances as well as her need to find a husband, and in all cases the economic (feminist) and sexual (queer) readings threaten each other in self-canceling fashion. In the first reading, the sisters' giddy dash to the altar (now their name, Dashwood, takes on added meanings) indicates—to us readers if never to themselves—the pathetically desperate circumstances confining women of that era (see also Gilbert and Gubar 86); in the second reading, sexual desperation refers to their desperado-style or outlaw sexual behaviors, with both the onanism and the lesbianism satisfied necessarily outside the bounds of matrimony. In both cases desperation is a productive, progressive term that steps away from our traditional understanding of Austen's happy, heteronormative endings, but each reading moves from there in completely different directions.[12]

HISTORICIZING AUSTEN

In a comment distinctly relevant to this project, Mary Poovey makes an observation whose every word I concur with, save one: "When an individual work by Wollstonecraft or Shelley seems morally or stylistically ambiguous, surviving letters or journals help provide a background for interpretation. . . . But the incompleteness and opacity of Austen's personal record often compound the notorious instability of her novelistic irony, thus leading us further into confusing (if delightful) ambiguity" (173). In fact, the ambiguities and opacities of Austen's politics, judging from the writing of several to be discussed here, do much more to frustrate than delight these politicizing writers; as even Poovey's argument in support of Austen's protofeminism fails to fully persuade, her profession of delight steps away from confrontation with the problems Austen presents to feminist critics. Due to these challenges, what counts as politics—and history—in an Austen novel is as variously defined as the theorists taking up the task. We can picture Austen at the center of a series of widening rings and note the way her historical reach has been widened as feminism itself has moved from a second-wave preoccupation with sex inequalities to third-wave emphases on world politics, influenced by new historicist, multicultural, and postcolonial theories.

Early feminist treatments of Austen focused their remarks on Austen's complicating of marriage plot, on the dark underside to the Cinderella stories that are the novels' ostensible main offering. As we will see below, the marriage plot as a locus of critical inquiry now belongs almost entirely to the lesbian or gay approach. Interestingly, recent feminist analyses of Austen's "unattached women" who trouble "the official mechanisms of cultural transmission and cultural memory" (Lynch 9) seem lacking not only in their bypassing of larger historical concerns but in their now obvious failure to queer the singlehood of Austen's spinster figures. Deirdre Lynch observes that Austen's novels "provide cultural spaces where we girls can all be girls together" (14) yet fails to nuance the term "girls" to include gay or effeminate Austen-lovers, let alone consider the possibility of actual girls "being together" in explicitly sexual ways. More often recent feminist writings have sought to debunk the "myth" that Austen wrote "contained," "domestic" novels, connecting them instead with the French Revolution, the Napoleonic Wars, and the slave trade in North America. Yet while discovering a statement on abolition in *Mansfield Park* clearly moves this text beyond the domestic sphere, does Austen's general mistrust of history or her knowledge of the literary marketplace indicate much awareness beyond the interests of her drawingroom and her career? On what occasions might these more narrowly defined interests constitute a political statement by themselves, and when do Austen's more political moments simply position her as politically conservative, even antifeminist?

At the back of feminist critics' minds might be a nagging sense of the declining strength of Austen's heroines throughout her career: Catherine Moreland, the heroine of Austen's *Northanger Abbey* (her first work though published after many of her other novels), is regarded by some readers as her most forthright and rebellious protagonist. "Unlike Richardson's Pamela," Carole Gerster notes, "Catherine does not attempt to hide her feelings . . . . [She] is guilty of Richardsonian heterodoxy by acting independent of artifice . . . [and] reveals she is not immune to sexual feelings" (118). Meanwhile, Julia Prewitt Brown determines that Austen's late *Persuasion*, as this absorbed the incipient sex polarities defining the Victorian era, presents us with Austen's most constrained and stereotypically demure heroine: "We see in Anne herself the sentimentalization of femininity that exists in wartime societies. Anne is more classically feminine than any other Jane Austen heroine" (165; see also Miller *Jane Austen* 68–76). While Brown argues that Austen herself "found the sexual stereotypes of postwar England divisive and burdensome" (165), her proof of this farsightedness—"in [Anne and Wentworth's] final reconciliation Victorian sex roles are reversed: the woman speaks, and the man relents"—is somewhat thin: Anne's climatic speech, regarding the special ways women love, can hardly be considered a breakthrough of sex stereotypes, while the image of the imploring woman and the "relenting" man, being only a reversal and not any sort of dissolution of sex dichotomies, seems to invite antifeminist readings of its own.[13] Additionally, Brown's argument that Austen was sufficiently unaffected by wartime protocols and her era's incipient Victorianism to see past these stereotypes has the side effect of returning her to the ahistoric register feminist critics now seek to rescue her from. If it is our intent to fully historicize Austen, we must face the possibility that she was not only a commentator, shaper, and improver of historical context but a disabled pawn (as are we all) of it as well.

Certainly, all of Austen's women present a markedly liberated improvement on the agitated Richardsonian heroine, ever in flight from a lunging rapist; they all wind up in excellent marital arrangements and—more importantly—they have all come into these arrangements through their own independent, "intelligent choices" (Gerster 128). Both Gerster and Poovey seek to politicize this independent choice-making: Gerster concludes her argument by noting that "In an Austen novel, the heroine's marriage is not to a ruling superior; it takes place realistically in a patriarchal society yet offers an unexpected alternative" (129). Poovey likewise considers "individualism's challenge to paternalism" (183), implicitly figuring the "individual" in this scenario as the rebellious daughter. Yet the gains made here must be qualified by our understanding that these are, after all, story characters enjoying zero real autonomy. With respect to the choice of marriage partners, the heroines *seem* to have so many options, but in fact the romantic path each takes is explicitly proscribed; one of the qualities separating an Austen heroine from an Austen-supporting female character is her refusal to be swayed in the wrong romantic direction for more than a moment if at all. And of course, the teleology of marital security defining all Austen novels has been the indicator of their antifeminism (not to mention heterosexism) for many contemporary theorists.

Mary Poovey's reading is staunchly feminist and clearly pro-Austen; specifically, Austen's ability to out-write both Mary Wollstonecraft and Mary Shelley is made prominent by references to her "genius," "narrative magic," and powerful "artistry," and these talents seem to equate for Poovey to a position commensurate with the less talented but more overtly feminist Wollstonecraft's. A tone of voice or turn of phrase that might connote Poovey's disappointment in Austen's politics is never found, a stylistic effect that clashes with Poovey's many acknowledgments that in fact Austen's writing always partially served the ruling social order. Thus, when the reader learns that Austen's novels constitute "the challenge to traditional values . . . and . . . part of a defense against this challenge" (172), she may not recognize that Poovey has just undermined Austen's feminist import by half. Later, Poovey notes that Austen "does not exclude passion from the novel" but instead "attempts to bend the imaginative engagement it elicits in the reader to the service of a moral education" (187). But shall we congratulate the novelist on this fence-sitting gesture, whose insidious conservatism might constitute a greater threat than the overt moralizing of other didactic writers of her day? Throughout, Poovey refrains from directly criticizing Austen's ideological duplicity, although it cries out for such critique.

Poovey's reading of "individualism" also goes in a surprising direction. Its troubling associations with industrial capitalism and economic and social self-interest are made to seem left-oriented relative to what Poovey claims Austen embraced individualism instead of: even more conservative economic modes such as aristocracy and patronage, as well as psychosexually inhibited pretensions to middle-class propriety. While the selfishness of, for instance, Mr. and Mrs. John Dashwood is mocked by Austen's ironic narrative tone, Poovey observes that the generosity and fairness Austen searches for at such moments are relatively rare in her works—where would Elinor and Edward be, after all, without "Lucy Steele's avarice?" (182)—and thus must not be part of Austen's feminist vision. Poovey calls into question such values, ordinarily hallmarks of leftism, as "moral" and "Christian" (184); thus her discernment of Austen's feminism requires the dubious rewriting of both capitalist individualism (now an element of social progressivism) and monetary or interpersonal generosity (now a minority opinion in Austen's works and, damningly, "Christian"). If such inversions seem more coercive than persuasive, it is likewise something of a straw argument to oppose propriety to romance (or even passion and desire) in Austen, since even her sensible heroines such as Elinor and Anne are as passionate as are her livelier, more impetuous ones. It is difficult to regard the romantic aspects of Austen's stories as hidden behind and in subversive conflict with so much middle-class propriety or, even more questionably, as reliable indicators of her feminist intent. Poovey posits that

> Jane Austen's irony enables her to reproduce—without exposing in any systematic way—some of the contradictions inherent in bourgeois ideology; . . . she endorses both the individualistic perspective inherent in the bourgeois value system *and* the authoritarian hierarchy retained from traditional, paternalistic society. (205)

Doing so, she demonstrates her acceptance of Austen's many discouraging capitulations to retrograde ideologies. Austen's endorsement of both the "bourgeois value system" and the authoritarian hierarchy of the old tradition cannot be seen by modern readers as anything other than doubly conservative, despite our historical awareness that in Austen's day these were opposing forces. That these failures to address the problems of her social context are defined as "enabling"—that is, beneficial to readers and a testament to Austen's skill as an ironist—indicates Poovey's support for this seemingly deeply conservative author based solely on her gifts as a writer and on her female sex. Near the end of the essay, Poovey offers the chilling image of Austen relating to her reader as "family"; as Austen manipulated this intense, Foucauldian intimacy to gently coerce her reader to subscribe to the status quo, so Poovey assumes that a sympathetic feminist readership receiving her argument will accept it on the basis of her own skills as a theorist and her gold-plated feminist credentials. Nevertheless, the effort does not succeed, and if anything, Austen seems more antifeminist in Poovey's assessment than in that of others less intent on establishing her leftist mindset.

In similar fashion, Johanna M. Smith and Devoney Looser maneuver through difficult textual territory to make their case for Austen's progressivism. For Smith, an initial consideration of the space opened up in *Pride in Prejudice* for the "oppositional reader" devolves into a discussion based largely on that reader herself—relieving Austen of the burden to create subversive space in her work. Smith refers to Michel de Certeau, who argues that readers come to oppositional understandings on their own, regardless of what an author may contribute (31). Thus, much of Smith's oppositional reading occurs without support from Austen herself; when, for instance, she questions Mr. Bennet's trafficking in women and the exclusion of characters from the comforting familial tableau at Pemberly at novel's end (36), this oppositional reading proceeds *in spite of* Austen's failure to note these contradictions herself. While the essay certainly contributes to the politicizing of "Austen," by this term we mean primarily the novels themselves, not Austen as an especially progressive author in her own right.

Looser sets out in opposition to "the myth of Austen's ahistoricism" (43), yet her argument succeeds primarily in demonstrating that Austen's relationship to history was almost entirely antithetical. Noting that in Austen's time, "history" often denoted something else (novels, narratives, romance, historical fiction), Looser acknowledges that references to history are sparse throughout Austen's canon and

often related to these other usages. Austen's early *History of England*
certainly demonstrates a familiarity with dates and highlights from
past centuries, but Looser notes the literary (not historical) sources
Austen accessed for her juvenile writing (46) and the "fierce royalist
loyalties" on display there (41). Additionally, what Austen culls from
her broader reading is decidedly girlish (the same as "herstory"?) in
focus—the romances, scandals, and bedroom exploits of famous men
and women—although Looser is counting (as do Poovey and Smith
above) on a receptive audience to regard this half-empty glass as half-full
instead.

Later Looser's reading of the "novel v. history" debate in *Northanger
Abbey* fails to deal with the primary challenge to critics interpreting this
text—that acceptable positions are espoused by both the protagonist
Catherine Moreland and her foil Eleanor Tilney: from a feminist standpoint, Catherine's promotion of "the novel" (as an emerging women's
genre) over (male-oriented) history *and* Eleanor's more complex and
accurate understanding of the value of historical context (and sophisticated awareness of the degree to which history itself is fictionalized) are
both viable arguments. Whether the novel itself supports as correct or
criticizes as naive one character's position or the other's is impossible to
determine. Certainly, both Catherine's and Eleanor's views are "historical" (i.e., political and potentially feminist) in a broad sense; in the
narrower terms with which Looser is dealing, however, only Eleanor
speaks for "history," so that Looser's argument rests implicitly with a
debunking of Catherine's antihistory position.

Can Austen, however, who feared and criticized the "histories" of
Sir Walter Scott in letters to her sister (Looser 38–39), and who was
intent to "justif[y] the novel" (Looser 49) in her first full-fledged
narrative exercise, be seen to stand apart from her heroine in this way?
Is the reader invited to take Catherine's part on every other occasion
save as she defends the novel (specifically the gothic genre) in the
course of a pseudogothic novel in which she plays the main role?
Eventually, Catherine, Eleanor, and Henry admit to their enjoyment
of gothic novels, leading the conversation even further from history
per se, until it is Eleanor herself who appears naive for thinking
Catherine is discussing "truth" when in fact she is narrating a novel
plot (Looser 52–53). Their shared interest in gothic literature unites
the three young radicals in an alliance destined to topple the conservative regime of the Tilneys' overbearing father, casting novels in a
light political and progressive (i.e., "historical") after all. Although
Looser criticizes the writings of Brigid Brophy and Gilbert and Gubar
for seeking to dehistoricize Austen, in fact her own work has a similar

effect; that it dehistoricizes inadvertently, in spite of its efforts to historicize, makes an even stronger case than could have Brophy or Gilbert/Gubar, for Austen's intensely equivocal position as an author engaged with history.

Feminist readings accessing that outermost ring of Austen's historical context—the slave trade in North America and especially the Caribbean, as this figures in the background of *Mansfield Park*—have demonstrated greater willingness to qualify their praise of Austen's views. Perforce, the very backgrounding to which such an important issue is subjected in the novel indicates a stance toward abolition on Austen's part that was less than fully formed; two writers on this theme, Moira Ferguson and Susan Fraiman, acknowledge the problem in their respective essays. Their emphasis on sex inequality instead of empire enable both to present primarily favorable assessments of Austen's novel; in both cases, they seek less to historicize Caribbean slaves and British women in their respective contexts than to metaphorize their relationship in more literary fashion. Both Ferguson and Fraiman, that is, read Sir Thomas Bertram's Antiguan plantation as a template for the "plantocracy" that is Mansfield Park; Sir Thomas himself functions as the "planter," while the main female characters (especially the younger ones) figure as the slaves.

That the chief evidence of Austen's concern for this colonial issue is also what might define her as ultimately insensitive to such external realities is a troubling contradiction lost on neither critic. Both acknowledge that reading colonized Caribbeans as mere metaphors for the "real" characters in the story can call Austen's motives into question as well as those of feminist writers presenting such arguments. Ferguson stipulates, "this is not to argue that the possibility of slave emancipation in *Mansfield Park* parallels a potential liberation for Anglo-Saxon women" (116), while Fraiman points to "the imperialist gesture [that] exploit[s] the symbolic value of slavery, while ignoring slaves as suffering and resistant historical subjects" (213). Interestingly, more direct language from Jane Fairfax in Austen's later *Emma*, regarding the black and female "slave-trade," is for Fraiman another example of Austen's imperialist metaphorizing (213), while Ferguson reads Jane's speech as proof of Austen's authentic political awareness (112). Despite these several much appreciated disclaimers, both critics occasionally employ the interpretive stretch, so as to demonstrate Austen's awareness of this issue and her desire to write in opposition to it.

Ferguson's target is Sir Thomas, whose wife she reads as the first of his several "captured slaves," yet to do so must implicitly reverse the wording of Austen's opening line—describing Lady Bertram's "lucky captivation" of Sir Thomas—without supplying sufficient grounds. Later, because Lady Bertram sees her husband off on his trip west with words to the effect that "she does not fear for his safety" (Ferguson 109), and because Sir Thomas comes home with stories of having been to a Creole ball, he must have been in Antigua, postulates Ferguson, fathering children with slave women. She reads Sir Thomas's "dead silence" in response to Fanny's inquiry about his trip as the novel's most obvious condemnation of slave-trading. Finally she blames the troubling Portsmouth/Mansfield dichotomy—Portsmouth being so impoverished and dispiriting a setting that the bourgeois sensibilities of Mansfield seem heaven on earth—on "the enormity of [Sir Thomas's] ideology" (Ferguson 108) when of course it is Austen who constructs the novel's various settings as well as Sir Thomas's bad attitudes. Fraiman blames readers themselves for imposing the dichotomy between the two settings, arguing that for Austen Mansfield is as bad as Portsmouth. We are to locate this critique, not surprisingly, in Austen's irony: according to Fraiman, because Fanny concludes her meditative defense of Mansfield with a clichéd expression—"a drop of water in the ocean"—Austen must be calling Fanny's entire declaration into question (210).

Finally it seems unnecessary to go to such lengths to develop a progressive reading of this novel, specifically the Mansfield/Portsmouth dichotomy. Both critics' failure to see this issue in materialist terms, that is, through the eyes of impoverished or enslaved subject herself, bespeak their entrenchment, however reluctant, within a bourgeois mindset. In fact, the degrading effects of poverty on both Fanny's home in Portsmouth and her once-genteel immediate family make the security and sustenance provided at Mansfield, however emotionally cold the setting, an obvious choice. In the metaphoric slave context employed by both critics—Fraiman even compares Portsmouth to Antigua—Mansfield in the materialist reading is not the dreaded plantation but the promised land of "the North" where racism (or classism) comes in more subtle, psychological forms but at least basic human freedoms are guaranteed. Investigating the relevant history, we would find countless stories of individuals forsaking family and familiar surroundings to make just this sort of crossing in the antebellum era. Instead of searching out a negative image of an ultimately gorgeous setting, I recall in this reading the ways in which Austen's stories always dwelt upon Cinderella's impoverished origins and thus also emphasized the sanctuary function of whatever fairy castle she ultimately found refuge in.

In each of these feminist attempts to historicize Austen, it is less the author herself than her literary legacy that submits effectively to the task at hand. On so many other occasions, the feminist reading might satisfy itself with having appropriated a neutral or oppositional text, but the rarity of Austen's example—not only as a woman writer but also as one of great artistic talent and canonical (i.e., "immasculated") status—invites the feminist critic to lay claim to both textual effect and authorial intent. Yet the difficulty of this added challenge shows itself in many of the writings considered here and, in some cases, threatens the success of the narrower, text-focused analysis.

QUEERING AUSTEN

The woman question also interests gay male critics of Austen, who consider her role as a powerful writer as this enlarges or diminishes the queer appeal of her work. Over the course of several essays D.A. Miller's response to Austen has run the gamut from acerbic critique to admiration. While the opening line of *Pride and Prejudice*— "It is a truth universally acknowledged, that the single man in possession of a large fortune must be in want of a wife"—is a source of enjoyment for most sexuality critics of Austen, Miller in "Austen's Attitude" ignores its pointed irony and instead rails against its prescriptive, unapproachable, epigrammatic style (1–3). He discerns at this point "conceit" and "insolence" in her tone, both of which make the dissenting reader feel "stupid" and "hateful" and which "propose excluding [him] from [his] entire [we can assume, gay male] community" (3), yet in later writing, it is this same Style (this time with a capital S) that he celebrates as constituting a kindred spirit to gay readers. Such readers, says Miller, come to Austen's writing in their youth, seeking "its genius for detachment," which would "sever us once and forever from all the particulars of who and what we were" (*Jane Austen* 2) and enjoy throughout life a powerful alliance with this rapier-like style. We detect in Miller's writings on Austen the love-hate sensibility of a devoted reader who is nevertheless intensely riled by the author's heterosexist tendencies. His reference to "taking Austen [to bed] with [him]" whenever he has needed a period of convalescence ("The Late Jane Austen" 223) suggests less a heterosexual affair between a male reader and woman author than a redefinition of Austen as a gay man. While only implied here, in "Austen's Attitude," she is explicitly likened to "the young man in the sweater bar" (who refuses to look Miller's way (2), to certain "gym rats" nervous about their bodily transformations (3), to a sadistically "withholding lover" (4), and to

Oscar Wilde (4). While Miller later, in *Jane Austen*, calls Austen's *style* "neutered," the equation here is between an aggressive "style" and a masculine form.

Interestingly, Miller's appreciation of Austen's strong, masculine style resembles to some degree the traditionalist observations of mid-century critics who only deigned to canonize Austen because she was a worthy descendent of Dr. Johnson, because her wit and strength blended imperceptibly into an all-male tradition. Both Miller's attack on Austen and his love of her masculinity are problematic from a feminist point of view, despite their valuable articulation of the gay male perspective. Conversely, Miller's smart feminist reading of the jewelry store scene in *Sense and Sensibility* (*Jane Austen*) depends in part on his adopting a homophobic attitude toward Robert Farrars who asserts his upper-class male prerogative to keep Elinor waiting for the clerk's assistance but is also so foppish and effeminate that he fails to notice her good looks, let alone his chivalrous obligation to step aside when she enters.

With his emphasis on female characters and meditations on social class, Joseph Litvak also provides feminist commentary on Austen in his largely gay-oriented readings. Three essays—on *Mansfield Park, Pride and Prejudice,* and *Northanger Abbey*—discuss the heroine's conflict with her various class milieus; in each, a controlling opposition is established by which to chart her failures and successes, but also by which, to some degree, to polarize the feminist and gay principles Litvak locates in Austen's novels. In the reading of *Mansfield Park,* for instance, "theatricality-as-subversion" (*Caught in the Act* 24) accrues to a queer perspective almost by default, due to its near-total failure to seduce and include the priggishly antitheatrical protagonist herself. Fanny, Litvak points out, "cannot act" and stays quietly in her room seeking "spiritual intercourse" with her reading "whenever the eroticism of the rehearsals [of the home theatrical] impinges too painfully upon her claustral sensibility" (20). Meanwhile, the conceptual opposite, "theatricality-as-convention" (24), engulfs Fanny entirely, as she is determined to be most herself when she "thinks in clichés" (24) and to be Sir Thomas's prime object of display for the admiring view of prospective husbands. Litvak notes "the shift from [sexualized] metaphors of infection and of seduction to [feminist-oriented] metaphors of debt and repayment" (24); while these ideas about women as risky but ultimately high-paying investments certainly permeate the story, they are in Litvak's reading no longer shown to be linked to anything specifically theatrical. The feminist reading is thus separated not only from what is subversive about theatricality but from theatricality itself.

His analysis of *Pride and Prejudice* (*Strange Gourmets*) dichotomizes sophistication, exemplified by Austen's lively heroine Elizabeth, and vulgarity, represented by the heavy-bodied male characters whom she disdains—and later, by the self-indulgent professional reader, who is then more narrowly delineated as "the gay man" whose homosexuality is a locus of middle-class disgust. Recalling the priggish Fanny of the previous essay, Litvak's Elizabeth is also ascetic in her slender, airy coolness; she functions finally as the obverse to the perversely indulgent gay critic, the essay's own protagonist. In Litvak's reading of *Northanger Abbey*, an early focus on Catherine Moreland gives way to consideration of both the "charming young man" mentioned fleetingly at novel's end and the attractive but underrepresented body of Henry Tilney. Of course it is Austen herself responsible for the novel's "scopophobia"; in addition, though he sympathizes that Austen is excluded from the "exercise of [literary] power," Litvak also faults her for borrowing too heavily into Henry's endearing qualities, "develop[ing his] archness and pleasantry into the 'irony' and 'wit' for which she is famous" (*Strange Gourmets* 54). In each of these remarkable readings, Litvak implies an irresolvable tension between the novels' feminist intent and queer subtext.

Earlier I reviewed the attempt of Terry Castle to construct a lesbian Austen from the details of her correspondence with her sister, noting the difficulty one may have making this case to a mainstream audience, although any audience may feel that the evidence is somewhat slim. Claudia Johnson makes a similar attempt and has similar difficulty, grounding her argument in Castle's controversial thesis then moving quickly and without the necessary sign-posting from the "lesbian Austen" to the importantly different "queer" (i.e., gay male) Austen. Johnson considers "the perceived queerness of many of [Austen's] readers, as this queerness has been played out . . . between macho and 'effeminate' standards of masculinity, and between academic and belletristic models of novel criticism" ("The Divine Miss Jane" 28). Clearly, the references here to macho and effeminate masculinities, as well as to professional and aficionado readers of Austen, signals an unannounced shift from questions of author-identity to those of reader-identity, from lesbian to gay (or pansifying) registers. As she reads a moment from Leo Bersani, during which "a butch number swaggering into a bar in a leather get-up" in fact "sounds like a pansy" and has "the complete works of Jane Austen" at home (qtd. in Johnson 25), Johnson might have called attention to yet another division within the ranks of the queer (i.e., gay male) Austen contingent —between "real" gay men who turn to Austen for the express purpose of inhabiting the persona of the sighing heroine and their academic counterparts bent on spoiling this fun through their antagonistic stance toward traditional romance plots in the novel. (See also Miller *Jane Austen* 4–5.) Throughout, the article swings between references to Austen's queer(ing) readers to her lesbian(izing) ones—the pansified Janeites who admired Austen for anything but a lesbian subplot and the he-men critics who queered her work in spite of themselves, through their assessment that "Austen was more of a real man—tough-minded, astringent, unblinking—than they were" (35). Ultimately, Johnson must count on an all-purpose category of nonnormative sexuality to make connections and form alliances that require but do not receive further delineation.

Clara Tuite deploys the umbrella term "nonreproductive" to enable similar transpositions in the response to Austen—from her biographer-nephew's original use of the term to indicate Austen's commitment to original (not "reproduced") writing to her actually childless state to a lesbian sensibility that Tuite suggests even her nephew is hinting at. Stronger evidence is sought out in Austen's stylistic influence on three "queer nephews"—Forster, James, and Firbank; that two of these three (Forster and James) roundly rejected this inheritance necessitates yet another interpretive stretch. In the discussion of Forster, for instance, Tuite sets aside his dismissive attitude toward Austen; his negative review of *Sanditon* is dispatched with a single reference to "Forster's attack." Otherwise, it is the canon, the closet, and "Augustan misogynist tropes of female authorship" (127–28) that bear the brunt of Tuite's critique. The only overtly gay "nephew" in Tuite's survey, Ronald Firbank, is read as having been influenced by Austen's *Sanditon* in the production of his queer-inflected novel *Valmouth* (1919). The impossibility of this lineage, however, is representative of the difficulty Tuite faces in tracing family lines at any point in her discussion: while *Sanditon* was written in 1817, it was not published until 1925, six year's after Firbank's novel debuted. Finally, Tuite's trope of literary inheritance means that the queer Austen must wait to be born in the queering influence she seems to have had on canonical and semicanonical male authors a century after her death, ultimately inheriting her queerness from three nephews instead.

In a discussion this time focused on *Emma*, Johnson again introduces feminist and queer arguments that pull the project in separate directions. Following a helpful review of antilesbian readings of *Emma* performed by mid-century male critics, she notes that the argument has survived to enjoy a decidedly subversive revision by contemporary lesbian theorists, due in part to the novel's own "amazingly [low level] of anxiety on the subject" of Emma's "wayward" sexual proclivities (" 'Not at All' " 150). Development of the lesbian reading, however, succumbs immediately to a discussion of Emma-as-feminist, as Johnson considers Emma's independence, "strong" handwriting (much admired by her husband-to-be), and intelligence (through contrast to her "vapid" sister Isabella). The antifeminist fix in which Emma finds herself near novel's end, "of having possibly to wait to be proposed to" (151) completes this unacknowledged transition from lesbian to (feminist) straight character, forming a less likely transition (than the lesbian focus would have been) to Johnson's discussion of the novel's nonnormative masculinities. Meanwhile, Johnson's dichotomies of proper and improper manhood are a study in tendentious contrasts: doddering Mr. Woodhouse (pansified by critics for decades) is simultaneously womanishly *and* chivalrously fixated on the situation of women, representing a family's scandalous queer burden *and* a dying patrician age. Mr. Knightley is likewise a fence-riding blend of antifoppism—he is critical of henpecked men and eager to silence bossy women—*and* suggestively "fraternal" feelings toward his manly fellow-farmers that coincides with a "passion" for Emma so subtle and cool it is more his homoerotic tendencies than her lesbianism that keeps her in the dark so long about his feelings for her.

Johnson's final emphasis is on Emma's admirable "mannishness," a state that would undo culturally imposed "feminine" weakness (like Isabella's) and connote a lesbianism refreshingly well handled by the story itself. But Johnson is oddly uncritical of what-all has been sacrificed in the process: "[I]t is not merely femininity that Emma's portion designedly lacks. It is effeminacy as well, as Emma's rebuke of Frank Churchill's double-dealing and trickery makes clear: 'Impropriety . . . has sunk him [says Emma], I cannot say how much it has sunk him in my opinion. So unlike what a man should be!' " (156). To what degree does Emma's feminism/lesbianism permit her homophobic sentiments (especially her equation of Churchill's criminality with his impugned masculinity) to go unchallenged by the feminist/lesbian reader?[14] Another interpretation of this passage (and this theme of "strong" women and men in *Emma*) might just as easily despair at Emma's parroting of Knightley's homophobic/misogynist pronouncements against Churchill, yet Johnson subsumes this moment, by means never fully demonstrated, under Emma's resilient lesbian perspective. Ultimately, the argument unites typically at-odds feminist and lesbian sensibilities by equating these with an "antieffeminacy" that reflects badly on them both. Because the men in this novel admittedly send a markedly mixed signal with respect to gender positionings, Johnson attempts to argue that nonnormative masculinities are a form of misogyny, a collapse of political opposites that not only undermines her own argument but threatens the platform upon which the projects of feminism and queer studies have been built.

JAMES ON THE COUCH

In much recent James criticism, the feminist approach is primarily the "straight" one, focused on the heterosexual entanglements of his various characters to the sometimes extreme exclusion of obvious queer shadings, relying often on a psychoanalytic approach. For instance, Kaja Silverman's discernment of the primal scene in James's novels seeks to explain their shifting homo/heterosexual atmospherics. Because this scene as determined by Freud is one of constantly changing identifications, James's many peeping protagonists are opened automatically to feminine and masculine (passive and active) sexual positionings, like the quintessential viewing child. Freud has likewise left us with a kink in this scenario that any queer theorist could warm to; in the *coitus a tergo* witnessed by the young Wolfman, identification with the receiving position marks the patient's homosexual tendencies, while the "straight" position (or "positive" Oedipal mode) is accessed not by picturing himself in the father's active role but by placing himself *behind* the father: "[there are] two desires which the Jamesian phantasmatic sustains—the desire to be sodomized by the 'father' while occupying the place of the 'mother,' and the desire to sodomize [the father] while he is penetrating the 'mother' " ("Too Early/Too Late" 165). Thus the viewing (male) subject perverts the heterosexual dyad no matter whether he chooses to cross sexual boundaries through identification with mother or through queering the original dyadic arrangement by making a threesome of it. Silverman herself determines this scene to include "three terms" in a perverse sexual "relay"; additionally, she notes that such scene-witnessing creates in the young male feelings of unawareness and disempowerment. As opposed to the Metzian theory (from film studies) that equates voyeurism with sadism, aggressivity, and control, Silverman argues that in the childhood stage (and as with many James protagonists) what is secretly viewed or overheard causes the witness to feel uninformed, excluded, and ridiculous.

These several assaults on normative masculine heterosexuality recommend the primal scene for wide application in Jamesian queer criticism, yet Silverman neglects such applications. Interestingly, her reading is part of its own three-term relay, positioned as it is between two related writings by Eve Sedgwick, the first of which ("The Beast in the Closet") Silverman responds to here, the second of which Sedgwick (in *Tendencies*) uses to respond to Silverman. Although Silverman mostly agrees with Sedgwick's queer reading of James's short story "The Beast in the Jungle," she suggests a psychoanalytic fine-tuning that in fact undermines Sedgwick's original queer interpretation. Eros gives way to theory in Silverman's primal-scene reading of Marcher and another man in the graveyard at story's end: here, the metaphoric act of the stranger penetrating Marcher "marks *the maternal point of entry* into the Jamesian phantasmatic—that turning, in other words, upon identification with the *'mother'*—and the latter [in which Marcher does the penetrating] the point of entry which occurs through which I have called 'pederastic identification' with the *'father'* " ("Too Early/Too Late" 166, emphases added). Silverman's wording not only literally interjects a female figure between two sexually engaged men; it almost comically recasts the scenario from the child witnessing parental sexual activity to first "mom" and then "dad" walking in on the illicit sexual activity of a "son" figure and his anonymous male lover. Gay male sexuality is also uncomfortably "identified with" pederasty in Silverman's assessment. While the psychoanalytic model works well to sexualize the witnessing done by multiple James characters, it is a tenaciously "hetero" sexuality that emerges from the model in each instance.

Despite the pointedness of their debate, Sedgwick's and Silverman's readings share several features. For instance, as Silverman determines that her project "enclose[s] homosexuality within heterosexuality" ("Too Early/Too Late" 165) so Sedgwick locates the index of Marcher's queerness *not* within Marcher himself or the man he meets, but within the narrative presence (and, in death, absence) of May Bartram, the straight woman whom Marcher fails to love and who, alone in the story, knows why. Like Silverman, Sedgwick borrows from the psychoanalytic paradigm to make this point, depicting May as the classic woman on the right side of knowledge: "it is always open to women to know something that it is much more dangerous for any nonhomosexual-identified man to know. The ground of May Bartram and John Marcher's relationship is from the first that she has the advantage of him, cognitively" ("Beast" 179). In fact, even her strong reading of Marcher's "cruisy" encounter in the graveyard (as opposed to Silverman, I am largely persuaded by it) employs the psychoanalytic paradigm—the Law of the Father substituting now for an earlier, more culturally inscribed homosexual panic and the sacrificed phallic mother who, in certain respects, shares the victim position with male-male desire in the boy's acquiescence to the Law ("Beast" 180–81).

Sedgwick challenges the heterocentrism of Silverman's argument, in her later reading of James's *The Wings of the Dove*. Despite the solid rationale for this challenge, her argument wavers on two counts— first, its lack of consideration on two occasions (*Tendencies* 78, 97) of the queer vectors in Freud's primal scene (discussed above); second, and more importantly, its inability to protect its several queering gestures from the encroachments of heterosexual reappropriation. She begins with Lionel Croy—the closet case with an "unnameable" secret, who is nevertheless "not seen to experience" same-sex desires at any point in the story (79). Croy's daughter Kate occupies the commodifiably feminine position toward which Lionel takes a queenie, "connoisseurial" interest (81), but is also a "handsome . . . breezy boy" (qtd. in *Tendencies* 83), now occupying a masculine/butch/ lesbian position instead. Sedgwick's persistently obscure reading of Kate's "sidedness" emerges at this point, perhaps to allow the reader to continue seeing her as lesbian despite her powerful heterosexual attachment to Merton Densher.

Merton is not only Kate's love interest (and later Milly's too) but is also transfixed, late in the novel, by the penetrating gaze of the Italian servant Eugenio; Milly enjoys (or suffers from) a "bi-gendered double vision" (87) that confines her upon ontologic fences such as the following: "Milly is not virilized by her desiring regard of Kate, but it leaves her vulnerable to being involuntarily assigned to a subject position she can only label male" (86). Milly's own queer tutor, Susan Stringham, is an "obsolescent but legitimated proto-lesbian" (79), and in an argument too multifaceted to rehearse here, Lionel is credited with a ripple-effect queering of most of the young women in the story. While her rapidly shifting feminine and masculine, queer and hetero characterizations are recognizable, viable features in the postidentitarian critical context in which Sedgwick writes, the contest between complexity and obscurity played out in this writing indicates the difficulties confronting the critical attempt to queer the last bastion in the field—a novel's heterosexual tendencies, either characterological or narrative, themselves.

Such textual resistance is exhibited best in Sedgwick's efforts to include a sustained lesbian reading of the novel. Knowing, as she surely does, that queer interpretations of James are overwhelmingly male-oriented, she seeks in the final moments of her essay to emphasize the lesbian figurations amongst the characters in the story. Working from the Wolfmanian premise that both "moms" and "dads" have anuses (and are thus, in the region of the anorectal complex, inter-changeable), Sedgwick insists that the multiple anal and fisting images in the novel in fact depict lesbian sexuality. Strikingly, however, the analysis is overrun with heterosexual male figures: her supporting sources are male (Freud, Pope, James himself, even Bob Dylan), and her coinage "fisting-as-écriture" (99) is removed in the reader's mind from its decidedly gay-male register only by reference to a heterosex-ualizing "obstetric hand" (a quote from Pope's *Dunciad*). The dying Milly Theale, whose "unspecified illness that can at certain moments be figured as if it were a pregnancy" (100), is anally probed—putatively to the delight of her lesbian desire (98)—by the healing hands of Sir Luke, later by the masculine Eugenio who plunges his hand into Milly's pocket. While for the protolesbian Susan Stringham "Milly represents a 'mine of something precious' " (101), all other references to Milly's "anal" (i.e., receptive) erotics function less to les-bianize her character than to resituate it along classically Freudian lines. While the novel thus makes it difficult enough to search out what is queerly male in its unfoldings, it seems positively immune to a viable lesbian reading, labor though Sedgwick may to accomplish such. To clarify what may have only been implied thus far, I am less interested to fault Sedgwick for failing to fully queer these texts than to gaze with fascination at the contest between closeted novel and queering critic in this struggle to expose its secrets.

In his reading of this same novel, Michael Moon faces similar obstacles and seems to have structured his analysis explicitly in response to these. He describes the essay's two sections, one theoret-ical and the other political, divided plainly into "Part I" and "Part II." In keeping with all the James interpretations we have surveyed so far, what is "theoretical" here will be women-centered, heterosexually ori-ented, psychoanalytically inflected, and feminist in tone; what is "political" will be historically contextualized, male-oriented, and dis-tinctly queered. As does Sedgwick's above, Moon's theoretical read-ing vacillates between opposing arguments; the wealthy women in this story are alternately victimized by money-seeking men and victimizers of these same figures by their superior wealth. The castrating gaze of the formidable Maud Lowder enables Moon's equation between wealth, visual terrorism, and access to phallic power, but beyond the largely unappealing Maud, the sexual entanglements of the younger, more attractive characters tangle Moon's reading as well. In an early moment, Moon reassigns "the 'potent' gaze that holds other persons (usually women) in check" from "males" to "simply a behavioral privilege of the rich" (429), yet moments later, the gaze reverts again: "in its presentation of [Kate Croy's] relation to her lover Merton Densher, the novel clearly manifests the prejudice in favor of the male inherent in the practice of visual terrorism" (430). If this is the case, however, how is that "Kate has inaugurated her relationship with Merton by looking him full in the face, frankly, not just by reflecting back his own long looks at her" (431)? In his desire to position Kate (and all women in the story) as victims, Moon ignores this seemingly singular expression of women's active sexual desire by insisting upon its "asymmetrical" subjugation to Merton's returning gaze.

Elsewhere, "The fundamental action the narrative unfolds is the *restitution* to Merton Densher of the phallus or phallic empowerment which he *initially* lacks" (429, emphases added), and Milly "*arrives phallicly empowered* to the considerable degree that rich women are in this novel" (431) yet later in the story "*undergoes phallicization*" during an interview with Dr. Strett" (432, emphases added). My seemingly picky inquiry into the temporal inconsistencies here—how can Merton have "restored" to him what he has been without from the outset? If Milly arrives on the scene phallicly empowered by her "thumping bank account," why must (and how can) she later "undergo phallicization" at the hands of Strett?—only responds to Moon's own ostensible goal in this section, to trace the path of the novel's phallic relay as "it" passes from one hand to the next. Finally, and with biographical knowledge of James's equal diffidence toward women and queer subject positions in mind, the reader senses this novel as resistant to the attachment of a solid feminist reading as it is to the queer interpretations sought after by Sedgwick above.

While readers familiar with Moon's work may have expected a consistently queer-inflected response to the novel, in fact the "queer half" of this article is itself significantly bolstered by a lengthy extra-textual investigation of the gondolier-as-prostitute for turn-of-the-century middle-class Venetian tourists. James's Italian servant figure Eugenio is from there reframed as this homoeroticized gondolier; although the analogy is suggestive—as a form of sexual innuendo similar to Sedgwick's masturbating girl, it cannot be otherwise—the moments in this novel with authentic queer potential seem fragile and fleeting as the dying Milly Theale. Considering the length of the novel, the paucity of examples Moon finds himself working with—a few intense gazes shared by Merton and some minor male characters—may cause us to question whether the novel is not winning this contest.

JAMES ON STAGE

Above I observed the ways in which not Freud's but Foucault's lexicon informed Joseph Litvak's exploration of James and the theatrical in *Caught in the Act*. Here I wish to expand that discussion by discerning certain obstacles to the queering of James, housed within the trope of the theatrical itself. In Litvak's panoptical theater scenario, to gaze (to direct, detect, stage, embarrass, be in on) is to assume the position of heterosexual mastery; to be seen (to be caught, exposed, pushed into the limelight, embarrassed, fooled) simulates the abjection of the receptive (i.e., gay) male. The metaphor recalls the director/actor dichotomy of Silverman's *coitus a tergo* scenario above. While the entire "act" is on stage before the viewing child in the primal scene, within the configuration itself, s/he who stands behind and directs and s/he who kneels before and takes direction are also constituted by oppositions between seeing and being seen, between sneak attacks from the rear and being taken by surprise. Litvak argues that James was more than capable of "catching *himself* in the act" on multiple novelistic and autobiographical occasions, in an authorial gesture that deconstructs binaries between straight and gay, top and bottom, good and evil, the player and the critic. He indicates that while James enjoyed the "top" position much of the time, he opted for the "bottom" role just as often and self-staged many moments in his work and life of his pants dropping around his ankles for his readers', and his own, pleasure.

Persuasive as this argument may be, it is also the case that, if James is self-selecting his position in both instances, he has never truly relinquished the director's seat. In fact to position James so masterfully behind (in fact, above) the multiple binaries read by Litvak accords him so much power that he begins to resemble less the savvy masochist than the homophobic heteromale, adopting elaborate drag for a sardonic laugh. Hugh Stevens's reading of James's satiric take on the Wilde trials (chapter 7) in part corroborates this view, and in separate writings Ellmann and Novick have also discussed James's paradoxical relationship to the stage and to Wilde. James's loathing of the low-brow masses was equaled by his disdain for those public figures who courted their attention. The mindless audiences who preferred Wilde's plays to his failed theatrical attempt were, according to Ellmann, too beneath his contempt to truly wound him (40–41); he liked them no better when they made a circus of Wilde's trial (Stevens 150), though his sympathy for the beleaguered Wilde was tempered by his deeply felt sense that Wilde had gotten what he deserved.

Novick also reports James's "initially hostile reaction" to Wilde's "public sexuality" (19); when he later notes that James "was always acting; in his notebooks, sketching out a fictional scene, he sometimes lapsed into the first person, jumping on to the stage and showing his characters how they ought to play it" (16), we note that James accesses the stage in this scenario primarily as director. Even as these collapsing binaries demonstrate Litvak's point, there remains the uncomfortable sense that they betray more plainly than ever James's sexual hypocrisy and cowardice. As valuable as are the many recent studies revisiting the sensual, sexual side of James, their introduction of the Wilde issue functions as effectively to queer James by association as it does to contrast Wilde's heroic self-realization to what almost appears as James's ethic of homophobia.

Tessa Hadley's study is primarily a feminist approach to James, yet her emphasis on Foucauldian-style "voluptuous imaginings of pleasure" (3) also classifies her work within the burgeoning canon of gay responses. She contends that her concentration on heterosexual love stories and the treatment of women in James's novels "is not unconnected to the new homoerotic perspectives on the writing. It is James's freedom from 'definitional frames' of hetero- and homosexuality that give him his special purchase on the whole urgent business of gender definition" (1–2). In Hadley's smart discussion of the difference between European (i.e., French) and English-language novels of the period, James emerges as a distinctly womanish figure— constrained within a prudish literary tradition dominated by woman authors and readers, as master of a "feminine and inward-turning" narrative style (11), and as practitioner of his own brand of feminine "delicacy" (12)—that is, of the restraint, discretion, modesty, and decorum by which he sheltered his personal life and marked the actions of his honorable literary characters throughout his career.

Yet this profile of James echoes the findings of Ellmann, Novick, and Stevens above; at his most gender-deviant in Hadley's estimation, James is simultaneously at his most erotophobic and thus conceptually opposed to the pleasure-seeking sensibilities of more self-accepting figures such as Wilde (not to mention Foucault). When Hadley traces the growth of James's pleasure-seeking impulse as this came to coexist alongside his strong sense of moral rectitude, she reads *The Ambassadors* (with its James-like protagonist) as paradigmatic: "no longer at the periphery but at the very heart of this novel the lovers, like lovers in the real world, take off their clothes and embrace. . . . [T]he writer who had always read Balzac and Flaubert no longer scrupled to name the simple facts that the French novelists had always told" (19). At James's most pleasure-accepting and sexually forthright, the paradigmatic scene is unabashedly heterosexual; returning to the traditional casting of the primal scene, exactly the dynamic Sedgwick questioned in Silverman's reading above, a heterosexual couple cavorts before the wondering eyes of nonparticipatory male. Relative to the robust, Balzacian sensuality on display in this scene, James's pose of diffidence or equivocality may constitute the queerer stance after all—that vague, diffuse *ecriture gaie* whose hidden truths are more queerly suggestive than the rampant heterosexuality unveiled here. While Strether is surely part of this scene for the reader, Hadley is correct that the heart of it is about straight sex; the Foucauldian semantic context in this case is not sufficient to reflexively queer James, and Hadley's reading leans well into the feminist register in its sex-positive exploration of straight sexuality.

For Love of Olive

The Bostonians is a key text for queer and feminist readers of James for obvious reasons. Centrally concerning the early women's movement, specifically its struggle for voting rights and the popular women's lecture circuit that significantly aided this cause, the novel presents not just one progressive, politicized female character but several, each exhibiting a range of repellent and riveting qualities that make them believable and meaningful. The plot involves the charismatic Verena Tarrant's conversion to (and lapse from) the women's cause; that she is almost convinced to take up the suffragist calling as a long-term commitment speaks impressively not only of the potential of her own character but of the persuasiveness of the feminist mentors she meets along her way. Perhaps the novel's most striking feminist statement, however, comes in the form of the novel's "hero," the simultaneously vanquished and victorious Basil Ransom, whose atrocious attitudes toward women are classic examples of feminism's raison d'etre. Basil is in fact so bad that "even" lesbianism might strike "ordinary" women as the more attractive alternative, and the intense relationship between Verena and her chief handler Olive Chancellor has been scrutinized for its lesbian content throughout the century. Meanwhile, Basil has no doubt struck many readers (and perhaps his author as well) as the ideal gentleman, and whether Basil is a heel or a hero (and whether or not James is in on the joke against him or against his female adversaries) depends once more on our discernment of an ironic distancing between author and character. If in fact it is only feminist theorizing that has succeeded in listening this irony into existence, or if—in the absence of such irony—it is simply feminist readers responsible for declaring Basil a monster, we can see how this feminist reading has in one respect enabled or formed the necessary first step toward the more developed lesbian interpretation.[15]

In both readings, meanwhile, it is Olive who commands critical attention; she is both a better feminist and better lesbian than her beautiful protégé may ever hope to become. Verena's ability to love seems as attenuated as her ability to commit politically; the novel makes plain her terrific appeal, but this is figured primarily as an aura she gives off—indiscriminately, in all directions—that generates a passionate response in any man or woman within its radius but that she is never able to reciprocate. Even though it helps greatly to include at least two women in the depiction of a lesbian relationship, and even though a feminist movement may be judged successful primarily by the number of "normal" women such as Verena it can convert and promote as spokespersons, she is a disappointment on both counts, while, for feminist, lesbian, and gay readers, Olive more than makes up for what Verena lacks. For while we might read Basil's pathologic attitudes toward women and failure to be touched by Verena's oratorical powers as twisted indicators of a self-hating gay subjectivity, in fact the primary gay treatment of the novel locatable for this study maintains a focus on Olive, as a sexually inverted analogue for the author himself. Olive's success in this novel, her relationship to her audience, her cause, and her desires, is of continuing interest for all of these critical approaches; specifically, whether and how she triumphs over Basil (in a battle of the sexes that works, I find, to reheterosexualize her character) or (along more queerly shaded lines) the traditional marriage plot he represents is a preoccupying theme. Her final appearance before an enraged Boston audience (and she has always averred that she cannot speak in public) is ambiguous in the novel itself; whether her moment in the spotlight ends in victory or defeat, her heroism is evident, giving these readers, all who for the most part admire her character, something to cheer about.

The relationship between lesbianism and misogyny in the early critical reception of this novel is seen to embroil even feminist defenders of its cause. Judith Fetterly surveys "phallic critics" who, reversing my argument above, read Olive's lesbianism as such an unpalatable threat that even a monster such as Basil figures as a rescuing hero. While critical of this attitude, Fetterly nevertheless rejects the "charge" of lesbianism as nothing more than an excuse to vilify the women characters and their politically productive relationships: "it is in the imputation of lesbianism, with all its assumed connotations, that the phallic critic feels he has irrefutable evidence for his reading of the book" (110). That lesbianism is described, not by the phallic critics but by Fetterly herself as an "imputation" (an accusation, an alibi, a disparaging figment of the imagination) positions it as something occurring primarily in the mind of women's worst enemy. Her feminist project thus depends upon a "debunking" of the lesbian "myth," generated by male phallic critics and standing in the way of our fuller understanding of both Olive and Basil.

Throughout the argument, Fetterly would rescue Olive from these false charges by focusing instead on her role as feminist reformer. Much more recently, David Van Leer takes the same tack by ruling against "*reduc[ing]* Olive . . . to her desires, making her [feminist] beliefs mere 'symptoms' of sexual deviance" (100, emphasis added).[16] Fetterly's emphasis on Olive's battle (over Verena, women's rights, the Civil War) with Basil (117, 119) also de-lesbianizes her character. While certainly Verena is the love interest for both figures, and while Fetterly at one point homoeroticizes Olive by depicting her as Basil's "rival" (144), her constant comparison of Olive and Basil links their names and qualities so as to heterosexually pair them. Olive and Basil are in fact passionately "engaged" in Fetterly's discussion, spending more discursive time in each other's presence than either does with Verena. And while Fetterly locates a Jamesian "irony" (127–28) at the heart of our proper reading of Basil as villain, it is Olive whom Fetterly insists is the "loser" in this story (131), with such confidence that her voice is at times indistinguishable from her phallic adversaries'. Likely she is depending upon her reader to listen for the ironic distancing between her feminist perspective and observations she is forced to mouth by characters such as Basil, authors such as James, and the phallic critics she targets; unfortunately, the alternative reading that would indicate this distance is never provided, so the impression made is that Fetterly's critique and the typical misogynist response are one.

Fetterly harps upon Olive's failure to win her heart's desire and— so that it is practically her own fault—work past the self-defeating attitude that weakens her feminist outlook. She "willingly evokes disaster" (132) and "engages in blatant exercises of power" (133), yet flops on her face in every instance, seeming to bring humiliation on herself. Significantly, this emphasis on Olive's powerlessness coincides with the first sustained mention of her lesbianism (132) so that the sadistic joy seemingly taken in Olive's failure as a feminist includes a large measure of homophobia as well. Elsewhere, "Olive believes ultimately neither in herself nor in women, nor in their cause or movement" (137). Such a sweeping condemnation certainly seems to be *the novel's* rationale for our eventual emotional leave-taking of Olive and her plight; here it is identical with the feminist critic's own.

Fetterly later compares Olive to Basil, in that "they both see as inevitable the patriarchal system," but to what degree do utter capitulations such as this only deepen the sense (and reality) of inevitability? In a final throwing-in of the towel, Fetterly observes that "Ransom is born to victory and to power, Olive and Verena to weakness and defeat, because this is the way things are and always will be" (150). She goes on to develop this argument at length, ending the paragraph comfortably espousing the message that women are completely doomed.

In such rhetorically controlled moments as these, the reader in search of a distinctively feminist argument must listen intently for an articulation that is ultimately missing. Instead of proposing an alternative or even articulating a complaint, Fetterly only describes the situation in attentive detail; we are returned by such a striking rhetorical gesture to the example with which this chapter began, in which a misogynist outrage is impossible to distinguish from a misogynist fantasy (which is in fact only reality— "the way things are and always will be"). While I thus fail to discern the irony in Fetterly's remarks, I do find it ironic that Fetterly at one point criticizes Olive's relentless focus on "women's suffering rather than on their suffrage" (136), while it is Fetterly herself who focuses on Olive's suffering, her qualities as a complete "loser," when many other readers of this novel have pointed to her important victories. Elsewhere, she criticizes the minor feminist characters Miss. Birdseye and Dr. Prance for each having "given up her sexuality in order to accomplish her goals" (141), returning to the equation between sexuality and fertility critiqued above.

Claire Kahane's more recent and more theoretical feminist reading in fact echoes Fetterly's response in several respects. Her emphasis, like Fetterly's, is on the novel's theme of feminism/reform, once more to the surprising exclusion of its obvious lesbian intonations. She likewise "engages" Olive and Basil in a battle of the sexes, between "male chauvinist and female avenger" (67), defining them through a series of binary oppositions: "North and South, freedom and slavery, speech and writing, the tongue and the touch, public and private" (67). Kahane notes that "the novel repeatedly sets up these cultural oppositions, binds them to the difference between masculine and feminine, and then provocatively flirts with their collapse" (67); while the flirtatious collapsing observed by Kahane indeed distinguishes her article from Fetterly's binarized approach, the effect produced is largely a feminizing of Basil (hysterically ranting against hysterical women) instead of a lesbianizing of Olive, who claims relatively little of Kahane's interest. In fact Olive seems to hold up half of the initial binary in this system (as feminist avenger), while it is the heterosexualized Verena and various members of her family who instigate the collapse of gendered and sexual identities.

It is not only Kahane's emphasis on the straight characters in the story that maintains the argument's heterosexual focus, but as with Silverman, and to some degree Sedgwick and Moon, in their Jamesian readings above, the psychoanalytic shadings that reinforce this effect. Especially reminiscent of Moon's reading of *Wings of the Dove*, here Kahane seeks to locate phallic power among these figures and encounters the same difficulties Moon did in maintaining a consistent reading. For Kahane, the voice is "the primary fetish" (70) but is paired with another fetish-figure, the hand (recall Sedgwick's reading of *Dove*) that is, as extended by the feminist characters, described as "cold and limp." Can something be limp and fetishized at once? Is the hand a failed, flaccid fetish and the voice its more turgid successor? Do women's hands somehow fail to compete with men's phallically infused voices? Kahane's overly open thesis moment—"Each of the characters is in some essential way defined by a relation to the speaking voice, a relation that also marks their sexual personality as phallic or castrated" (70)—perpetuates the confusion. Basil's rant against this "chattering, canting age" makes him verbose and effeminate, while Verena's father is good with his hands in traditional manly fashion. Yet Mrs. Tarrant is "humiliated by her husband's inability to speak" (70), so it seems that those who speak enjoy a phallic cachet after all. Yet is it his inarticulate ways or his henpecking wife that signifies Mr. Tarrant's castrated status? Matthias Pardon's ubiquitous speech places him in the category of the verbose and effeminate, so a silent man and a verbose one both seem to have fallen victim to the castrating knife. Ransom considers "holding one's tongue [to be] a masculine attribute" (71), yet he represents "the 'feminine' principle" by hailing from "the warm, earthly, sensual South" (72). From this welter of mixed signals, Kahane extracts an argument at chapter's end "that equates speaking with potency and silence with being raped or castrated" (79), a productive observation that is only half-supported (and thus largely unsupported) by the preceding argument.

Like Fetterly's, Kahane's queerest moments occur at the end of her argument. She describes Olive wanting to "unveil the father's guilt" and relates this to even more suggestive novelistic effects: "To be quiet and not to touch—these prohibitions on the voice and the hand are also narrative prohibitions on revealing the sadomasochistic ground of sexual relations that James's narrator both uncovers and covers over in a recurrent and classically hysterical act of playing secrets through textual allusion" (75). But do Kahane's references to paternal guilt, sadomasochism, and open secrets bespeak a queer subplot or not? Is this argument's own supposed allusion to the queer counterreading so obvious as to not bear mentioning or so far from the author's mind that she would never dream of referring to it? Later Kahane describes "highly allusive suggestiveness" in James's description of Marmion with its "sour fruition" and "bare stone dykes" (77), but for unspecified reasons does not name the lesbianism at the heart of these allusions. Kahane's reference to Marmion as "feminist enclave" leads the reader to ask: for Kahane, once one has said "feminist" has one also said "lesbian"? Is feminism worth naming since it continues in sophisticated allusive mode, while direct references to lesbianism might strike the reader as a déclassé ton of bricks? At the end of her argument, Kahane locates in the impending marriage of Basil and Verena a "most subversive ending to a heterosexual marriage plot"—a claim I find provocative. Here it seems to be that horrible straight characters entering disastrous heterosexual unions constitute a stronger challenge to the marriage plot than do a novel's coded queers. I argued above that we had Basil the bachelor to thank for this story's strikingly attractive alternatives represented by both feminist activism and lesbian romance; while my point there was to indicate the misogyny that necessarily founds the feminist project and the feminism that in part enables the lesbian counterpoint, here Kahane fixates on Basil and his marriage to the vapid Verena as loci of cultural subversion to the comfortable exclusion of the important alternative challenge Olive represents.

My largely critical response to the two preceding feminist arguments should indicate my feeling that the lesbian reading of *The Bostonians* is the most obvious and necessary of the three we might select here, obvious in a way that creates interesting problems for Terry Castle's analysis. The ostensible theme throughout *The Apparitional Lesbian* is the (homophobic though subversively recuperable) ghosting of the lesbian figure—especially in canonical works by male authors; at the end of her chapter on Sylvia Townsend Warner, Castle stipulates that properly eroticized lesbian fiction is locatable only (when it is locatable at all) within a marginalized, experimentally styled, lesbian-themed countercanon. In a later chapter, however, James's certainly canonical *Bostonians* is hailed as an "important lesbian novel" (152); and not only is James's text clearly canonical, but its heroine Olive, at least in Castle's adroit handling, is so certainly lesbian that she barely belongs to the category of the apparitional.

In an effort to deepen her potentially self-evident observations, Castle embarks on an analytic course and makes particular use of the interpretive stretch: after several paragraphs highlighting the novel's many lesbian moments, Castle claims that "lesbianism is no more than a ghost in *The Bostonians*" (170). As did Hadley, Castle also reaches across the Atlantic, this time to compare *The Bostonians* with Zola's risqué but influential *Nana*. In fact, the parallels between texts isolated by Castle are many and persuasive, and are deployed to effectively solve a persistent problem in queer approaches to this novel:

> By setting up a train of discreet yet compromising intertextual links between Verena and Nana on the one hand, and Olive and Satin on the other, James manages to suggest the *effect*, if not exactly the reality, of a reciprocal lesbian desire. To the degree that Verena and Olive seem unconsciously to mimic their indecent French counterparts—at times to even appear to be 'possessed' by them—so their relationship itself comes to seem haunted by a ghostly Zolan carnality. (165)

Thus while at first one seems to not need to go outside James's own household (specifically, his sister's "Boston marriage" with Katharine Loring) to locate the lesbian analogue infusing the story, in fact Castle has made the trip to France for good reason—to infuse the text with an unspoken eroticism that would seem to finally embody these American ghosts with a sexuality that can also be read as a "haunting."

Later, however, Castle admits that "Olive is as *unlike* Zola's trashy Satin as anyone could possibly be. Satin is, after all, a fairly minor character in *Nana*, and one ends up caring very little about her" (172). If Satin's part is in fact so very small, the reader then wonders whether Nana has other female lovers in the novel, whether *Nana* is very much of a lesbian novel after all. This concern grows when Castle posits that in fact it is Count Muffat who makes the better Olive analogue, although the grounds for comparison—the Count's tragic qualities (176)—seem somewhat flimsy and problematic on their own. The argument that Olive is a meaningful reflection of both Dorothy Strachey's Olivia and Djuna Barnes's Nora is also tenuous: when Castle asserts that a doll found on the bed of Nora's ex-lover is an echo of the "doll-dressing" Mrs. Farrinder refers to in order to dismiss Olive's love for Verena (182), we seem to have arrived at the opposite pole of the obviousness of Olive's lesbian qualities, where the ice is so thin that these qualities' very obviousness is called into question. Again, I am most persuaded by what turns out to be this writing's most slanted reading (regarding *The Bostonians* and the ultimately nonanalogous

Nana), but also so fully swayed by Castle's well-selected quotes from James's novel that they in fact speak for themselves (i.e., threaten the very need for any sort of critical support). Ultimately, because of this effective work with the novel itself, the interpretive stretches do not undermine Castle's contention that Olive is an authentic, fully drawn lesbian character.

Persuasively, Castle notes that even though the women's affair turns out more tragic than erotic, "the question of female same sex desire" cannot be ruled out "simply because Olive and Verena's relationship ends badly" (170). She discerns real heroism in this tragic outcome, in a move similar to Joseph Litvak's gay-inflected reading of this text, during which he locates a distinct eroticism in Olive's final public humiliation. In keeping with Litvak's overarching theme of embarrass-ment as (masochistic) fulfillment, Olive is here poised on the same threshold between constrained observation and erotically charged per-formance that Litvak has discerned in other of James's characters and the author himself. If in fact Olive finds not only humiliation but excitement on the public stage, our question might regard the coinci-dence of Litvak's and Castle's projects: does Litvak's reading position Olive as lesbian just as effectively (perhaps even more effectively) than Castle's does? Does it cast her as more generically, almost abstractly queer, as "what remains, on stage and in the text, after the brutal bina-risms of heterosexuality have been imposed" (*Caught in the Act* 234)? Or does the reading tend after all to reserve Olive for the role of Jamesian (i.e., gay male) analogue, primarily in service of Litvak's larger project of identifying a gay sensibility in James and his works?

The bulk of Litvak's argument establishes concise similarities between Olive and James. Not only do both share a teasingly liminal relationship to stage and sideline, ever hovering over the possibility of "coming out" and the terrific risks and thrills this move might entail; both, says Litvak, fully recognize and utilize their authority on the margin: "there is no more reason to assume that Olive is simply betrayed into publicity than there is to assume that James, in the passage from *A Small Boy and Others*, is the dupe of his own self-deconstructing rhetoric" (*Caught in the Act* 230). Meanwhile, Litvak's effort to eroticize Olive's moment on stage works to ultimately de-eroticize what other-wise engages her in the novel, her relationship to Verena, who is treated here primarily as Olive's opprobrious counterpart, the real "dupe" in the story who falls easily for Basil's heterosexist fairy-tales. As Litvak reads the final moments of the novel, in fact, Olive's erotic self-expression has no chance until Verena is whisked off-stage; her sexu-ality is both a solo act and the center of a large, orgiastic event, but the twoness effected between Olive and Verena in their private moments is not accommodated in Litvak's handling.

Clearly, his reading offers a distinctly queer eroticism; of all the critical treatments she has received so far, here Olive sees her best chance for getting off, but whether this is an effect produced by and/or conducive to lesbian sexuality, or whether she has had to sacrifice this sensibility to adopt James's own (purportedly gay male) sexual positioning remains an open question. In addition, considering the politics of humiliation as these play out between a male author and his female character, Litvak concedes that "James's cross-gender identification with Olive cannot constitute a lesbian-feminist politics and poetics" (*Caught in the Act* 223), Once again, a critic has identified a "lesbian-feminist" whose politics and poetics work in cross-canceling fashion with the gay male and/or his eroticized counterpart: has the lesbian reading suffered by association with its overly politicized, acutely desexualized feminist alter-ego? In light of Castle's plenty-eroticized reading, and her ultimately favorable assessment of James's authorial handling of the novel's lesbian characters, is Litvak inaccurately classing a more sex-affirmative lesbian approach with the de-eroticized political focus of the feminist reading? Finally, it is the case that both the lesbian and feminist approaches tend to signal, sometimes even emphasize, the failures and losses imputed to Olive (and Verena) by James/the novel, while Litvak minimizes both the adversarial author/character relationship and this pervasive sense of loss—but primarily by transforming Olive into a gay man. Comparing all three approaches, Olive as feminist and/or lesbian is ultimately a "loser," yet as gay man she comes out on top (or, to her masochistic delight, on bottom)—a combination that undermines the novel's lesbian eroticism and also reinstates the triumphant-male scenario that feminist and queer theorists of James work constantly to dispel. To turn public embarrassment into an occasion for socially subversive eroticism may finally be a luxury enjoyed primarily by men, who can rely on an understanding of their social superiority to transform such moments into self-staged erotic play. If we can only fully eroticize Olive by casting her as a gay male analogue, we must certainly acknowledge the value of such a sexualizing interpretation but realize as well that we have lost ground, in separate and differing ways, on lesbian and feminist critical fronts.

CONCLUSION

Scene from a novel: a beautiful and well-positioned heroine—yet strange, brooding, and wise beyond her years (Fanny Price? Olive Chancellor?) — poised on the threshold of marriageability shrinks from the opportunity, scandalizing family members and social connections. Her unorthodox behavior might signal a latent feminism or lesbianism, or an antisexual moralism that classifies her amongst her own arch-conservative agents and advisors; in any case, this dissenter from a relentlessly heterosexualizing cultural milieu is marked as a sexual rebel likely to draw the interest, perhaps even admiration, of contemporary readers in lesbian, gay, and feminist studies. Olive, who is certainly "passionate" about many things, is perversely unwilling to capitalize upon her youth and beauty to make the gains she might; Fanny insists upon marriage to Edmund—a perfect match, we realize, when his fussy quibble with Mary Crawford's response to scandal marks him as a prig of equally fanatical proportion. Shall these two sexophobes come together in a marriage as convenient and asexual as any embarked upon by a gay man and lesbian woman in the Regency period? Shall a watered down religiosity and paranoid sexphobia reclassify them as the perfect straight couple after all?

In a climactic moment, the shy and silent heroine is shoved onto the public stage, forced to function as an object of erotic interest for a threatening, anonymous, sexually undifferentiated audience, and causes an unforgettable "sensation." Whether or not this stage is akin to the auction block, and whether said auction block serves as insidiously humble tool of an overarching slave economy or a delightedly mounted prop in a densely orchestrated sexual scene depends significantly on the theoretical inclinations of whoever performs the reading. Throughout this chapter, I have sought to demonstrate how the layerings of literary language make simple assumptions about a novel's politics or sexuality impossible to ascertain, while critical responses to these complicated texts can be just as layered and ambiguous. I have pointed with interest to the occasions on which categories necessarily maintained have collapsed in these critical readings. Attending to the difference between progressive and reactionary intentions and outcomes; between political and sexual forms of cultural subversion; and between gay, lesbian, and feminist perspectives in fiction and criticism, I have noted how attempts to interpret complicated texts can result in equally complicated, sometimes convoluted critical response. I have contended that "queer" should not (always) presume to speak for "lesbian," that "lesbian" is not just another word for "feminist" (and vice versa), and that arguments seeking to have it both ways by simply redefining what is feminist, queer, or homophobic in cultural representation must be questioned.

In my readings of Austen and James, I have noted not only how feminist, gay, and lesbian readings of the same passage from a novel may be separate and contradictory but also how any one critic's observation (e.g., regarding Basil Ransom's heinous misogyny) may be seen to indicate the novelist's (or critic's) feminism *or* anti-feminism. I have shown how textual irony and the intensely charged air of a novel's sexuality or politics creates a situation in which each reader hears a different tone of voice in the same narrative moment, and how this tone will always be open to question in the ultimately silent medium of literary representation. I have sought to distinguish the feminist or queer author from the feminist or queer stories s/he tells and the feminist or queer readers s/he reaches, suggesting that each point on this line of communication likely represents a different point on the political and sexual spectrum and that the radical politics or sexuality of the critical or popular audience does not guarantee similar proclivities in the text or especially the author. I have, meanwhile, sought less to fault individual writings for failing to maintain boundaries than to demonstrate the discursive breakdown endemic to the project of conducting textual interrogations, arising from the indeterminacy of literary language itself. Elizabeth Grosz, in a passage closely bearing on this entire project, writes: "there isn't really a clear-cut distinction between [gay, lesbian, or] feminist and mainstream texts and . . ., moreover, one and the same text can, in some contexts, be regarded as [gay or lesbian or] feminist and in other contexts, as [homophobic or] non- or anti-feminist" (*Space, Time, and Perversion* 18).

In the previous chapter, I described the inverse relationship operating among feminist, gay, and lesbian approaches to the interpretation of culture and find here that the sophisticated critical sleight of hand by which a feminist author or character becomes a gay becomes a lesbian one (not to mention by which a potentially reactionary literary figure is handily transformed for consumption by a leftist academic readership) replicates that same cross-canceling phenomenon. Mutually exclusive counterreadings impose themselves on a shared text with surprising quickness and ease, indicating that such slippery usurpation is one of the main hazards (and opportunities) of gender/sexuality-based reading practice, with each being much more willing to take (and command) the stage than shrinking Fanny or Olive ever was. While we might read indeterminacy as a recipe for gridlock or critical relativism, in fact the marked (sexual? political?) tension characterizing this situation energizes the relevant fiction and their authors with each reopening, while it ever intensifies and (to borrow a favorite term from *Mansfield Park*) improves the critical debates surrounding them.

CHAPTER 5

WHY WE WATCH: LESBIAN, GAY, AND FEMINIST APPROACHES TO FILM

APPROPRIATING BETTE

In *Flaming Classics*, Alexander Doty records an exchange with a straight female student, who asks about favorite icons of gay male film fans. At his mention of a particular screen diva from the classical Hollywood period, the student reportedly interjected, "Don't take Bette Davis away from us, too!," and Doty describes his frustration at this response: "Before this, I hadn't thought of gay culture . . . as taking anything away from anyone. . . . Was I ever naive: I guess most people out there really are lifting up their leg or squatting to mark their popular cultural territory" (53). One of Doty's contributions to the discussion of film's intersection with sexuality studies is his firm rejection of the "appropriator" position for gay and lesbian viewers. For Doty, to position oneself as queer appropriator of straight-identified Hollywood cinema, as multiple gay and lesbian film theorists have done, is to concede the original rights to these images, narratives, and meanings to the heterosexual hegemony, a concession Doty refuses to make. In the quote above Doty bisexes the pissing-pet image to refer not only to the straight male filmmakers and filmgoers notorious for their territoriality but also to the women who have been squatting in this field for decades, claiming their feminist squatter's rights, and likely including the student whose remarks initiated the discussion.

Since Doty speaks against turf-marking with respect to specific stars and films, he would surely welcome Patricia White's lesbian-centered analysis of Davis's persona and filmography, even as this may significantly impinge for its duration upon Doty's own. For instance, does the "strong, independent," celebrity-heroine that inspires White complement or cancel out Davis's drag queen persona, which Doty (along with Michael Bronski and Brett Farmer and many others) in part responds to?[1] Is White's admiration for the Davis characters' seeming indifference to men a necessary component of or a complete negation of her persona *as* male—as the campy, bitchy, over-the-top diva recognized easily by a culturally adept gay audience? Does the "strength" and "independence" almost always attached to references to Davis[2] resemble more the strength and independence of the long-suffering heroine of melodrama, whose longing to lay aside those qualities for the right man coincides with the underlying falseness (and overarching illusion) of the drag performance, or that of the protofeminist whose presumed heterosexuality would present another challenge (or even barrier) to White's own reading? In much contemporary gender/sexuality–based film criticism, female figurations—characters, celebrities, narratives—interest all three of the critical camps in this discussion. While the feminist and lesbian focus on women is not surprising, gay film theory turns with equal frequency to the feminine (and not only the effeminate) in film—from Bronski's and Farmer's emphasis on gay identification with female stars to Lee Edelman's and D.A. Miller's *analysis*, if you will, of Grace Kelly and Elizabeth Taylor, respectively. Additionally, gay film theory's developing response to "feminist" film analysis—a term addressing both straight and lesbian contingents on different occasions—is another point of contact among the three schools. Despite this seeming symbiosis, however, the focus here, as it has been throughout, will be upon the structurally necessary (and/or the politically mandated) moments of discord among the positions advanced by these fields of inquiry.

HISTORICIZING THEORY

While I take up in greater detail the significance of Bette Davis, and the critical favorite *All About Eve*, toward the end of this chapter, I return here to the original exchange between Doty and his evidently straight, feminist-identified student, to consider what I feel to be the most striking feature of her comment: that as straight feminist film analyst she would seek to lay textual claim to (and express a fan's appreciation for) a celebrity such as Davis when the feminist theoreticians publishing most prolifically in her field have abandoned such a position long ago. How, in fact, may Davis be said to "belong to" a group of thinkers and writers for whom her persona and films (let alone her strength and independence) register barely a blip on the collective discursive screen? Certainly feminist theory's more recent interest in textual analysis, supported by the related fields of semiotic-inspired apparatus theory and psychoanalysis, has presented an entirely different set of concerns for feminist writers thinking about film, while Laura Mulvey's seminal injunction to deploy the "destruction of pleasure as a radical weapon" (58) has led feminist film theorists to resist the temptation to gush, to occupy the position of the "scholar-fan" so proudly taken up by Doty and other gay and lesbian film analysts. Indeed, as bracing, enlightening, and rigorous as feminist film theory has come to be, rarely if ever could we call it lighthearted or fun, and such a contrast in tone between straight and gay approaches serves as an index for other significant points of departure. Thus an important focus here will be the relationship to psychoanalytic film theory forged by all three of these critical camps—gay and lesbian theory's overt rejection of or semiwilling interaction with the practice, feminist theory's utter domination by it.

The perceived "lightness" of nonpsychoanalytic approaches to film creates an impasse for various workers in this field—gay and lesbian critics seeking to imbue their scholarship with their love of these, in fact, overtly homophobic classic films, and feminist film theorists who are likely equally passionate about the films they analyze, yet who might exclude a personal response, and the cultural studies–based approach more receptive to it, lest their work be considered not just light but "lite." Indeed, the dominance of the psychoanalytic approach across the field since the mid-seventies has caused feminist film theorists to engage with each other in contests of discursive one-upmanship, to the point where some writing is so densely theoretical that it barely speaks of film at all. Old-style radical feminist B. Ruby Rich has argued for decades that the feminist emphasis on psychoanalytic theory leaves behind the question of women's oppression as often as (I argue) it forgets the subject of film, and the curious tendency of psychoanalytic theory, to be gotten absolutely right only when it is talking about itself, will be considered in detail below. (Rich *Chick Flicks*, see also Gubar 163.)

Indeed, Rich's work, and that of gay film critic Thomas Waugh, for example, constitutes a form of film *history* that may be contrasted to feminist-style film *theory*. Their respective efforts to archive, record and simply remember the rapidly fading ephemera of the early women's and gay liberation movements—this women's studies conference, that anticensorship rally, yet another run-in with the homophobic mainstream—constitute an essential record that theorists of every generation should be prepared to maintain and build on. Yet as essential as is the reporting and remembering done by critics such as Rich and Waugh, it tends almost always to compare unfavorably—as lightweight, as analytically thin—to the high-powered paradigms being generated most often by the straight feminist approach, a negative impression created by the weight of psychoanalytic film theory itself. Thus we may note how psychoanalytic theories speak not simply *for* themselves but, however subtly or unintentionally, *against* other, less rigorous forms of film analysis, how the very articulation of such theories diminishes the preferred mode of many gay and lesbian cultural analysts. Strikingly, Rich's roots in second-wave feminism engender a woman-centeredness in her writing that ignores distinctions between straight and lesbian feminists, positioning all in sisterhood against a (straight or gay) male opposition. Rich's own mid-life transition from straight to lesbian identification seems to have reshaped this perspective little if at all, so that ironically, Rich is now in the position of reminding straight (and lesbian) women film theorists to place "feminist" concerns in the foreground of their criticism, yet marking herself (and her antitheory approach) all the more plainly as "the lesbian" in this debate.

Ellis Hanson has considered this analytic divide in similar terms, specifically targeting Vito Russo's cultural history of classical Hollywood, *The Celluloid Closet*, for joining the "lesbian and gay campaign for so-called positive images . . . [of] politically correct ladies and gentleman" (7). Hanson names the entire cultural studies approach "a critical perspective [that] can be judged by the quality of the thinking it produces and the quality of the art it inspires, and in this regard *The Celluloid Closet* is not very impressive" (7). Hanson's own gay-but-theoretical perspective helpfully challenges the dichotomy I construct here, although the references to Russo indicate the tendency of gay and lesbian film analysts to (at least until very recently) lean toward the cultural studies approach. Also in contrast to a point I made above, Hanson accuses Russo and the cultural studies field of an anticamp, easily offended seriousness that contrasts with theory's search for "pleasure" in cinema: "In decrying Hollywood homophobia, we [as cultural studies practitioners] concern ourselves with only one gaze: the ubiquitous, prefabricated, gullible, voyeuristic gaze of homophobia. . . . Meanwhile, our own pleasure, the elusive gaze of delight, is left curiously undertheorized and at times inadmissable" (8).

Reading the arguments of Lee Edelman and D.A. Miller (anthologized in Hanson's collection) below, however, I will argue the reverse of this position, noting that both authors, working adroitly within the psychoanalytic paradigm, come to their task revved by a sense of outrage at the homophobia of not only classical Hollywood but of feminist theory as well. Hanson himself later concedes that a central issue for feminist film theory is "misogynistic violence and objectifica-tion of women in classic cinema" (13), an accurate formulation that decisively works against the notion that these theories promote feelings of "pleasure" and "delight." While Hanson claims that both approaches are evident in his own work, his largely protheory position skews his perspective against cultural studies; his reading of Russo seems overly harsh and at times completely off the mark, and the fact that there exists a delightfully entertaining *film version* of Russo's text, when the movie deal for Hanson's erudite and hyperliterate aggregation of theories will be surely a long time coming, speaks to the essential *enjoyability* of Russo's work, as well as its ability to be enjoyed by a wider range of gay, lesbian, and feminist audiences than Hanson's work will likely ever enjoy.

Finally, the documentation done by Rich and Waugh constitute a small fraction of queer film criticism focused on history. An even more important historical factor—filmgoing audiences, including these film-loving theorists themselves—has drawn attention to a central question characterizing the gay/lesbian cinematic experience: in light of Hollywood's patent and virulent homophobia, what specifically do gay and lesbian viewers derive with enjoyment (and also, of course, deep sadness) from going to the movies? The practice of queer appropriations of classic Hollywood texts (despite Doty's provocative quibble with the term) has been profitably explored by film historians such as Russo, Elizabeth Ellsworth, and Michael Bronski; subversively editing storylines, foregrounding queerable (or already queered) char-acters and situations, and mentally revising or deleting the film's inevitably heterosexualizing final 10 minutes (or in the case of *Personal Best*, its second half[3]), gay and lesbian audiences have been able to wrest pleasurable readings for themselves from resisting texts. Finally, what Judith Mayne in *Framed* has unfairly dismissed as a game of "finding the lesbians"[4] is a critical strategy successfully deployed only from the queer perspective, whose engagement with films' meaning occurs on this remarkable subtextual level. What, after all, does it profit a viewing audience to set off in search of the "straight girl" in the story, when her overdetermined presence everywhere in film is often the source, according to feminist film theorists, not of subversion but of oppression? By contrast, the veiled traces of queer inflection in film deserve careful, sustained critical attention, creating an interest-ing analytic occupation that not surprisingly has diverted queer readers from unifocal engagement with more abstract theoretical approaches.

If the work of critics such as Rich, Waugh, and the audience-based cultural analysts forms an observable opposition to the entrenchment of theory, perhaps even more interesting are the efforts of gay and lesbian critics at midpoints on this spectrum whose love-hate interface with psychoanalytic theory is a shaping feature of their work. Important in this group are queer textual analysts such as Edelman, Miller, and Teresa de Lauretis, all of whom engage deeply with the terms and terminology of psychoanalytic theory, so as to hack incisively at its homophobic roots. Both Edelman and Miller emphasize anal symbology in their filmic readings to counteract psychoanalysis's heterocentric obsession with the phallus and the strictly demarcated either/or of sexual difference. De Lauretis considers the relationship between desire and identification in her work, yet concludes that the deployment of identification as a concept in film theory is homophobic. I will return to these arguments below but here note that writings in this vein tend thus to be both intensely psychoanalytic and antipsychoanalytic at once; while we may determine that their critique of the homophobia of psychoanalytic theory places them closer to the "history" end of the spectrum, stylistically and thematically their debt to psychoanalytic theory is large enough that they in fact constitute a subfield of the "theory" category instead.

Contrasting these are various gay- and lesbian-focused film studies expressing initial interest in psychoanalytic theory, yet reverting at some point to more traditional audience–based approaches. Representative of this trend, recent books by Patricia White and Brett Farmer engage with psychoanalysis in their introductory moments, noting the threat of heterocentrism but arguing that this theoretical approach properly handled is ultimately well suited to queer readings. White "urges that psychoanalysis be retained" (xvii), and Farmer argues that "psychoanalysis can be invaluable for analyzing homosexual desires and their complex effects on both psychic and social life" (12). Farmer's aim to include theory and history ("psychic and social life") coincides with White's delineation of the concept of "retrospectatorship"—a term that suggests a Freudian *nachträglichkeit*, a Lacanian mirror stage, and cultural-based themes such as nostalgia, fond memories, and subversive revisioning all in one.

Both texts refer in their early pages to two psychoanalytic terms key to theories of spectatorship, identification and desire, that nevertheless lead both authors almost immediately back to the question of *audience*: whom do we want to *be* in this movie? Whom do we want to *have*? Certainly, the mixing, shifting vectors of projection and identification that surely accompany gay and lesbian filmgoing experiences make for a more interesting story than the cut and dried divisions in allegiance film seeks to hand down to straight viewers. Still, results can be predictable, as in multiple recently published studies identification and desire form a conceptual swinging door from one critical register to the other, lending more cultural studies–based approaches the sheen of high theory, introducing more practical issues into otherwise abstract arguments, and/or, as in the case of White and Farmer, generating texts that connect a largely audience-based approach to the "value" of psychoanalytic theory along a narrow passageway. White's study engages with Freudian theories and introduces psychoanalytic themes primarily in response to straight feminist film theorists, but is involved primarily in her own intriguing and helpful round of "finding the lesbians" when she turns to the films themselves.[5] Farmer deploys the concept of "fantasy," that all-important "setting" providing a subversively wide range of identity positions for the fantasizer, a model well suited to the ever-shifting nodes of identification occupied by gay and lesbian film viewers. Despite his appropriately theorized opening chapters, however, it is, as with White, the introduction of specific films and stars themselves that cause each subsequent chapter to split between a theory-based prologue and a cultural studies-style close reading, again both valuable in themselves but less than a total integration of the psychic and social aspects of queer desire. Even the work of Edelman and Miller, positioned by myself closer to the theory end of the spectrum, must be seen to narrow its point of engagement to a psychoanalytically generated anal/phallic opposition; once situated inside this model, it is a terrifically insightful version of "finding the faggots" that the reader is invited to join in each case.

Significantly, de Lauretis demonstrates the least interest, among all of the gay and lesbian theorists under consideration here, in the classical Hollywood period and is likewise most suspicious of any aspect of queer viewing practice described as "identification." In multiple works, she has argued for the need to define lesbian sexuality through the lens of object choice instead of de-eroticizing identificatory practice, leading Carole-Anne Tyler to the assessment that for de Lauretis "identification negates alterity" and "is implicitly and essentially heterosexual" (175). In *The Practice of Love* de Lauretis emphasizes the modern/art film (specifically, Sheila McLaughlin's *She Must Be Seeing Things*), while her complex interaction with continental structuralist philosophies reflects her focus on *avant garde* international films in early works such as *Alice Doesn't* and especially *Technologies of Gender*. And indeed, when gay and lesbian theories focus on arthouse cinema or even popular films classified as drama, the emphasis is often on desire instead of identification. Jim Ellis's appreciation for the queer oeuvre of Derek Jarman, as well as Valerie Traub's and Judith Mayne's readings of *Black Widow*, are instances of this. Meanwhile, Hollywood comedies and musicals often impel the analysis toward questions of *identification*—both the identifying of a film's covertly queer characters or contexts, and identifying with (and often laughing along with) figures on screen whose status as object of erotic contemplation is obscured by the outlandishness of their gender performances—*Oz*'s cowardly lion, the butch Jane Russell character from *Gentlemen Prefer Blondes*, Doris Day's Calamity Jane. The comic texts featured in these readings exude a layer of camp irony likely indiscernible to original audiences, now creating a de-eroticizing distance between modern viewer and archaic text.

The various discrepancies between identifying, identifying with, and psychoanalytic identification are similar to the (mis)use of "desire" in some writings by gay, lesbian, *and* straight feminist theorists: a character's or audience member's "desire *for*" an erotic screen object may have little to do with the *echt* Lacanian usage that links this term with concepts of absence, lack, castration, and death. In both cases, the stringency of the terms in their strictest psychoanalytic sense limits their appeal to certain gay and lesbian cultural analyses of film, seeking to subversively humorize or eroticize a Hollywood film *and* the critical apparatus interpreting it, and the difficulties involved with successfully (that is "correctly") applying the terms emerge.

The issue of "correctly" employing psychoanalytic theory seems relevant here, since the analytic concepts constituting this field have proven notoriously difficult to receive from their original disseminators (specifically Freud and especially Lacan), while rivers of ink have evidently necessarily flowed toward the correction of ubiquitous misinterpretations. The discussion as it applies to feminist studies and film is well initiated by Constance Penley's influential mandate that feminists get the theory right:

> To put it bluntly, none of these essays [in Penley's collection *Feminism and Film Theory*] belong to the "what if" school of feminist criticism: What if women had an Electra complex to complement the male's Oedipus complex? What if the crucial psychical relation to the body were not to the phallus as a symbolic organ but to the real of the mother's body? What if there were no such thing as penis envy but rather "womb envy"? . . . These "what if's" are no more than the signs marking the well-worn dissident paths of a reductive biologism, sociologism, or mysticism of the feminine. (2)

As difficult as it may be, Penley implies, for feminists to swallow the phallocentrism of the psychoanalytic mode, it is useless to construct parallel alternatives that not only mysticize an eternal feminine but, more importantly, it would seem, also damage the integrity of the original model. What Penley warns against, in other words, is the temptation to derive, to take the opportunity offered in the very slide from its original term—from the Oedipal son to the anti-Oedipal woman—to tailor the argument for feminist purposes but sacrifice the basic rightness of the theory in the process.

Meanwhile, Judith Mayne has insightfully rejoindered this argument by pointing out that the shift of psychoanalytic theory from therapy session to movie theater already constitutes just such a slide or derivation, after which insistence upon a purist approach is theoretically pointless and tinged with homophobic intent. Mayne argues: "what I find striking in Penley's account is the unexamined premise that what film theory had adopted was some pure definition of psychoanalysis. Wasn't film theory already a 'what if' about psychoanalysis, namely, what if psychoanalysis were adapted to read films, not people? What if psychoanalysis became not a medical practice but a cultural one?" (*Framed* xv). Mayne has struck upon a phenomenon I find endemic to psychoanalytic theorizing: the inevitable reduction or oversimplification suffered by "theory" as soon as it is applied to any other consideration but its own. Are, for instance, the Real, the Imaginary, the traumatic, and the unconscious so easily accessed by certain films and thrust so plainly upon spectators, when Theory informs us that these psychic components are buried beneath deep layers and long years of denial and repression, forever removed from ordinary waking existence? (See Kaplan "The Case of the Missing Mother" 131.) Does the mere fact of a woman in the director's chair mean that women have now entered the Symbolic in some newly empowering way, that the reign of the phallus has been effectively threatened and the laws of sexual difference mitigated? (See Doane "Woman's Stake" 220–21.) It seems that to *apply* psychoanalysis, or theory in general, in any way is to fall away from its original tenets in significant ways, a move that always opens itself to the charge of misreading but may be better understood as nothing more and nothing less than reading itself.

Later in her introduction, Penley indicates an underlying factor in the need to get theory right. Seeking to correct the tendency in the early writings of Pam Cook and Claire Johnston to construct just the sort of "biologized, mysticized" woman Penley speaks against, she argues finally that "*there is no feminist advantage* in positing either a historically unchanging feminine essence or a monolithic patriarchal repression of that essence" (5, emphasis added). While we might feel that Penley's strict exclusion of an Electra complex or womb envy creates just the sort of monolithic patriarchy she questions, the larger point of interest is how cozily coincident correct psychoanalytic theorizing seems to be with "the feminist advantage" at this moment. Will theory always support politics (by, according to Penley, supporting history) in this way? When it fails to do so, which factor should determine the direction taken by the argument? What will happen, as Penley seems to suggest in the first quote retrieved here, when theory creates an oppressive phallocentrism that certain feminist theorists feel unfairly constrained by? What will happen when such feminist theorists attempt to loosen those constraints by emphasizing the threat posed "when the woman looks"? Must not the theory purist respond that, since women's exclusion from the Symbolic denies them access to both desire and the gaze, and since (according to Raymond Bellour, as read by Bergstrom "Enunciation and Sexual Difference" 173) women's cinematic look is always immediately co-opted by the gaze of male character or viewer, the "woman's look" is either impossible or completely meaningless?[6]

David N. Rodowick has sought to correct the several ways in which Laura Mulvey has gotten the theory wrong *because* political constraints necessarily limited her: "The playing down of masochism is also interesting in Mulvey's essay. However, rather than being a misreading, this is better understood as a point necessitated *by her political position*. She hesitates—and not without justification—to characterize the position of the female subject as masochistic" (198, emphasis added). As opposed to Penley's happier conceptual intersections, good psychoanalysis is at odds with good feminism in this case; and Mayne, we recall, says that good film analysis also places certain demands on this equation that are bound to distort the other two. Returning to Mayne's assertion, that psychoanalytic film theory is already a derivation of the original therapeutic model, we must ask what will happen if elements of the psychoanalytic paradigm are purposely gotten wrong (appropriated, misread, deemphasized) in the service of valuable feminist (or gay or lesbian) film theorizing? Will psychoanalysis as a therapeutic method be affected by misuses such as these? Will the ability of those who like to get it right be limited by the work of those who intentionally do not? Will the misogynist and homophobic "realities" that psychoanalytic theory (and classical Hollywood cinema) are said to primarily represent be reshaped to some degree if one day it *is* shown satisfactorily that it matters when the woman looks? As a field of inquiry shaped around the analysand's necessary bracketing of much fundamental common sense ("I guess I *do* want a penis. . . . I suppose I *must* hate my mother. . . . I know very well, but all the same"), psychoanalysis is at its core a subject open to question, and the effort to close down productive, analytic, and politically enlightened variations on the theme, especially those hailing from gay and lesbian perspectives, seems itself highly questionable.

Delineating this spectrum of approaches to film, I have attributed to the gay and lesbian camps the most mobility between poles, noting that many of these theorists employ a mix of theory and history or balance questions of text and audience in a dynamic manner. Feminist theoretical approaches may seem narrow by contrast, burrowing deeply into specific questions and limited in their movement by this very depth. Indeed, certain feminist film theorists have sought to open a space for history within a film paradigm evermore fundamentally defined by theory. Penley, for instance, critiques the "essentialist notion of 'femininity' or 'Woman' " that is "ahistorical and asocial, and suggests a set of traits not amenable to change" (5); one can therefore surmise that the collection of essays she introduces with this comment attempts in each case to move away from ahistorical essentialism while staying rigorously theoretical, that is to productively historicize theory.

In another influential collection, Mary Anne Doane suggests that "we need to look more closely at what 'theory' is or might be and what 'history' denotes in opposition to that term—for it is 'history' which promises to find away around the theoretical impasse" ("Remembering Women" 49). Doane criticizes Baudry's "non-ideological subject" who "escapes . . . both ideology and history" ("Remembering Women" 55), as well as his deployment of Plato's cave allegory, noting that "he can activate a 2000 year old scenario in the analysis of the cinema precisely because the psychical force he examines is characterized as ahistorical" ("Remembering Women" 55). Ultimately, for Doane, "the validity of psychoanalysis would . . . be linked to the style of its confrontation with history" ("Remembering Women" 57). As do some other theorists (e.g., Rodowick 194), Doane introduces the instance of the *case* history, the individual analysand-as-text, whose symptoms, traumas, and memories are fundamentally structured by temporal and historical concerns. While Doane concedes that individual, private "memory" is not perfectly analogous to the collectively experienced world events constituting "history," she correctly argues that individual and collective memories are linked throughout psychoanalytic theory and that history is, after all, little more than the aggregation of individual memories constructing it. She concludes by urging feminists to resist the "process of troping," the tendency to read into individuals an abstractive, universalized meaning, and cites Sally Potter's explicitly feminist film *The Gold Diggers* as a similar urging to resistance. Both Penley and Doane, therefore, raise the difficult question of theory and its opposition to history, both, however, with the intent to demonstrate or at least suggest a successful integration of the two.

Yet both of these arguments leave questions unanswered and resist a set of demonized concepts—essentialism and biologism—that in fact offer core support and, I would argue, rich analytic opportunity, for the psychoanalytic model. Penley, for instance, might have applied her charges of essentialism and ahistoricity to almost every contributor to her collection; what film analysis from the mid-1970s through the mid-1990s, after all, has refrained from some reference to monolithic abstractions such as the "to-be-looked-at" woman or "the male gaze"? Certainly, Laura Mulvey's seminal work contains (and coined) multiple such references, and while she and her contemporaries refrain from employing the capitalized "Woman," the universalizing gestures their arguments make are only inches from what is connoted in this stylistic device. We might, in fact, argue that the color-, class-, and culture-blindness inherent in such universalizing *only* becomes perceptible when we move the discussion away from theory toward history, or away from questions of texts to those of audience, at which point one's historical context entirely informs the viewing experience. Are not the founding scenarios of psychoanalysis dependent, in fact, upon an "essential" ahistoricity, presuming the universal experience of having been breastfed, having witnessed the primal scene, having undressed with children of the opposite sex when only some or none of these may be part of "historical" subjects' individual pasts? Can it possibly matter, after all, and is it not essential that it not matter, whether bombs were falling or Paris was burning at the moment of our entry into language, at the formation of our first identifications and neuroses? While certainly bombs falling throughout a child's formative years could have a psychological effect, "theory" has assigned itself the task of defining the normal (and normalizing) scenario while it is "history" that represents what is pathologic to this standard model, what runs outside the theoretical boundary and complicates its ability to predict and diagnose. (See Berger 22–24.) As indicated above, my contention is that theory cannot and should not reshape itself to accommodate every event and generation; theories are valuable to the degree they *are* universally applicable.

And Doane's critique of Baudry's "2000 year old scenario" only reminds us that Plato's 2000-year-old counterpart Oedipus has reduced the complexities of family dynamics throughout the ages and around the world to a single mechanical model; again, when the model turns out to so handily illuminate the plight of Oedipus *and* Hamlet; their vastly different cultures, eras, and political situations; and all of us less famous examples coming before, between, and after, what is gained by gratifying the impulse to "always historicize"? With respect to cinema, it is true that each film text has its origins in a specific historical moment and bears the mark of that moment's politics and aesthetics, proudly, in every frame, but is it not also the case that any film worth remembering, that is theorizing, is a film with a certain timeless and universal significance, that memories and theories themselves do most of the work of immemorializing film in this way, and that the only consummately historical films are those we have consigned to history—completely forgotten because of their inability to renew themselves for new generations of filmgoers? It seems especially difficult to consider film in general—the mechanics, technology, and viewing experiences characteristic of all filmgoing—as "case history," as these aspects return us even more firmly to the realm of the universal, although again I contend that theories doing this sort of work are exactly as ahistorical as they need to be. Certainly film seems as fully analogous to theory as it does to history, casting hypothetical characters in representative situations, providing viewing audiences with ways to think about their worlds and themselves; therefore, the marriage between theory and film (another form of theory) might be productively maintained without the intervention of history at all, and perhaps theory knows itself best and does its best work when theoreticians acknowledge this.

Likely this effort to historicize psychoanalytic theory stems in part from feminist theorists' tacit understanding that at the root of multiple core psychoanalytic concepts—the castration threat, scopophilia, the phallic mother, we could go on—lie a series of anatomic verities—the penis, the womb, the eye, the brain—that cause contemporary discourse severe anxiety. Specifically in the register of film theory it seems "essential" that men have penises and eyes and that women's relationship to these organs be productively oppositional in some way; meanwhile, so great is the fear among feminist theorists that biology will be reapportioned to them as destiny that psychoanalysis's roots in biology are rarely if ever positively incorporated into the argument. We have heard above, for instance, from Penley's staunch antiessentialist position; Rodowick refrains from accusing Mulvey of "biological essentialism" as this would be "to write off her argument" (194).[7] For the purposes of this study, however, it seems productive to consider the "universal" tendency of men, regardless of sexual orientation (and whether this tendency be biologically or culturally instilled, or both), to experience sexual stimulation through the eye and the "universal" tendency of women (again, straight or lesbian) to be less stimulated in this manner (often women's erotic investment in touch is noted in opposition).[8]

Certainly women's relative disengagement with the visual register in part motivates and enables suspicions of representation—the unrepresentability of women, the impossibility of nonvoyeuristically representing lesbian sex—voiced by straight and lesbian feminist commentators; an area of inquiry derived from this observation might involve delineating the differences between lesbian and straight women's resistance to representation (in the senses of being themselves unrepresentable, unable *to* represent, or not wanting to be represented). More significantly, gay men's avid cruising habits and consumption of sex culture in the public sphere (and of course in movie theaters) indicate at least as active an investment in the gaze as has the straight male spectator identified by the psychoanalytic film paradigm. When both gay and straight men are acknowledged to "universally" enjoy a greater erotic kick from merely looking, multiple questions emerge: What are the differences between the way gay and straight men gaze? (An example might be the excited response of the typical heterovoyeur versus Ellis Hanson's admiration for the "killer cosmetics" and other erotically appealing aesthetics of the thriller *Bound.*) Does the gay gaze include the voyeuristic (sadistic) aspect characteristic of the straight male gaze? Only when it encounters male objects on film? (Again, for Hanson, the male cast members of *Bound* seem to have barely registered.) How might the recognition of a shared gazing tendency enable gay film theorists to confront elements of misogyny in their theorizing, or challenge the homophobia inherent in straight male viewing practice? How might feminist film theory decide to modify its approach, following upon the realization that, relative to the male film character who subversively returns the male spectatorial gaze and even relative to the lesbian character whose "to-be-looked-at-ness" may fall outside the narrative structure, the heterosexual heroine, not to mention the feminist theory focused upon her, is *least* equipped of all three to deflect or contain the oppressive male gaze? (See also Farmer 131.) Despite the universal tendency to avoid essentializing, biologizing, and universalizing in contemporary theory, such gestures would allow for the breakdown between categories of sex and sexual orientation that has been so productively begun in more poststructural contexts. Especially, once more, in the case of psychoanalytic theory, so "essentially" informed by bodily function and bodily definition, the resistance to the body threatens this basic layer of structuration and misses opportunities to politically deploy its arguments.

DESIRING WOMEN

The theory/history debate may be seen to divide the approaches of feminist and lesbian critics *within* the psychoanalytic paradigm as well, as these schools ponder the question of the desiring woman. For lesbian film analysts, it is vital to consider questions of women's desire on screen and in the theater, while for feminist theorists it is psychoanalytically mandated—and, to quote Penley once more, to great feminist advantage—that women's desire be unrepresentable. Pam Cook and Claire Johnston posit that in film, "woman is not only a sign in a system of exchange but an empty sign" (27); elsewhere, Doane contends that,

> in order for representation to be possible, . . . a stake is essential. Something must be threatened if the paternal prohibition against incest is to take effect, forcing the gap between desire and its object. This theory results in a rather surprising interpretation of women's psychic oppression: her different relation to language stems from the fact that she has nothing to lose, nothing at stake. ("Woman's Stake" 222)

Her "different relation to language"—that is, her placement on the wrong side of the Symbolic—thus freights the position of the woman filmmaker (or film actor or audience member) with hazards and impossibilities. The tenets of the psychoanalytic model dictate that women be read as barred in this way and that this exclusion from the Symbolic be understood to index and enable countless other forms of sexed oppression isolable in the social sphere.

Meanwhile, multiple theorists have echoed Doane's realization that "we know that women speak" ("Woman's Stake" 223) and have sought to delineate women's hidden but vital points of access to desire and language. Mulvey along with Annette Kuhn and Molly Haskell have sought this access in various "women's genres," exploring the transvestite and masochistic options in the process, while E. Ann Kaplan and Linda Williams have highlighted the role of mothering in classical cinema as offering women access to the pre-Oedipal/imaginary realm where women's voices, bodies, and desires have been left behind. For Kaja Silverman "the phallus is always the product of dominant signifying and representational activities, activities which are vulnerable to interruption and transformation" ("Historical Trauma" 113). Transferring the phallus from the register of theory to that of history, Silverman argues that WWII-era films such as *It's a Wonderful Life* and *The Best Years of Our Lives* disrupt the process of male subject formation, forcing male viewers to confront their own foundational lack in a crisis of identity. Doane (in "Woman's Stake") herself joins this attempt, citing feminist films such as Laura Mulvey and Peter Wollen's *Riddle of the Sphinx* and Sally Potter's *Thriller* as having succeeded in assigning to women the "stake" they require to enter into language. Elsewhere (in "Film and the Masquerade"), she deploys the concept of the masquerade to counter women's paralyzing "lack of distance" from their cinematic image.[9]

Have the obstacles presented by so many disabling psychic monoliths been surmounted in these instances, creating common ground for straight and lesbian film theorists who can now share in the project of delineating women's desire in film? Certainly, in all of the arguments referred to above, the remarkable ease with which deep psychic structures seem to be rearranged, challenged, and dissolved by cultural discourse may strike skeptical readers as simply too good to be true. Silverman's analysis, for example, of postwar amputees in William Wyler's *The Best Years of Our Lives*, argues that male subject formation is significantly affected ("traumatized") by such films, that "the spectacle of male castration may very well result in a destructive questioning of the dominant fiction" ("Historical Trauma" 114). Yet can films about war and postwar disillusion be said to adequately reproduce the trauma of actual battle, amputation, and community ostracization experienced by GIs, or must we assume that films such as *The Best Years of Our Lives* only affected such male viewers whose own traumatic memories were triggered during the viewing episode? We know of course, that soldiers throughout modern history traumatized thus are not looked upon by the larger social collective as conduits to improved understanding of the sexes' shared castrated status within the Symbolic order but are instead diagnosed—with shellshock, tripwire syndrome, posttraumatic stress—as standing outside this social order and led toward "cure" as quickly as possible. Silverman's envisioning of "destructive questioning" of the social order brought about by such traumatizing cinematic experiences therefore seems to be primarily this—an optimistic vision regarding specific cultural representations that could undo a psychic order so much larger, older, and more entrenched than itself.

Likewise, Doane's efforts to theorize a path around the constraints of the psychoanalytic model betray a tone of insistence that undermines. She refers, for instance, to "the necessity of *assigning* women a specific stake" ("Woman's Stake" 223), to "theories which attempt to *define or construct* a feminine specificity," and to "theories which *provide* the woman with an autonomous symbolic representation" ("Woman's Stake" 226, emphases added)—indicating an intense political motivation yet a troubling lack of empirical support. Elsewhere, "Womanliness is a mask which *can be* worn or removed," and "the effectivity of masquerade lies precisely in its potential to *manufacture* a distance from the image, to *generate* a problematic within which the image is *manipulable, producible, and readable* by the woman" ("Film" 433, emphases added). Certainly issues emerge even in Riviere's original essay, "Womanliness and Masquerade," that complicate the agency suggested in this reading: importantly, the discrepancy between the "intellectual" woman who inspires the concept of masquerade and "women" in general is never clarified;[10] this discrepancy, more significantly, mirrors the break between the masquerade actively donned by intellectual women and "genuine womanliness," which would seem to belong to all women—will-she, nill-she—while Riviere later posits that these are "the same thing" (38). Does Doane also observe the power to wear or remove the masquerade accruing to only intellectual women? (She locates subversive examples in art films—and not popular films—that would be viewed by better-educated audiences.) Should such "universal" theories of women's psyches be tailored to specific IQ levels in this fashion? The trouble emerges from Doane's, and from Riviere's own, attempt to extrapolate a general finding (the theory) from the anecdotal evidence related to a specific patient (the case history). Finally, the shortcomings of these several attempts to revise the theoretic status quo in the name of the speaking, desiring woman only reinforce the tenacity of the theory itself, and point to the differences that characterize feminist and lesbian approaches to psychoanalytic film theory.

THE LESBIAN AUDIENCE

If these feminist attempts to theorize (or historicize) around misogynist impasses seemingly endemic to psychoanalysis seem weakened or doomed by the solidity of the theory itself, lesbian film theorists navigating similar waters have as much or even more difficulty, due in part to the ways psychoanalytic theory automatically deflects the lesbian alternative. Doane reminds us that in the psychoanalytic paradigm, woman's "closeness" to her image on screen is the very mechanism producing a suffocating identification between the two and negating the possibility of woman's desire. If desire is indeed predicated upon distance, the relationship to the like is always one of identification, a dilemma inherently frustrating to lesbian film theorists. Approaches to solving this dilemma take several forms—forging an equation between identification and homophobia, as has been presented by Teresa de Lauretis (see also Tyler); emphasizing *other* demographic differences between the women in a lesbian relationship, as Barbara Johnson (163; see chapter 2) has done; acknowledging that desirous relations between women are all but successfully repressed in classical film, as does Judith Mayne (*Woman at the Keyhole*); or moving toward the cultural studies approach, where desire can slide toward its association with "pleasure" and where closeness between women signifies subversion of the patriarchy, not succumbing to it—but at the cost of abandoning the psychoanalytic model. In each case, the results are creative and productive yet leave intact the line of demarcation separating the feminist and the (necessarily complicated) lesbian deployment of psychoanalytic theory.

In her early work on "Feminism and Women's Cinema," Judith Mayne divides her argument between the feminist perspective (with its antipatriarchal occupation of the oppressed position) and the lesbian one (with its anti-patriarchal occupation of the subversive position). Her dilemma centers around the ultimate effectiveness of the spectacle as disruption, how quickly it is reincorporated into the patriarchal structure, what productive damage has been caused before this moment occurs; while she at first rejects the "utopic" impulse "to 'rescue' the classical Hollywood cinema for feminism, [and] to affirm ambiguity as an inherently radical or progressive gesture" (*Woman* 24), her reading of the noir classic *The Big Sleep* in fact proceeds along these lines. If Mulvey's focus is the inevitable recuperation of spectacle's disruptive powers,[11] Mayne highlights, under the influence of de Lauretis, those all-important moments before, yet ultimately acknowledges, in accordance with Mulvey, the overwhelming tendency of the patriarchal discourse to prevail.

In *The Big Sleep* Mayne reads "the sisterly bond as the obstacle" (25) whose very repression by the narrative "invites the hypothesis of similarly forbidden relationships between other, male likes" (*Woman* 26). Yet her move to the much more overtly lesbian, modern cinematic narrative *Black Widow* (a text de Lauretis might be much more interested in analyzing than she would be *The Big Sleep*), signals her return to the position taken at the beginning of the discussion—a position against the "romanticization of marginality" (*Woman* 25) and in closer alignment with Mulvey's own. While Mayne acknowledges that in *Black*

Widow, the relationship between the female protagonist (Alex) and another woman is "decidedly homotextual" (*Woman* 46), "it will be the work of the film to draw the projected image—Alex's fascination with Catherine—into proper alignment with the law" (*Woman* 47). Mayne calls the conclusion of the film "silly" and deems the story as a whole to be "part of the institutions of commercial cinema" (*Woman* 48). Curiously, this pessimistic reading is supported by her own tendency to deemphasize the queer shadings of *Black Widow*—she refers only briefly to "several scenes . . . quite explicit in their delineation of lesbian attraction" (*Woman* 48) and does little to develop a definition for her coinage "homotextual,"[12] so that in places her own text seems as constrained by repressive forces as is the ultimately disappointing film she examines.

Valerie Traub's equally mixed assessment of this film includes those "several scenes" referred to briefly by Mayne; and while Mayne uses psychoanalytic film theory to elucidate the repressive workings of patriarchy "behind the screen," Traub for the most part sees psychoanalysis and patriarchal homophobia as partners in crime—as equally responsible for a damaging cultural "conflation of gender and eroticism" ("The Ambiguities" 129), even though this key concept of gender remains undefined throughout the article.[13] Traub points incisively to the pertinent semantic discrepancy dividing questions of text from those of audience, psychoanalytic from cultural studies–based approaches, homophobic from queered readings of film: the sliding emphasis in "wanting" from verb to adjective, desire to lack (125). Thus, argues Traub, while a lesbian audience for *Black Widow* may focus on the story of Alex's *desire* for Catherine, the homophobic text itself, supported by the cultural and academic apparatus producing concurrent readings, fixates on the ways in which Alex *lacks* what Catherine has—beauty, power, wealth, femininity. Traub polarizes the concepts of lack and desire across the hetero/homo divide (and often uses "pleasure" as a synonym for the latter word), when the standard psychoanalytic handling would regard the terms as nearly interchangeable and fundamentally dependent upon each other.

Traub borrows briefly from the psychoanalytic paradigm, reading a "mirror stage" moment for Alex looking into a mirror, yet blames both the film itself and "Lacanian psychoanalysis" for encouraging the slippery shift from desire to identification— "if Alex wants Reni, she must also want to *be* Reni" ("The Ambiguities" 125)—that so effectively diffuses the film's potential lesbian energy. Despite her early assertion that "my methodology is both informed by and contestatory of psychoanalysis" (117), her approach is primarily a cultural studies–style elucidation of lesbian figurations in the film. In a final move similar to Mayne's above, Traub's very engagement with theory seems to cause her to ignore or misread the subversive potential of this "real lesbian" element, faulting lesbian audiences for "enact[ing] precisely the conflation of gender and eroticism endorsed by the film" whereby "identification *with* Alex becomes desire *for* Alex" (129). Note, however, the significant reversal overlooked by Traub: where perhaps the film itself, aided or not by the Lacanian apparatus, would deflect the lesbian signification by encouraging the move from desire to identification, it seems that the move in the opposite direction executed by the lesbian audience—being enjoined by the film to identify with Alex's masculinized gaze but deciding to perceive her as the object of desire instead—constitutes yet another insult to "correct" theorizing but a remarkably effective subversion of the homophobic film text.

LESBIAN PANIC

Feminist film theory has failed in large part to recognize what some lesbian film theorists (e.g., de Lauretis *Practice* and Hoogland, chapter 6) see as a solution to psychoanalytic theory's antifeminist impasses—the lesbian Real that represents a radical alternative to "woman's" entrapment by the Symbolic. Despite calls to "denaturalize" women's position within and before the filmic text (e.g., Cook and Johnston 34 and Cook 54) and the taking up of textual examples (especially "women's films") that cry out for an integrated feminist-lesbian approach, feminist psychoanalytic film theory tends to ignore or even denigrate this alternative perspective. Jacqueline Rose's reading of Hitchcock's *The Birds*, for instance, seems in part predicated on repression of the film's lesbian elements. While "delusional" and "paranoid" have elaborate psychoanalytic definitions, relayed by Rose with dazzling impenetrability in the opening moments of her essay, they have political shadings as well—those deemed insane have been victimized by aggression and are socially powerless—and when "the woman" (for instance, *The Birds*'s heroine Melanie Daniels) is assigned this position, feminist film theorists such as Rose are bound to challenge this assignation through psychoanalytically inflected dissection of it. Significantly, Melanie's most delusional (e.g., catatonic) state is reversed at the hands (literally) of her future mother-in-law, Lydia, who cures her with a loving embrace. Yet Rose reads Melanie's smile at her moment of recovery/recognition in Lydia's arms as instead "scarcely perceptible" and as a mark of her persistent delusion, a "response to the holding of the mother" (152).

Lydia is defined by her inability to "give . . . love" to her son Mitch (qtd. in Rose 151); by the end of the film her emotional attachment to Melanie (and Mitch's young sister Cathy) is clearly stronger than it has ever been to Mitch; the birds themselves elicit this relationship and the loving language the women share with regard to "being careful" (qtd. in Rose 151) in the film's climactic scenes. But Rose defines these instances of caring between the women as a "diluted" opposition to the consummation of Mitch and Melanie's sexual relationship (151), presuming this union, along with the heterosexually defined mother-son dyad formed by Lydia and Mitch, to occupy the entire stage. To the degree that the birds themselves represent a lesbianizing element in the film, it is significant that the obviously butch Mrs. Bundy, who is read by Rose as "desexualized" because of her "age and physical appearance" (150), reassures panicky diners in the Bodega Bay café that there is nothing especially "abnormal" about the birds after all.

Mary Ann Doane's investigation of "femininity as absence" in Max Ophuls's *Caught* and Hitchcock's *Rebecca* misses similar opportunities. While the female characters of *Rebecca* have been insightfully lesbianized on multiple occasions[14] in the years since Doane's article, "*Caught* and *Rebecca*" has received little if any attention by these same theorists, with the queered reading to be derived primarily (and to be entirely derivable) from Doane's own feminist-only approach. She begins with the "assumption"—the film's? her own?—that with the "positing of a female spectator . . . it is no longer necessary to invest the look with desire in the same way. A certain despecularization takes place in [women's] films, a deflection of scopophilic energy in different directions" ("*Caught*" 197). Both films open with images of women gazing at images of other women, with the women in *Caught* admiring styles (and models?) in a fashion magazine, even murmuring desirous intentions of "taking" this one or having that one "for me" (qtd. in Doane "*Caught*" 198; see also Lewis and Rolley). Doane reads this gaze, in standard fashion, as transformed from desiring to identifying: "Binding identification to desire . . ., the teleological aim of the female look demands a becoming and hence a dispossession. She must give up the image in order to become it—the image is *too* present for her" ("*Caught*" 199). While certainly the films themselves are primarily responsible for disfiguring the women's gazes thus, it is worth considering the degree to which Doane's own reading, which might have challenged the transformation by maintaining the aspect of desire a moment longer, steps immediately into line.

Both films depict bad marriages to wealthy men, revealing, in Doane's encouraging phrasing, "a rather fragile binding of drives in the heterosexual unit of the harmonious couple"; but the ways in which an absent woman queers her vacated position go unremarked in both the films and Doane's response to them: Rebecca is absented (murdered) for her "unnarratable!" transgressions against her marriage vow (see White 67), while in *Caught* Leonora is absented from all-male environments that barely noticed her in the first place. Within her marriage she is excluded from the high-powered industrial sphere occupied by her husband and his large contingent of male associates—as Leonora herself breathlessly realizes, "so many men" (qtd. in Doane 200)—and after the marriage her absence from work leads to a telling exchange between her boss and his male associate. Doane describes the tight symmetry of the shots that frame one man and then the other— "a sustained cross-cutting between Hoffman and Quinada, alternating both medium shots and close-ups" (*"Caught"* 208), while at one point in the scene Hoffman suggests that Quinada "forget Leonora" (*"Caught"* 200–01). The stills included in Doane's article reveal the men lounging in their respective doorways across the noirishly darkened office that contains her desk; Leonora's absence has literally enabled the eroticized exchange between them, yet the homoerotics of this homosocial triangle are not noted by Doane.

From the opening moment of both film and criticism, when the response of women viewing women was transformed from desire to identification, class transgression has obscured the possibility of sexual transgression in Doane's reading.[15] *Rebecca*'s Mrs. Danvers, frequently outed by lesbian and gay viewers for her obsessive devotion to the dead Rebecca, functions for Doane only in a "revers[ed] . . . hierarchy of mistress and servant" (212) that connotes the class transgression of the Joan Fontaine character. In *Caught* Leonora is separated from the "mink" that has come to insistently symbolize "marriage" by the physician who utters tellingly, "If my diagnosis is correct, she won't want that anymore" (qtd. in Doane *"Caught"* 210). Evidently, this ingenious doctor has managed to cure Leonora of her desire for mink (that is, marriage), but the obvious sexual alternative is replaced by the film (and without hesitation by Doane's reading) by the economic one; she prepares to marry Dr. Quinada, a member of her own class, who presents her with a cloth coat. The class-inflected reading—of Leonora as she continues to function as an object of exchange between her first and second husbands—coincides well with Doane's feminist project, yet the emphasis that would suggest Leonora's escape from this system of exchange, as well as the male homoerotics brewing beneath the surface of this homosocial triangle, are necessarily canceled in the process.

SHARED ISSUES

I have examined the issue of the desiring woman within psychoanalytic theory from three angles—feminist resistance to this possibility based on adherence to the tenets of psychoanalytic theory, lesbian insistence on this possibility through various forms of resistance to the theory itself, and a pseudosynthesis of interests in the case of feminist psychoanalytic readings on the threshold of acknowledging the lesbian alternative that nevertheless fail to do so. In a final approach, I consider another but more balanced exchange, this one giving voice to lesbian and feminist theorists in separate writings on topics of shared interest, specifically the import of motherhood as a theme in classical films and the film career of the lesbian director Dorothy Arzner. While feminist film theorists ignored Arzner's obvious lesbian orientation in their initial feminist-only readings of her work, lesbian theorists have been "outing" motherhood in recent writings on film. Specifically, the intense devotion and erotically charged generational divide characterizing the bonds between mothers and daughters queers what has been treated as asexual (at least pre-Oedipal) and sacrosanct by traditional feminist film theorists. Both discussions exhibit patterns of shifting emphasis and moments of outright disagreement; in the case of filmic images of motherhood, both perspectives deserve separate consideration, while neither approach to Arzner seems to fully account for this director's striking perspective.

Two films from the studio period, *Stella Dallas* and *Now, Voyager*, have received attention from feminist and lesbian film theorists considering motherhood in popular film. Significantly, Patricia White, reading E. Ann Kaplan and Linda Williams, has been instrumental in queering the mother-daughter bonds in these classical films when straight feminists from the psychoanalytic perspective have declined this option. Once again, the feminist emphasis is on oppression—for instance Kaplan's reading of *Now, Voyager*'s demonized and loveless Mrs. Vale—and the lesbian emphasis on desire—for instance, White's focus on the pleasurable and suggestive relationship between Charlotte Vale (played by Bette Davis) and her surrogate daughter Tina. Defending such unsympathetic images of motherhood from the antimaternality of the film itself, Kaplan argues that we are set up to feel negatively about Mrs. Vale due to mothering philosophies of the time, at the root of which were anxieties about women's developing role in the workforce during the war. She describes Charlotte herself as something of a patriarchal dupe, "flourish[ing] because of her submission to Dr. Jaquith" ("Motherhood" 130), while White promotes the lesbian shadings of Charlotte's situations and blames Kaplan's own text for causing us to hate Mrs. Vale (White 126). In fact White's criticism seems a bit unfair, as White herself later acknowledges that Mrs. Vale is readable as one "who misidentifies with patriarchal power and is tragically cut off from the daughter's recognition" (127); likely these theorists differ on the proper approach to Mrs. Vale because of related disagreements over how to read Charlotte.

Elsewhere, Kaplan in "The Case of the Missing Mother" determines the mutual devotion of mother and daughter in *Stella Dallas* to comprise the greatest threat to patriarchy in the film. To counter this, says Kaplan, the film enlists our support for the upper-crust point of view that the tacky, working-class Stella should sacrifice contact with her daughter, Laurel, to ensure a better life for her. While she closely reads the famous sleeping car scene, during which Laurel creeps down into the lower berth with Stella in order to comfort her following an insult, to depict this mutual bond, Kaplan's reading is the least lesbian of the three considered here; employing suggestive phrasing such as "getting so much pleasure for herself out of Laurel," "that Laurel returns Stella's passion," and "kisses her tenderly, snuggling up to her under the covers," Kaplan's own terminology lesbianizes the relationship between the two while the argument itself is without reference to the queer valences of this scene. Interestingly, Linda Williams's analysis of the film, provocatively titled "Something Else Besides a Mother" (a quote from the film) and containing multiple references to female homosexuality, skips the shared-berth scene as she reads moments immediately before and after instead (491). While her intended emphasis is on the intensity of the relationship between Stella and Laurel's stepmother, Helen Morrison (107), and while she argues that the film's mother-daughter bond is intimate "but not . . . lesbian" (104), White later describes Stella and Laurel as "gaz[ing] at each other with the blind eyes of lovers," depicts this scene as an image of "two adult actresses caressing each other," and refers to Hollywood gossip about Stanwyck's alleged lesbianism (104). A large photo of the scene, with the women embracing in bed together, accompanies the reading. Significantly, the (homo)sexual shadings of motherhood are manifest in psychoanalytic theory (de Lauretis *Practice*), yet not as fully explored in straight-feminist psychoanalytic readings of mother films as in less theoretically inflected analyses by lesbian film critics.

The films of Dorothy Arzner represent a tempting challenge to feminist film theorists of all critical approaches and sexual perspectives. One of few women directors in studio-era Hollywood, Arzner is praised for having produced an oeuvre worth attention from feminist theorists, and yet the texts themselves remain frustratingly resistant to the subversive readings sought there. It is presumed (or at least intently hoped) that Arzner directed "as a woman" and was speaking about the role of women to her female audiences in ways that contradicted, however subtly, the prevailing ideology emanating from other Hollywood productions. Feminist theorists such as Cook and Johnston have insisted upon the presence of a "women's discourse" identifiable beneath the surface of her otherwise mainstream films; even Jacquelyn Suter, who argues that this discourse is ultimately unable to survive any of Arzner's individual texts, works from the premise that such a discourse at least initially exists.

In support, critics have imposed a feminist intent on Arzner's quirky style. Cook and Johnston in separate writings consider this women's discourse as a locus of rupture and contradiction, describing the films' overarching narratives (the "male discourse") as "fragmented and incoherent" (Johnston 39), as lacking "smooth flow from one scene to another" (Cook 50) and as "distancing" (Cook 51). Johnston argues that it is only the missing women's discourse that, when added back in by discerning readers, "provides the principle of coherence and generates knowledge" (41) in Arzner's films, while Cook applauds Arzner's recurring gags that "do nothing to further the flow of the narrative" (52). What is striking in these arguments, especially to readers (including this one) lacking first-hand experience with Arzner's work, is the seeming effort under way to rescue with political intention what in fact seem to be structural defects in Arzner's films that threaten their ability to stand the test of time. Such "active reading" (Cook 46) indicates the dilemma feminist theorists struggle with in Arzner's work—the project of salvaging a women's artistic career that may be less than entirely salvageable.

Even more challenging are the decidedly antifeminist heroines populating Arzner's texts—especially the self-sacrificing Cynthia of *Christopher Strong* and the seemingly ridiculous Judy and Bubbles from *Dance, Girl, Dance*, two of the most frequently analyzed Arzner films.

Cook has creatively determined a "displacement of identification" at work in these texts, acknowledging that Arzner's heroines are "not fully and finally identif[iable]," although again positing the claim that this is all for the best, as it causes women viewers to "focus attention on the problematic position they occupy in their world" (47). Cynthia's airborne suicide on the occasion of her crisis pregnancy is "actively read" by Johnston to indicate both the failure of women's discourse to triumph over patriarchal ideology and "survival in the form of irony . . . [as] in itself a form of triumph" (44). Similarly, Judy and Bubbles's catfight before an excited burlesque audience is read by Cook as "call[ing] into question the processes by which women's desires are presented as a spectacle for consumption" (48); Judy's love-starved collapse into the arms of a ballet impresario at film's end is likewise an "ironic reversal" intended to "encourag[e] us as spectators to recognize the all-important problematic of the difficulties of the working through of female desire under patriarchy" (48). Meanwhile, Janet Bergstrom has effectively challenged the presence of such "irony" in Arzner's work, suspecting it is only locatable within certain critical responses, never the films themselves ("Rereading" 84). (See my discussion of this term in chapter 4.) Reading these scenes through the writing of their defenders, the flustered, fainting femmes starring there seem inadequately transformed by the feminist treatments they receive; it remains extremely difficult to separate Arzner's directorial imprint from the classically oppressive gaze of male Hollywood auteurs.

As Arzner's "feminist gaze" and "women's discourse" remain little more than tantalizing specters for these writers, it is plausible that Judith Mayne's effort to isolate a lesbian gaze in the films would have better success. Arzner's famously masculine wardrobe, hairstyle, and bearing have marked her fairly obviously for modern audiences as lesbian-oriented, while these same qualities create a curious blindspot in much feminist criticism, which Mayne correctly critiques in her work. Mayne's argument takes up the same filmic characters and situations popular amongst the feminist theorists and determines them to be representative of Arzner's films' two main lesbian traces—their emphasis on communities of women and the marginal lesbianized figure. Thus Mayne focuses not on Cynthia's pregnancy but her status as "virgin" early in the film, describing this as a "euphemistic catchall for a variety of margins in which she is situated, both as a woman devoted to her career and as a woman without a sexual identity." Ultimately, says Mayne, "the acquisition of heterosexuality becomes the downfall of Cynthia Darrington" (*Woman* 112), and Cynthia functions as one of Arzner's "marginal lesbians"—not so much a lesbianized figure marginalized in the film (she is played by Katharine Hepburn in a leading role) as a woman whose potential lesbianism is that which would marginalize her character and is marginalized by the overriding heterosexual narrative. Developing her "communities of women" argument, Mayne's focus is on the dancers in the burlesque house of *Dance, Girl, Dance*; she reads the catfight between Judy and Bubbles as encouraged first by an excited *female* member of the audience, then as an on-stage "extension of their conflicted friendship, rather than as an alienated site of performance" (102). Mayne deems the exceedingly problematic conclusion of the film to be a "heterosexual romance . . . but only after it has been mediated by relationships between women" (103). While Mayne's delineation of Arzner's "lesbian gaze" may suffer as much beside these films' strident heterosexuality as may readings of her "feminist gaze" beside the films' blatantly sexist portrayals, her emphasis on Arzner's lesbianism brings us much closer to what I would deem the proper labeling of Arzner's directorial perspective—that of the theatrically inflected *butch*, whose erotic investments include not only a self-dramatized masculine pose but also the solicitation of hyperfeminine performances from erotic objects around her. Arzner's "butch gaze" seems to occupy a position of political subversion indistinguishable at this complicated level of representation from the classically straight-male directorial gaze, but seems to represent the most viable interpretation of these traditionally feminine, ultimately helpless heroines. Thus it is only in Arzner's butch persona, her physical presence and her tendency, as Mayne has noted, to position herself for photographs in relationship to her hyperfemme leading ladies, where we find the subversively antitraditional "missing element" that saves Arzner's films from the designation of Hollywood-as-usual and marks her contribution to feminist/lesbian culture.

(MORE THAN) FRIENDS

Mayne introduces the "controversial . . . connection between lesbianism and female friendship" (*Woman* 103–04) in film, and the issue resonates across much of what I have been considering in this chapter. Especially considering how images of "communities of women"—sisterhood, female friends, and even the "strength and independence" of a character such as Bette Davis—have been said to mark the lesbian element in popular film,[16] the question arises as to how to locate "the feminist" in these same texts, now that its traditional representations have come to mean something else: since classical film never offered overt representations of lesbianism, instances of lesbian identity and desire must occur at the subtextual level, and perhaps a film's feminist intent must be locatable elsewhere, in the overall vision of a "women's picture" or a woman director. We might even argue that Hollywood is much more (sexually) lesbian—due in part to the voyeuristic interest of male viewers—than it has ever been (politically) feminist, so that only rare actual feminist elements will ever be isolable in popular narrative.[17] Note, however, how this argument credits the male gaze with creating the lesbian element in film and canceling these same elements' potential as feminist instead—just as this same gaze read a feminist gesture as lesbian ("she must be a dyke") for its very exclusion of the male agent from the scene.

In her writing on the relationship between theory and history Mary Anne Doane suggests an image from Sally Potter's "explicitly feminist film" ("Remembering Women" 61) *The Gold Diggers*, of one woman rescuing another during a crisis moment. Her vision of "Julie Christie [a]s saved from the cinematic scene, saved from the confines of the apparatus by another woman—Colette Lafonte—riding in on a white charger" ("Remembering Women" 62) is feminist *and* lesbian, although, I would argue, not simultaneously.[18] Specifically, two competing forms of strength are located in the women's actions (and even letting oneself be rescued by another woman takes fortitude within the Hollywood sign system): if these women are read as lesbians, their strength and subversive qualities derive from their enacting of mutual desire, at great personal risk, in a sex-phobic and homophobic society; conversely, as feminist "sisters" they subvert the classical Hollywood paradigm by *not* acting upon desire, by foregoing involvement in what Carolyn Heilbrun terms "the erotic plot" (48)—the enforced cinematic formula joining the woman to her love interest by story's end. They (as characters and as women) are seen in this sense to turn their backs on the love relationship—a sacrifice the lesbian reading of this same scene does not entail—to model a sisterhood that is powerful and particular in its very willingness to leave behind the prospect of sexual love. (See also Moore 145.)

My argument regarding these mutually exclusive readings of women on screen accords with Teresa de Lauretis's critique of "the lesbian metaphor"—a device that seeks to queer popular film but obscures the lack of actual lesbian cinema in the process—in the straight-feminist writings of Julia Kristeva, Kaja Silverman, and

Nancy Chodorow. Elsewhere she rejects the watered-down woman-centeredness locatable even in some *avant garde* women's films, insisting upon depictions of overt lesbian sexuality as the only indicators of authentic lesbian cinema. In a similar vein, Valerie Traub faults the filmmakers of *Black Widow* for defusing women filmgoers' erotic response through psychoanalytic sleight of hand: because Alex wants Reni, she "must also want to *be* Reni" (125). Contra theorists such as de Lauretis and Traub, although with arguments that also reinforce the identification/desire dichotomy, lesbian theorists emphasizing an "anti-voyeuristic" perspective (e.g., Becker et al. 37) advocate for films presenting lesbian lifestyles that do not depend on frankly rendered love scenes for "proof." Lesbian desire in these readings obscures and (because of the voyeuristic male interest it draws) threatens larger lesbian identities and limits the range of "identifiable" lesbians to only those sexually performing as such. Andrea Weiss's critique of *Silkwood*, in which the point of view shifts homophobically away from the lesbian character Dolly toward the heterosexual couple Drew and Karen at the moment Dolly's lesbianism threatens to become more than furtive, nocturnal sexual activity, exemplifies this approach (60–61; see also Russo 146, 187).

Yet de Lauretis, Traub, and others critiquing a homophobic tendency to water down authentic lesbian sexuality (whether this be defined as sexual activity or an overarching lifestyle) ignore widespread engagement of "the lesbian metaphor" by multiple *lesbian* theorists in search of lesbian subtexts in films about sisters (Mayne's *The Big Sleep*), mothers and daughters (*Stella Dallas* and *Now, Voyager*), or best friends (e.g., *Thelma and Louise*).[19] These critics seek to eroticize identificatory (sisterly, asexual) relationships between women on screen, not to substitute superficial lesbian tendencies for frank lesbian erotics but to infuse an otherwise superficial relationship with the charge of this lesbian eroticism. Yet whether such a gesture constitutes a watering-down or a juicing up of a film's lesbian potential, in each case, surface-level, asexual sisterhood gives way to (or successfully represses) subtextual lesbianism. Finally, the lesbianizing of women's bonds is a productive and necessary approach to film analysis but one that cancels the subversive potential of what we may have otherwise identified as "purely" feminist. When the nonsexual aspects of feminism are read as subversively as the erotic qualities of "the lesbian metaphor," both interpretations may seem viable, although film theorists of both orientations will have to choose between them.

IDENTIFYING DESIRE

If the bonds between women on screen are much more easily read as identificatory *or* desiring but not both, the issue is certainly more complicated when considering the shifting interests of the audience members themselves. To at last introduce the third member of this discussion, gay male film theory's identification with (and of) women on screen demonstrates well the complications involved, taking as it does at least three forms—traditional identification *with* screen stars eliciting from gay viewers feelings of adulation for the stars and affirmation for themselves—and two modes of identification *as*, in other words, the identification of women *as* the locus of homophobia in the film (harshly critiqued, despite the misogynist overtones of such a project) or *as* the locus of gay desire, to the degree that women function as stand-ins for absented queer male characters (with again a necessary roughness in the transformation of screen diva into desirable "asshole"). In fact, much of the gay response to women on screen partakes of the traditional identification-with; recent influential writings that depart from the role of adulating fan require consideration at the outset.

Significantly, gay theory has taken up the question of desire in viewing practice with an ease and effectiveness escaping feminist and lesbian theory. Early in this chapter I aligned the contributions of Teresa de Lauretis, D.A. Miller, and Lee Edelman, three text analysts who have employed psychoanalytic paradigms to support their queer perspectives on film. In addition, Miller and Edelman, like de Lauretis, deemphasize the significance of identification in their filmic readings, locating gay desire everywhere, even in heterosexist classical-era Hollywood films. As opposed to the cultural studies approach, which defines female film icons as loci of worshipful identification, theorists such as Miller and Edelman gleefully subject formerly sacred stars to in-depth proctological examinations of their viability as indices of queer desire.

While Miller has elsewhere conducted his analysis of the mostly-male cast of Hitchcock's *Rope*, newer writing by himself and Edelman approaches a much more ubiquitous phenomenon in classical Hollywood, the spectacle of the woman, and queers this most unlikely of figures for the gay desiring gaze. Both authors emphasize the backside—of stars' bodies, the psychic make-up—as opposed to the forward facing, frontally invested dichotomies of sexual difference that heterosexualize sexual relations, psychoanalytic theories, and popular cinema. Since even Elizabeth Taylor (Miller's point of interest) and Grace Kelly (whom Edelman reads) have backsides and anuses that, with the proper chiaroscuro lighting, might be indistinguishable from a desirable man's, these female stars function in these psychoanalytically shaded arguments in ways radically departing from their role in feminist and lesbian film theories—no longer as women but as an iconicity and desirability that deploys itself for those least likely to cathect upon such qualities in women.

In Edelman's reading of *Rear Window*, Lisa Fremont (Grace Kelly), or more specifically her "ring that can be found behind" ("*Rear Window*'s Glasshole" 84), is just one of many holes and rings orbiting the evermore anxiety-ridden L.B. Jeffries (James Stewart). Edelman's reading is sharp, but the sharpness of his attack is directed at Lisa herself (not the writers and director who brought her to life), as it is she who bears the "other cut," the forwardly placed vaginal slash that distracts men so effectively from their anal anxieties and coincides with presentation of Lisa's designer gown, beautiful face, Hitchcock blondness, and upper-class name, in short her total spectacle. Equally culpable, from the argument's first sentence, is "feminist, psychoanalytically oriented theorization of narrative cinema" (72), guilty of discursively modeling this heterosexist either/or, of working "complicitously with the seductions of dominant cinema" to reinforce the phallic regime (72). Positioned in tandem thus, feminist film theory and Lisa Fremont lend each other the agency, complicity, and culpability that either on "her" own could more easily deny. But can the character Lisa decide for herself the role she will play in a story being told about her at so many male-occupied levels of viewership? Should feminist theorists follow Edelman's lead, renounce the phallic economy their theories inadvertently support and emphasize films' repressed anality, yet do so by vilifying women on screen, for contributing to straight men's phobic backlash against all nonselves?

Lisa is in fact rescued here from her status as perpetrator, but only to take up the status of victim when she is aligned at the end of the article no longer with misguided feminist theory but the murdered Mrs. Thorwald. The actions of both the voyeuristic Jeffries and the dismembering Thorwald "aim to find the cut in the woman, or to find the woman cut, in order to cast out, project, or excrete the cut that threatens to rupture the Symbolic's signifying structure from within" (91). In the relay between the scene of repressed anal sexuality and the frustrations and rewards of capitulation to the Symbolic, woman is no more than a pushing-off point, the background against which men struggle with the homoerotic and homophobic aspects of their psychic selves. Ultimately, the anal emphasis that so closely defines the libidinal economy of gay *men* promotes a phallocentrism of its own, that is, a return to heterosexist power differentials, that can express queer desire only at the expense of the woman's cinematic presence.

In similar fashion D.A. Miller in "Visual Pleasure in 1959" spies the anality behind the phallicity in the homophobic film version Tennessee Williams's play *Suddenly Last Summer*. Again the woman functions as a pawn in the homophobic, intramasculine relay—as Miller (and the story itself) defines her, a "front" for the homosexual escapades of the perverse and mysterious Sebastian. Significantly, Cathy has more subversive agency and less culpability than had Lisa above, as she models not the pubic absence that Lisa so proudly displays but the protruding breasts that signal the phallic thereness of a beach boy in tight white swimming trunks in shots intercut with images of Cathy. Later it is her "crouching buttocks" (110) that are suggestively exposed to a group of these same boys, hungrily reading through her backside Sebastian's own queer desire; she is most threatening as "Gay Male Woman" who fails to embody for Man "the possibility of a peremptory refusal of homosexual desire" (115). At the end of the film, her hybrid gayness reveals itself in her neurotic unwillingness to get up from her chair, an ass-covering move that reminds us Edelman's Jeffries, who clings stubbornly to his convalescent seat.

A feature distinguishing both Edelman's and Miller's arguments from traditional analyses is a willingness to violate cultural categories, physical boundaries, and sacrosanct attitudes toward female stars that radically shifts the mood of the writing. Brett Farmer's more recent work, like that of Edelman and Miller, adopts a sophisticated psychoanalytic framework but returns readers to the reverential atmosphere sheltering gay audiences and their adored female stars. Where Farmer chooses camp-comic films for analysis, Edelman and Miller select dramatic thrillers; Farmer comments on perennial gay favorites such as Judy Garland, Katharine Hepburn, and Mae West, while Edelman and Miller target sex-goddess icons who have traditionally appealed to straight male audiences. Farmer reads women stars' and gay men's shared style of "excessive gender performance [that] confound[s] the borders between masculine and feminine" as cultural subversion, while Miller attributes the blended physicalities of Cathy and Sebastian to the film's homophobic intent. Interestingly, both writers use similar terms to describe this phenomenon: for Farmer, Mae West's radical appeal derives from her status as " 'gay man trapped in a woman's body' " (135), while Cathy as "front" to Sebastian's "back" becomes first a "female gay man" comfortably reinforcing homophobic gender demarcations and then a "gay male woman," no longer able to ease men's homophobic anxieties. Farmer reads Laura Mulvey appreciatively (187), when Miller challenges her "homophobic" assessment of men gazing at men.[20] Not surprisingly, Farmer's own reading of *Suddenly, Last Summer* continues to respectfully maintain boundaries. His focus on Violet Venable (played by the venerable Katharine Hepburn) depends upon this character retaining her female (maternal) status, while the only dividing lines he blurs are those separating the dead and scandalized Sebastian from the clotural and heterosexualized Dr. Cukrowicz (played by the 1950s gay icon Montgomery Clift).

Citing the influence of Leo Bersani's theory of anality as enabling the gay subject to "demolish phallic maleness" (208), Farmer notes that such "psychosexual violation and refiguration" (209) has come to characterize this subject's response to multiple cultural productions. Quoting from the stringently irreverent fanzine reviews of Boyd McDonald, who has subjected celebrity royalty such as Elvis and Pope John Paul II to eroticized speculations about their "soft" and "white" bodies, body parts (especially asses), and cinematic performances (for Elvis, scenes shared with other men), Farmer determines McDonald's writing to assume "the status of an aggressive assault on the phallic male image" (216). To the degree that *women* are rendered by the fetishistic male gaze as one more version of this phallic male image, we can see that Edelman's and Miller's readings partake significantly of this "logic of male phallic violation" (217) depicted by Farmer and exemplified by McDonald's scathing assessments. Importantly, McDonald's methodology—"Using what he terms 'the same harshly sexist and ageist standards that are applied to women in pictures'" (Farmer 216)—raises questions for Edelman's and Miller's approach. While Farmer considers the "thrills" of "subjection" and "particular pleasures generated in this act of queer erotic objectification" (218), can the same love-hate arrangement be said to inhere in the queer erotic objectification of female stars, or will the "harsh sexism" this style mimics and critiques somehow return in force now that actual women are being violated—albeit by different perpetrators for markedly different reasons—once more?

In the introduction to the collection housing the work of Miller and Edelman, Ellis Hanson's approach seems similarly predicated upon a disturbing anti-"feminism." This term is in quotes because this article ostensibly rejects a (presumably homophobic) feminist approach that in fact only disguises the real target of his disdain—a specifically *lesbian* contingent in queer studies, producing crunchy granola readings of "correctly" lesbian texts. Hanson criticizes not only the "bland," "prescriptive," and "amateurish" example set by Sheila McLaughlin's film *She Must Be Seeing Things*, but by obvious implication also favorable assessments of this work by lesbian theorists such as Teresa de Lauretis, who treats this film extensively in her influential *Practice of Love*. Hanson takes issue with de Lauretis elsewhere in his introduction, but refrains from naming her among the politically correct, aesthetically boring theorists he has in mind when attacking the cult status of McLaughlin's film. Hanson thus hides his critique of "affirming and crunchy" (21) lesbian readings behind an assault upon a much more acceptable adversary—(presumably homophobic) feminism—in a moment of ostensible queer solidarity against the homophobic/feminist mainstream.

The kind of lesbians (and gay men) Hanson *does* like are the snazzy and stylish "violent criminals" (9) populating progressive films from the thriller genre such as *Swoon*, *Poison*, and *Bound*. These gorgeously dressed villains with their cut physiques and "killer cosmetics" (1) remember film's mandate to be aesthetically enthralling, with properly politicized attitudes and agendas backgrounded. Hanson considers at length the lesbian characters heading the cast of *Bound*; his appreciation for their erotically charged performance verges curiously onto the typical male voyeur's, yet Hanson fails to consider the area of overlap, as well as the significant differences, between his own positive response and *Entertainment Weekly*'s panting assessment of Gina Gershon as a " 'fierce hot patootie' " (qtd. in Hanson 1). While Hanson himself likely noticed the women's bodies beneath the make-up and welcomed the representation of frank sexual activity enabled by them, his comparatively p.c. emphasis on the cosmetics, lighting, and atmosphere (as opposed to the mainstream fixation on the actresses' " 'patooties' ") distinguishes Hanson's subversively queer— he watches these women but is not turned on in the traditional manner—minority perspective from the majority of male viewers who come to the film with a completely different mindset. This majority response is, of course, the one that lesbian theorists have worked so effectively to counteract with their own positive reception of films by lesbians and, most importantly, *for* lesbians, that most men (even perhaps, if Hanson is a reliable indicator, most gay men) will simply not find sexy enough. Hanson's implied thesis, that films as stylish and arresting as *Bound* comprise political statements in themselves, may be true *only* for spectators sharing his specific sex/sexuality position on the spectrum; Hanson's silence on the issue of this limitation and his insistence that "feminists" stop spoiling the fun and join him in this eroticized appreciation for stylish films resembles the sacrifice requested by Edelman above of his gay-affirmative feminist readers.

argues heterosexual women must employ transvestism or masquerade to obtain. This "natural" distancing mechanism (in fact, a direct effect of Hollywood homophobia) enables both identificatory and desiring responses to women stars.

Introducing the important butch/femme distinction in lesbian viewing practice, Weiss sees butch identification with male stars as freed from the need to undergo "what film theorist Laura Mulvey has called a 'masculinization of spectatorship' " (42) yet acknowledges that "for a 'femme' the *problem* of spectatorship . . . remains largely a matter of speculation" (42, emphasis added). Weiss's determination of the femme mindset as a "problem" suggests that the femme lesbian shares the limitations of the straight woman's spectator role; Clare Whatling complicates the question by describing her own femme response to Weaver's Lt. Ripley in *Alien*—a desiring response directed toward Ripley's butch and *femme* aspects, as well as to the other femme characters in the story. While (and, likely, because) for Whatling, desire vectors outward toward butch *and* femme cinematic elements, desire and identification are a combined, though certainly not unified, response to film for her. As opposed to de Lauretis who challenges lesbians' identificatory responses to film, and who criticizes Jackie Stacey for muddying the waters between identification and desire in the first place (*Practice* 120), Whatling employs the arguments of Stacey to describe a pathway to lesbian desire *through* identification processes of "feminine fascination" with women stars (Whatling 62), insightfully positing near the end of her book that lesbians' "chameleon understanding of identification and desire might also read for a heterosexually identified spectator" (Whatling 164). Patricia White, also drawing to some extent on Stacey's work, succinctly phrases this phenomenon: "Our relationships to stars go beyond identification. . . . Simply put, when you recognize your lesbianism through movies and movie stars, you identify your desire" (36).

Despite the challenges presented here to the fixed dichotomies instituted by heteromale ideology and perpetuated faithfully by the Hollywood cinematic formula, all three gender/sexuality studies schools work within this paradigm as they continue fixing their gaze upon the filmic spectacle of the woman. All three, however, work from within *outward*—seeking to redefine the significance of women on screen in their respective, mutually exclusive ways: heterosexual feminists by *resisting* the identificatory relationship, gay theorists by *reveling* in it, and lesbian theorists by *eroticizing* it. What feminists fight to achieve "distance" from, gay men and lesbians draw closer to, through emphases on identification and desire, respectively; while gay men's enjoyment of identification with women stars constitutes its own subversive subject positioning, feminists and lesbians must complicate this relationship to avoid the ensnarements of sexism and homophobia, respectively. Finally it is the lesbian subject position that seems to most effectively challenge not only patriarchy's insistence upon sexual difference but also psychoanalytic theory's insistent dichotomizing of identification and desire; following the cinematic code's own mandate, that women in film shall be gazed upon and desired, lesbian viewers need only give voice to the special way in which they occupy a "masculinized position" to throw the entire model into question. Meanwhile, all three have tended to forego theorizing the spectacle of men in film—the desirability as straight or gay object choice that could radically redefine cinematic practice—or seeking out other ways to move beyond the psychoanalytic film paradigm instituted in early writings by Laura Mulvey and other feminist film theorists.

ALL FOR *EVE*

In the two films, *All About Eve* and *The Silence of the Lambs*, whose analyses conclude this chapter, powerful central female characters mark each as a "woman's picture," although the term has shifted significantly—from something desperately feminine to something powerfully feminist—in the 40 years separating their debuts. For the earlier film, feminist, lesbian, and gay readings are uniformly positive; for the more recent one, feminist and lesbian assessments remain favorable, yet the text's intense approach to issues of women's independence, sexual deviance, and the relationship between sex and death has caused a primarily critical response from the gay male perspective. In *All About Eve*, Eve's intense attachment to Margo indicates an important feminist *or* lesbian subtext; in *Silence of the Lambs*, Clarice's primary feminist *or* lesbian quality (her portrayal by lesbian icon Jodie Foster aside) is her marked erotophobia or asexuality, her total lack of interest in the men whose several spheres she intrudes upon. Eve's and especially Margo's bitchy personality traits are embraced by feminist and gay viewers (although for separate reasons), while the indifference to men that informs Clarice's character reflects the antimasculine features of the film itself: specifically, its array of unattractive, often villainous, males, is reinforced by the various sexual perversities defining them. Bette Davis's beloved drag queen, Margo Channing, gives way to Jodie Foster's homophobic Clarice Starling; feminist, lesbian, and gay viewers can unite in their appreciation for

Davis's work, while the three camps are forced to take up embattled positions in relation to the merits of the later film, with charges of sexism and homophobia leveled not only against the film but also against the contesting factions of its academic audience.

My reading of *All About Eve* is inspired by Patricia White's lesbian treatment of the film and numerous gay-oriented appreciations of the Davis persona, but must rely upon speculation as to what feminist theorists *would* find important in Davis's role and this film, due to the complete lack of discursive interest in either in recent decades. Feminist theory's turn toward the abstract and esoteric psychoanalytic mode has required a simultaneous turn toward appropriately complex filmic examples—from Hitchcock, Tourneur, and feminist filmmakers such as Sally Potter and Laura Mulvey; rare is the truly popular text analysis, such as Cook and Johnston's early work with the films of Raoul Walsh and Elizabeth Cowie's psychoanalytic reading of *Coma*. With *Silence of the Lambs*, feminist interpretations locatable in mainstream film reviews bolster the academic discourse issuing from all three camps. Both readings, therefore, will develop from my own interface with the primary texts and by my fashioning of gay, lesbian, and feminist responses as have been learned from my readings in the critical methodology that constitute this chapter. Yet again one interpretation often signals the limitation or even cancellation of one or both of the other two.

Almost no consideration of classical screen divas coming from the gay perspective fails to include a moment to adulate the "archetypal model for the bitchy gay queen" (LaValley 62), Bette Davis. Al LaValley singles out *All About Eve* as "the key gay cult film" (62), while Michael Bronski praises "the sheer theatricality of Davis" ("Judy Garland" 205), and Brett Farmer includes her on his list of "great stylists of temperament and mannerism" (114) beloved by gay audiences. Multiple theorists point appreciatively to the capaciousness of Davis's larger-than-life celebrity persona and screen roles; she is a supremely imitable Hollywood figure, making her a perennial favorite of drag performers across the decades, and spans the gender spectrum from butch lesbian to bitchy queen to shrinking southern violet, all roles fantasmatically inhabitable by a gay sensibility. This broadness opens onto the humor, even the "not-intended-to-be-comic" performances (Doty *Flaming Classics* 81), found everywhere in Davis's work, and the cynical sneer she brought to so many of her roles mirrors fundamentally the wryness, bittersweetness, and irony that defines the camp aesthetic and the quintessential queen's outlook on life.

These qualities of largeness and humor are not, conversely, the focus of available lesbian readings of this film, which emphasize instead the intimate/erotic intensities shared by the women characters in the film (not only Davis and her costar Anne Baxter but also the supporting characters played by Thelma Ritter, Celeste Holm, and Barbara Bates) and the drama (as opposed to the comedy) evinced by the film through the insinuation and playing out of these eroticized relations. Vito Russo criticizes the homophobia behind the queering of the supporting role played by George Sanders— "a symbol of sophisticated decadence . . . presag[ing] the gay-as-alien images of the 1950s" (95)—as well as the minimizing of the overt lesbian tendencies of Eve, originally conceived as a lesbian character (94). Patricia White argues that the women's "intensely invested relationship, . . . what goes on 'between women' " (204), is the subject of the film, and determines this relationship to inextricably join the enigmatic, anonymous Eve to Margo, the publicly adored star. White describes Eve's "stealthy itinerary" (204) as mirroring the devotional, identificatory agendas of ordinary film fans and considers the significance of "the content of Eve's secret [a]s lesbian" (204), again emphasizing the dramatic, startling, almost thriller-type aspects of the film. Jackie Stacey—in a reading designed to address "the specifically homosexual pleasures of female viewership" ("Desperately Seeking Difference" 450) but defining desire between Margo and Eve as only "incomplete identification" (459)—refers to the eroticized "pleasures of spectatorship" but also "its dangers . . . as an intense rivalry develops between them [and] Eve emerges as a greedy and ambitious competitor" (457). (See also Straayer 44.) The shift from the gay to lesbian perspective, therefore, entails not simply a change in emphasis from identification to desire but a new rendering of the film's very mood, genre, and subject matter—from camp comedy to erotic thriller.

Stacey's reference to Eve and Margo as "dangerous competitors" marks for me a viable strain of feminist analysis, in part inspired by Doane's focus on class in *Caught* and *Rebecca,* considered above. In the story, the socioeconomic distinctions between the women pits them against each other in their battle for and against various men. As Doane isolated a homosocial triangle of exchange between men in *Caught,* here it is the women at various stages of their careers struggling for the romantic and professional attention of the men. In an early moment from her analysis, Stacey describes Margo as "step[ping] down from stardom into marriage" (457), as Eve ascends to the position of celebrity Margo once occupied; with this telling choice of words, Stacey indicates that the husband figure represents a downturn in the career of the "woman" (no longer the star) destined to join with him, as the financial security he is traditionally considered to offer is here irrelevant beside Margo's independent wealth. What he offers instead is the conventional love relationship, the traditionally outlined "womanhood" that Margo resists conforming to until the end of the film. From camp comedy to erotic thriller, we move to melodrama and romance, although it is in no way a permanent move, as this ever-shifting narrative transitions constantly from one mode to another.

Early in the film, a relationship is established between Karen (Margo's best friend, played by Celeste Holm) and Eve (an adoring fan waiting at the stage door) that is warm and supportive although popping with questions due to confusion between lesbian and feminist interpretations. Specifically, we are compelled to ask what Karen sees in Eve, this girl Karen is "looking for" without ever having spoken to her: would her relationship to this younger woman be Oedipal-maternal, feminist-sororal, lesbian-erotic? Does she envision Eve as young ward to her governess (she's referred to as such by Margo), a potential locus of sexual interest, a potential threat to her own relationship with Margo, a juicy tidbit to bring home for Margo to nibble on, a fellow-outsider to the theatrical world Margo rules over, with whom she might form an alliance? At various moments in the film, the answer is "yes" to all of these questions, and the rapidly changing status of this relationship creates much intrigue in the film, as well as mirrors the complicated bond between Margo and Eve. For certainly, Margo is to Eve all of these things and more and at a much higher emotional pitch; even their first encounter is intimate in a way that could position them as sisters or lovers with equal ease.

As Karen ushers Eve into Margo's dressing room, it is not some state of boudoir dishabille that creates this sense of intimacy but Margo's willingness to receive Eve in her postproduction, utterly deglamorized state, face shiny with cold cream, hair plastered beneath the headgear that enables her to don a stage wig, yet resembling the dressing one might apply to a patient fresh from the lobotomy table. Despite the potential in this arrangement for the youthful and luminous Eve to outshine Margo, mention is made throughout the scene of Eve's drowned-rat condition—her baggy coat and funny hat, her sob-story past, and pathetic hanging about the stage door—while no mention of the star qualities exuded by Margo, evident even in this reduced state, is necessary. The striking physical and psychological opposition between the women reminds us of the differences described above by lesbian theorists seeking to eroticize the likeness between lesbian characters in popular film; the pretense of Margo's superior glamour and beauty, supported

by both Margo and Eve, as well as the circle of well-wishers forming
an audience in the dressing room that night, creates the feel of an
elaborately staged scene that further eroticizes the situation. In the
thick of Margo and Eve's densely imbricated relationship—they soon
share a home and daily schedule as Eve becomes Margo's personal
assistant—Eve jumps to perform Margo's most demeaning chores
(carrying coats, mixing martinis), while Margo sadistically delights in
transforming Eve into whipping girl.

While the pseudo-sororal bond connecting Karen with Eve denotes
a feminist element, the primary connection between feminism and
this text is the more-than-necessary critique elicited by the film's
inherent misogyny—the situations that pit the women against each
other in desperate competition for marriage or survival. Even the
master/servant games indulged in by Margo and Eve have an economic
interpretation; Margo seeks to limit Eve's mobility and desirability by
treating her as a menial servant and forcing her to remain in low-
profile, deglamorized jobs. Elsewhere, however, these moments of
anti-feminist pitting-against—Eve challenging Margo or Karen for
rights to their respective men—are yet thoroughly entwined with lesbian shadings, creating more intriguing questions for the audience to
consider. As Eve interrupts the kiss between Margo and Bill at the air-
port, is it jealousy of Margo or of Bill that motivates her act? When she
sweeps Margo's white, frilly costume across her arms, bearing it back
to the dressing room moments after her mistress has stripped it off,
are we to picture one bride carrying another across a threshold or a
triumphant adversary bringing Margo's dead body (or dead career or
dead love relationship) to the funeral pyre? In the climatic ladies room
scene at the end of the film, shall Eve's firm grasp on Karen's wrist,
which forces Karen back down on the couch beside her and initiates
the blackmail scheme between them, be read as a touch of homoerotic
bondage or the shackles that keep women of this era bound to the
men who control their financial destinies?

Much has been made of the young woman character who "calls
herself Phoebe" and enters the story in the final scene, after Eve has
won the annual award for best actress in theater, now fully supplant-
ing Margo in her role as "immortal star of the moment." As Eve (now
evidently channeling Margo) drowses on the couch, cocktail and cig-
arette in hand, throatily commanding her new protégé (played by
Barbara Bates) to get the door, Phoebe steals into Eve's room, dons
her glamorous evening cape, and takes up Eve's freshly bestowed
award. In a tryptic mirror in Eve's room, Phoebe's even more youthful form is reproduced countless times, and the thesis—that Phoebe

represents the next Eve, just as Eve became the next Margo—is obvious. Once more, however, feminist and lesbian readings contend for prominence here, although the film is simultaneously at its most antifeminist and antilesbian at this point: if banal and undesirable "likeness" has been fought against by lesbian theorists pointing toward the eroticizing differences between women, what is to be made of the "just another starlet" theme that dissolves what is special and particular about each of these characters (and each of these actresses as potential objects of lesbian-erotic contemplation) at the end of the film? From the feminist perspective, this theme may remind viewers that women's essential interchangability (as bodies, as breeders) is what keeps them in such fierce competition with each other, that their ever shortening shelf-life as sexual commodities only intensifies this crisis, and that their ultimate expendability in the marketplace threatens not just their social positioning (as wife, as "woman") but their very survival.

Yet as clearly as the film suggests a trigenerational connection between Margo, Eve, and the newly ascendant Phoebe, the sense of a break between Margo (as nostalgic "last of her kind") and Eve (the first woman, or in this case the first "nonwoman") provides a homophobic atmosphere of decadence or decline, from golden-era Margo to iron-age Eve to the already-jaded Phoebe. The contrast is well discerned in the outcomes for Margo and Eve: Margo leaves the story on the way to the altar surrounded by laughing, loving friends; Eve is stuck with the dandified, dangerous Addison DeWitt (George Sanders) and the already-scheming Phoebe, two thoroughly unappetizing love interests. In a chilly seduction scene between DeWitt and Eve earlier in the film, DeWitt is clear about his lack of love for Eve, but what is more evident is his utter lack of lust for her; and his effete qualities add much to the menace of his character. Both DeWitt and Eve are therefore trapped and villainized specifically by their queer shadings; Margo, who has always figured more as the object of Eve's pursuit than vice versa, escapes both Eve's clutches and the taint of lesbianism by story's end, while the three queers (Phoebe included) are left to each other, and the legitimate theater is doomed.

Yet the queer shadings of DeWitt's character are infrequently noticed by gay readers of this film (save Russo's comments as referred to above), with Davis's performance the focal point instead. While the lesbian and feminist readings of this film concern the various directions its plot takes, the ways its central questions are resolved, the gay response pertains primarily to its outer layer—its style and mood, its pacing, atmosphere, and comedy—that rises above the drama unfolding below. While Margo's every wry glance and flipped wrist is a source of camp enjoyment for attuned viewers, the kinetic birthday party scene contains many of Davis's best lines ("I hate men!" and the classic "Fasten your seatbelts. It's going to be a bumpy night!") and offers her the moments of triumphant flourish, deadpan wit, and drunken bathos that span the range of camp emoting. Especially the moments between Bill and Margo burst with hilariously overdramatized action; Bill grabs Margo, flings her about, pins her to the wall or bed; Margo struggles against the power of his love with grand gestures and a resolute sense that he is falling in love with Eve. When he storms out, Margo plays the abandoned victim to near-distraction. Davis's character simmers with this sensibility in every scene, and the drama, pathos, and eros anchoring the lesbian and feminist approaches to this film is more than balanced by the queer-camp elements illuminated by the gay reading.

In fact, we can align the three approaches along a plot- and style-based spectrum that shades one mode so subtly into the next that the three are interestingly, however contentiously, united by this film. Specifically, the lesbian erotics intensify the relationships between Margo and Eve, Karen and Eve, and Eve and Phoebe and include the titillating S&M components—emotional cruelty, physical bondage, and exaggerated master/servant relationships—that simultaneously structure the "competition" reading constituting the feminist response: when power struggles are played out over issues affecting only the women characters, the emphasis remains on "play"—cat and mouse games that draw the women to each other and could certainly code the interactions as homoerotic for a lesbian audience; when men or money are introduced, however, the "scenes" between the women shift from play to reality, while players become potential victims threatened with social isolation or economic ruin. These catfights between the women—over the men, starring roles, fame and wealth—rise to a level of comic theatricality beloved by gay viewers of this film. What had been seductive one moment and threatening the next, expands into overblown hilarity, presided over by the delightful Davis whose snide and incongruous throw-away lines create high comic moments.

Beyond her classic poses and delivery, Davis's physical self in this film is a striking hybrid of butch confidence (her strident stance and walk, her deep voice), conventional femininity (the long, glossy hair and graceful figure), and overly made-up, drag-style masquerade (necessary to counter to the degree it could Davis's rapidly aging facial features). Significantly, age is an issue throughout the film, as

Margo's eight-year seniority to her boyfriend and director Bill
(although, again, her appearance makes her seem much older than her
stated "40") adds to the insecurity Margo increasingly feels around
the youthful and vibrant Eve. Lloyd Richards, Margo's playwright,
keeps writing plays featuring heroines too young for Margo to play,
while Karen (Lloyd's wife) seems older than he by at least half a decade
as well. Thus both Margo and Karen figure to some extent as the
pathos-laden aging queens so recognizable to gay audiences, leaving
them vulnerable to the backstage treachery of Eve (who tries to seduce
both Bill and Lloyd in the course of the story). Again, from one
moment to the next, the ways in which the women characters threaten
and become threatened by each other shifts from lesbian-erotic "play"
to triangulating/misogynist competition to free-for-all camp theatricality, transitioning the film from one mode of audience appeal to the
next and palpably, constantly transforming its entire atmosphere.

SILENCING DISSENT

Pertinent to most readings of *The Silence of the Lambs* is consideration
of four figures—the psychopathic and homosexualized serial killer
Jamie Gumb, the effete yet fascinating Hannibal (the Cannibal)
Lecter, the asexually feminist heroine Clarice Starling, and the possibly closeted (and thus hypocritically homophobic) lesbian/feminist
icon bringing Clarice to life, Jodie Foster. Within this spectrum of sexual irregulars is something for filmgoers of every sex, gender, and sexual orientation to love or hate: feminists are so enthralled by Clarice's
powerful character and Foster's powerful performance that the queering of both male killers barely registers; in the words of "feminist"
critic B. Ruby Rich, "Please excuse me if my attention is focused not
on the killer but on the women he kills" ("Response" 49). Conversely,
gay critics are enraged by the film's homophobia—Gumb's queer-
coding with respect to dress, makeup, and pet poodle; Lecter's over-
board oral fixations (Diana Fuss's observation) and overly refined
manner; Foster's tight-lipped unwillingness to out herself as a
lesbian—that disincline them to praise the strong central female character on mere feminist grounds. (See also de Lauretis *Practice* 117.)
While Douglas Crimp has argued that feminist and gay readings of
this film "do not have to be mutually exclusive" (311), in fact he
rejects sympathetic feminist readings (specifically, the one produced
by Rich). For him, Rich's very voicing of support for Foster's on- and
off-screen personae exacerbates the homophobia perpetrated by the
film itself.[21]

Crimp reads the concluding moment from Rich's review—when she defends her position by acknowledging "guess I'm just a girl"—as a claim of allegiance with the feminist (i.e., straight/homophobic) camp as opposed to the "gay" enclave to which she also belongs. Michèle Aina Barale determines that Rich's self-girlification is meant to purposely raise eyebrows as she styles herself a " 'girl-feminist' . . . being 'bad' in her gender loyalty" ("When *Lambs* and *Aliens* Meet" 100). Yet I contend that Rich's lesbianism is revealed in her very choice of terminology; as offensive as "girl" can be when referring to an adult heterosexual woman, more recent associations of lesbianism with the word girl ("odd girls," "guerilla grrls," "girl power") should ring a bell for both Crimp and Barale; Crimp asks "where has the lesbian gone" in Rich's argument, when Rich's word choice indicates her own queer status and queers her impassioned defense of Foster (now lesbianized as the recipient of Rich's attention).

In a glowing review of Foster's career, Rich (in "Never a Victim") defends Foster from the "Hinckleyesque" attacks perpetrated by gay activists during the debut of *Silence of the Lambs* (58), securing Foster in her heterosexualized (at least privatized, sacrosanct) closet of personal relationships, yet outing her effect on at least one female fan (Rich herself) as specifically lesbian by its very intensity. In this instance, Rich allows aesthetic appreciation and erotic appeal to influence her response to the film, ignoring the political mandate to review favorably only "crunchy and affirming" images of gays on screen. Here I quote and recontextualize Ellis Hanson's injunction to "feminist" (i.e., certain lesbian) film critics, to expand their range of positively received queer cultural figurations beyond innocent, wholesome, or otherwise communally sanctioned types. Since Hanson's argument does not include *Silence of the Lambs*, we can only speculate as to whether he would deem the queer villains depicted therein stylish enough to deserve gay and lesbian film critics' favorable response. Similar to Rich, Martha Gever likens Larry Kramer not to a Hinckleyesque stalker but the almost-as-offensive Oedipal father, a "self-appointed daddy," attempting to police Foster and her character. In her gender-focused reading, Judith Halberstam "resist[s] the temptation to brand the film as homophobic because gender confusion becomes the guilty secret of the madman in the basement" (40), arguing that the problematic Gumb character himself "challenges the heterosexist and misogynist constructions of the humanness, the naturalness, the interiority of gender even as he is victimized by them" ("Skinflick" 51).

Yet Halberstam is somewhat alone in her recuperative reading of Gumb, since even feminists who like the film for other reasons often concede this character's homophobic and, of course, brutally misogynist presentation. Supported by these reservations, the complaints of Crimp, Kramer, and other gay-oriented reviewers are clearly justified: Gumb's body is filmed from obscure angles and chopped into sexualized parts to heighten the effect of his frightening strangeness; his deep voice adds to the freakishness of his effeminate physical appearance and especially his aspirations to become, in whatever way he can, a woman. In a scene that irritates many, multiple extended closeups of Gumb applying lipstick, teasing the ring in his nipple, and prancing before a camera in his basement draw out and draw upon voyeuristic fascination. It is as if the film's own lens cannot seem to get enough of Gumb's pink lips and erotic self-contact, culminating in a pose he strikes with genitalia hidden between his legs. The scene has no bearing on the larger narrative; as "exposition" its contorted erasure of the male character's anatomy exposes only his freakish depths. Straight viewers are fascinated and stunned, gay ones bored or offended.

Yet it seems necessary to question many gay critical assessments of Gumb's character as "stereotypically" gay. In fact the ways in which this enigmatic figure steps outs of (by thoroughly entangling) effeminate and macho/misogynist typology may be even more troubling than a "classic" version of either extreme. While Gumb's poodle (named Precious), silk scarves, eye makeup, and camera-posing suggest a typical effeminate sensibility, these elements are thrown into question by his hypermasculine qualities: I have already mentioned his deep voice, utterly lacking in camp inflections, while Halberstam points out that Gumb "is a confused mosaic of signifiers. In the basement he resembles a heavy metal rocker as much as a drag queen" (41). Janet Staiger, who shares the critical opinion that Gumb embodies "stereotypes of gay men" (144), that "Gumb is effeminate," points out elsewhere in her discussion that he is a "working-class lout" (145). Gumb's criminal nickname—Buffalo Bill, due to his habit of skinning his female victims—reinforces the masculist qualities of his persona. Surely it is his propensity for intense violence that moves him most clearly away from the stereotypically effeminate gay male: often in these readings Gumb's serial-killer status is linked to public misperceptions of gay men purposefully, diabolically spreading HIV/AIDS, while Staiger reads in the film "wide enforcement of the notion that effeminate men are psychopathic serial killers" (152). But this is a notion that is years outdated if it has ever existed at all: surely the contemporary perception is that effeminate gay men wear tennis

sweaters knotted over their shoulders and worry too much about
color schemes. They may hit you over the head with their purses, yet
this is always played in mainstream (i.e., homophobic) media for comedy, not violence. They are not even sexual (or viral) threats since, as
Leo Bersani points out, "parody is an erotic turn-off, and all gay men
know this. Much campy talk is parodistic, and while that may be fun
at a dinner party, if you're out to make someone you turn off the
camp" (208). At the level of representation, it is *masculine* gay men
who are eroticized and demonized (by and for straight and gay
audiences) in popular literature and film. The classic recent example is
the vampiric Gaetan Dugas, whose (hyper)masculine charms make
him an erotic focus *and* a detested reservoir of HIV infection in
Randy Shilts's *And the Band Played On.*

In the irresolvable contradiction that makes up his gendered
identity, gender/sexuality critics must acknowledge that Jamie Gumb
is exactly what we have been clamoring for in our critiques of mainstream cultural texts: a narrative figure that does *not* rely upon stereotypes and familiar formulas to make itself readable to an audience. Like
an ordinary human being—despite the fact that he is read repeatedly as
the personification of evil—Gumb is a difficult-to-theorize mixed bag
of "typical" and incongruous traits. His gender-bending qualities, in
addition to what Halberstam, for instance, reads as his victim role—
exacerbated by the film's own comment that he was denied sex reassignment surgery by medical authority—should make him sympathetic
to the gender/sexuality studies audience but instead he is almost
universally reviled.

For while Halberstam appreciates the ways in which this character
throws gender identity into question—proving that it is "only skin
deep" (48), it is equally viable to criticize the arbitrary nature of his
gendered identity and the gender-sexuality rationale for his heinous
crimes: reading Gumb as the macho/misogynist character he primarily is, his effeminate bits of stage business seem little more than this—
unsavory attempts by the filmmakers to deepen his freakish
hatefulness by resorting to those qualities in masculine subjecthood
most terrifying to straight men—feminine ones—since his "straight"
physical qualities have already well taken care of frightening women
viewers (Halberstam 41). In the film, Dr. Lecter warns Clarice that in
fact Gumb is not a transsexual, and Halberstam's interest in Gumb's
skin fixation, persuasive as it is, reminds us that this "deviant" is much
more interested to transform the surface of his being—when of course
both men and women have skin—than to add or subtract those parts
that interrupt the surface by sticking out—breasts, buttocks, Adam's

apple, penis—as is typical for the *normal* preoperative transsexual. Thus, just as feminist theorists read in the act of rape not sex (let alone lovemaking) but pure violence against women, so Gumb's desire to flay his victims may be read as nothing more than an excuse to murder them painfully and disfigure them thoroughly. His utterly gratuitous criminal behavior matches his utterly gratuitous effeminate shadings, and he is readable as pure violence, not as sex at all—while remaining profoundly problematic—simultaneously for a change—to both feminist and gay male analytic perspectives.

While Gumb's character is abhorrent to almost all analysts of this film, it is the feminist perspective that has called attention to the queer shadings of Hannibal Lecter, sometimes to deepen a critique of the film's homophobia but often to suggest that Lecter is a subversive (because sympathetic, attractive) queer character even if Gumb is not. Indeed, Lecter is ingenious, witty, charming, elegant, dandified, and effete; his striking portrayal by the charismatic Anthony Hopkins received equal (and equally enthusiastic) attention to Clarice/Foster from the mainstream press, and Andrew Schopp observes that Lecter's profile improves throughout the "Hannibal trilogy," so that by the series' end he is readable as its hero. While Diana Fuss draws out the psychic shadings of Dr. Lecter's oral fixation, denouncing the "psychoanalytic morbidification of homosexuality" ("Monsters of Perversion" 188), Elizabeth Young acknowledges Lecter's "camp artistic sensibility" (27), and Julie Tharp calls "the epicurean, classical music aficionado, and artist . . . dangerously feminine" (111).

But why has Lecter not been favorably aligned with those gay-coded "fascinating, insidiously attractive Hitchcock villains" (206) identified by Robin Wood, or the "stylish villains" touted by Ellis Hanson in his appreciation of queer-inflected modern thrillers?[22] Why does Douglas Crimp sneer at Lecter's campy one-liner, "Oh, Senator . . . love your suit" (Crimp 310) when a similar lavender-shaded comment by a bachelor character in another film might have drawn appreciative recognition? Might gay viewers of this film even find interest in Janet Staiger's argument that the "boyish" Foster herself, with her deep voice, androgynous character, and intense relationships with older men functions, according to Carol Clover as " 'a homoerotic stand-in' " (qtd. in Staiger 147)? Likely for these viewers, the Gumb character is offensive enough to spoil any inclination to seek out aesthetically interesting gay portraiture elsewhere in the film. That he is played not by an attractive, iconic star such as Foster or Hopkins (or Ralph Fiennes who is a villain later in the Hannibal series) but by the relatively obscure and nondescript Ted Levine makes him an even more distracting target for vilification, perhaps blocking from view the admirable performance of Hopkins as a wickedly delightful index of camp humor or Foster's Clarice as a Ganymede figure in several of the film's "man-boy" love relationships.

The Silence of the Lamb's women characters are as fraught with interpretive dilemmas as are its men. Many feminist critics, beginning with Rich above, praise the strength and intelligence of Foster's Clarice Starling. Young congratulates Clarice's "competence and confidence" (11) among her fellow FBI operatives, and hangs much of her contention regarding the film's feminist stance upon its tendency to depict scenes from her perspective. Taubin reads *Silence* as a feminist film, while Donald sees "the depth and strength of . . . character" (351) in Clarice's unflinching appraisal of a photo of one of Lecter's victims. While Judith Halberstam contends that "Starling is no match for Lecter" (39), she applauds the film for "refus[ing] to reduce the female to a mass of mutilated flesh" (40). Many in fact appreciate the way Clarice holds her own within the all-male environments she negotiates; Tharp calls her "truly the New Woman, the modern professional counterpart to [*Psycho*'s] Lila Crane (108); analyzing a mutilated body, she "quickly establishes the difference between herself and the body . . . by setting herself up as an authority" (Halberstam 43).

Meanwhile, Corey Creekmur and Alexander Doty speak against the film's homophobia *and* its misogyny (6), and Stephanie Wardrop observes the film's "technique of 'quid pro quo,' providing a scene that reinforces patriarchy for every scene that seems to challenge it" (105). I am equally inclined to call into question the film's so-called feminist aspects. With respect to the issue of Clarice's "strength," it is the case that the he-men cops and doctors the film surrounds her with evince a lockjaw indifference to obviously disturbing situations that looks contrived and defensive. I disagree with Young that Clarice adopts male qualities of strength and intelligence "without falling into male mimicry" (11); in fact, her studied copying of the men's unnaturally unfazed responses hardly secures our sense of her confidence or strength, yet normal reactions of disgust to the more gruesome aspects of her work would put her at another kind of disadvantage. Certainly Foster's performance succeeds in part by the vulnerability she brings to her encounters with her FBI mentor Jack Crawford, Dr. Lecter, and Jamie Gumb, although her frequent attitudes of subordination, anxiety and/or terror undermine our expectations of her bravery and strength. As Crawford's student there is little she can say, and nothing the film does say, against his patronizing shielding of her from their case's various crisis moments. As he gathers with backwoods sheriff's deputies in the mortuary of the town of one victim, Crawford leads his fellow officers into the back room to discuss the gritty sexual details of the case, while Clarice is left to wander the emotion-laden environment of the funeral parlor where memories of her tragic past overwhelm her. As her other father/teacher, Lecter solicits these same painful memories for sadistic enjoyment, but is his lack of an excuse that much worse than Crawford's defense that he had to exclude Clarice so he could "blow smoke" (whatever that means) for the deputies? Later in the film, Clarice is sent by Crawford on multiple solitary errands, seemingly removed from the action, and then stumbles into the thick of it by accident. While she eventually achieves heroism in this coincidental fashion, the pure accident of her achievement coincides with and in part justifies Crawford's paternalist coddling.

And can we picture a male actor playing this film's final basement scene in the wild-eyed, panting, frantic manner in which Foster was directed (or perhaps directed herself) to handle it?[23] While no doubt such a situation would be actually that terrifying for anyone, male or female, having to contend with it, films rarely structure coherent narratives around such a frank response: what FBI trainee so obviously psychologically unequipped to handle this traumatic situation would turn up for the next day of schooling, let alone stick around for the graduation ceremony? If the film decides, after all, to take the "reality" tack, where are the equally realistic aftereffects of such a scare—the debriefing, counseling, depression, paranoia, and substance abuse? Certainly a woman hero, still a fairly rare entity in the thriller genre, creates interesting options and dilemmas yet being worked out by contemporary actors and filmmakers; in this textual example, the softness imposed upon Clarice's character counters the strength in subtle but incongruous ways.

Perhaps even more troubling is the film's negative rendering of Gumb's several female victims. Their physical largeness is necessary to the plot (Gumb is collecting skins for a "woman suit") but makes freaks them as well, as Hollywood always does to large women, in this case aligning them with the film's other freaks (Lecter and especially Gumb) and thus subtly blaming them for their own victimization. Especially the main victim Catherine, whose pluck and wit many reviews have correctly praised, is also an exceedingly unattractive character from her first moment on film; banging her steering wheel as rock music blares from the radio, staring open-mouthed as Gumb works the ruse of struggling with a piece of furniture in a van, her character exudes trashy stupidity, in striking contrast to her classy, businesslike mother, a Republican senator from Tennessee. Finally it is only dress size that separates this brassy daughter from the elegant professional identified as her mother; the film suggests that this size difference has shifted the daughter several rungs down the social scale as well and sapped every bit of grace and sophistication in the process. And while no one was likely hoping for a wilting damsel for Clarice to rescue at film's end, Catherine's abrasive, ungrateful attitude—she calls Clarice a "fucking bitch"—hardly depicts the sororal bond that might constitute an authentically feminist moment, let alone the erotic charge that might connote a lesbian one. (See also Young 17–18.) The film fails to depict Catherine's actual moment of heroism—the cleverness and dexterity that enables to her turn the tables on Gumb by taking hostage his beloved poodle—creating another accidental or dumb-luck scenario that weakens our inclination to admire this already difficult character. Finally Catherine is a composite of the worst of both worlds—strength that comes across as abrasive (and, when dealing with a maniacal killer, quite foolish) and weakness manifested by the film itself through her "freakishly" large size and diagetic absence from her own moment of heroism. Young has called helpful attention also to her scenes' lesbophobic qualities, which open themselves to then nervously deflect the subversively romantic prospect of Clarice rescuing Catherine and Catherine showing gratitude (18).

Yet Catherine as an index of the film's antilesbianism may be the exception rather than the rule: when reviewing the spectrum of unattractive male figures scattered everywhere in this story—through the film's own pathologizing of Gumb and the feminist critique of even good villains such as Lecter, "good guys" such as Crawford, and the well-meaning but shortsighted men who made this film—a sort of default (i.e., naturalized) lesbian sensibility emerges. The deputies at the funeral parlor, her fellow FBI trainees, the smirking doctors and wardens preventing her from doing her job are all depicted as consummate pricks so that Clarice's wholesale rejection of every sexual advance is fully supported by the film (Young 11). Even Scott Glenn's Crawford is overly pomaded and tightly laced into his three-piece suit, and Hopkins is frumpy and washed out in his prison pajamas. By contrast, Clarice's interactions with Ardelia, the only other woman FBI trainee, and with the best friend of the first murder victim bring a spark of warmth, however flickering, to her face (Klawans, Tharp 109, Young 26). Foster, Kasi Lemmons (the actress playing Ardelia) and Lauren Roselli (the actress playing the friend of the first victim) are all beautiful women; the eye is drawn to them and their physical proximity to each other, and women's erotic appeal as traditionally emphasized in Hollywood film finds worthy recipients among none of the male figures included in the story, only various of its minor women characters. While the feminist and gay male approaches to this film are fraught with intriguing interpretive quandaries, the lesbian reading is attractive for its straightforwardness; it completes the equation set up by the film's extreme darkness, by the horror compelled by its utter strangeness and the truth it whispers regarding the depths of the ordinary human heart: in a world (again, our own?) where all men are this bad, all women turn naturally to each other for emotional comfort and physical love.

CONCLUSION

In this chapter, I observed divergent approaches among feminist, lesbian, and gay respondents to film. The number and variety of sticking points considered—psychoanalysis v. cultural studies (and related themes of text v. audience and theory v. history), identification v. difference, identification v. desire, the absence or presence of "the desiring woman" in film, the homophobia or queer subversiveness of "the lesbian metaphor," and the numerous, conflicting modes of identification with (or desire for) women on screen—are meant to indicate the rich variety of argument and counterargument energizing the field at this point, and the sheer hopelessness (not to mention the detrimental result) of unifying the discussion in any way. I hope my readings of the feminism, queerness, misogyny, and homophobia circulating through the frames of two important and popular films (as well as critical response to these) have demonstrated the inverse nature of these mutually exclusive approaches in a manner coincident with my fiction treatments in chapter 4 and in accordance with my initial definition of this dynamic in chapter 3. As the medium more and more warmly embraced by a culture evermore more subject to the reign of the visual, perhaps film much more than fiction leads us to the widest understanding of counterpointed relations among gay, lesbian, and feminist sensibilities in the world beyond the bounds of academic discourse. Again, there is little if any regret in my realization of the three groups' always triangulated, triangulating connections to each other; I contend that productive communication amongst them requires deep understanding and broad acceptance of each other's unique modes of analysis and interpretation.

CHAPTER 6

CONCLUSION: DIVIDING LINES, TIES THAT BIND

There is little solidarity among the sexually oppressed. Lesbians dissociate themselves from the "public sex" of gay men. Gay leaders dissociate themselves from pedophiles. Paedophiles can see little relevance in feminism. And the ranks of feminism are split asunder by divisions on topics such as pornography, sadomasochism, and sex itself.

Jeffrey Weeks, *Sexuality and Its Discontents* (1985)

By what criteria can we say that a text is feminist, or feminine? How is a feminist text to be distinguished from the patriarchal or phallocentric mainstream . . . ?

Elizabeth Grosz, *Space, Time, and Perversion* (1995)

[I]t is becoming impossible to tell the difference between prejudice and its representations, between, then, homophobia and representations of homophobia.

Judith Halberstam, "Skinflick" (1991)

Noting the early date of Jeffrey Weeks's rather dismal report, presented in the first epigraph, on the many issues polarizing lesbians, gay men, and feminists, one might wonder whether "the ranks" of sex, gender, and sexuality practitioners have yet begun to close, whether they have realigned or redivided themselves over different issues, whether "solidarity" and "splitting asunder" have themselves been revalued in discursive and political contexts. Significantly, Weeks's focus is not on texts, where much of my own attention has turned, and not even on academics, but on "ordinary" men and women whose sexual and political interests position them against the cultural mainstream and, Weeks cannot help but lament, against each other.

I set off my reference to ordinarity in the preceding comment not simply because the term unflagged would tend to distinguish unaffiliated sexual minority members from their "weird" counterparts in academe (perhaps the subject of some other writing) but also in order to emphasize the ways in which battles for gay and women's rights have been in part fought for the right to claim normality, centrality, even, if wished, mundanity for identities consistently marked as extreme, pathological, or contagious by the phobic majority. Also, of course, ordinarity is called into question because of Weeks's striking inclusion of "the paedophile" within his population of the sexually oppressed. For many, even in sex-positive academic and political circles, including the pedophile within the category of the oppressed emphasizes this figure's victim status in ways that problematically obscure his role as victimizer of others. For many, he is definable as neither ordinary nor oppressed, yet he presents an image of illicit, dangerous sexuality that is forever being thrust upon ordinary lesbians and gay men by those intently searching for excuses to hate and fear them. Significantly, Weeks has dropped this spoiler into the very center of his ranks, perhaps indicating his own solidarity with the NAMBLA (North American Man/Boy Love Association) cohort or perhaps merely indicating the dimensions of controversy and courage that constitute the field of sexual rights—as he saw them back in 1985 and as they continue to define the terrain today.

Pertinent to the issues that have preoccupied this project is the ambiguity attached to the term itself. Like many of the loaded words and phrases I have interrogated in this book, pedophilia indicates a range of sexual practices and markedly different forms of sexual interest in "boys," which are universally offensive only to those who refuse to consider the enormous physical, emotional, and psychological differences between a boy of five and a "boy" of fifteen. Significant differences also constitute the interest itself—between the damaged psychosexual makeup of those who seek out the physically prepubescent for sexual gratification and the much more routine preferences of those especially turned on by extremely young men. The tendency on the part of both the phobic mainstream and even many within left-wing academe to ignore these important differences and classify a wide range of harmless private sexual practice as socially unacceptable or even criminal is the focus of much important writing in sexuality criticism. My own intent throughout this book has been to explore the divergent, conflicting worlds of meaning contained in various semantic shades, word choices, gendered identities, sexual displays, and reading and viewing practices.

The two comments from Grosz and Halberstam, appearing five and ten years after Weeks's, step away from both the controversy of outlaw sexual figures and the controversies dividing sexual practitioners and attend instead to the dilemmas and aporias constituting the phenomenon of representation itself. Grosz ponders the uncanny resemblance between feminist and patriarchal texts (or perhaps feminist and patriarchal shadings within the same text), while Halberstam wrestles with the near impossibility of distinguishing a film about homophobia (i.e., *The Silence of the Lambs*) from homophobic filmmaking itself. Both theorists implicitly suggest that long-favored weapons in the feminist and queer theorist's arsenal—resistance and appropriation—cut both ways after all: what is thought to have been subversively wrested from the antifeminist, homophobic canon may be finally impossible to maintain in its state of resistance. For Grosz, the adversary is not even simply a male-oriented countertext or male-oriented counterinterpretation, but "the mainstream" (culture, literature, language as "universally" defined) itself. Halberstam indicates that lesbian and gay film theorists confront modern films that are perhaps so thoroughly antagonistic to their efforts to favorably interpret them that the critical field has become a minefield.

While we may hear in each of these three epigraphs the plaintive tones of those who write to dispel the trouble they describe, it is perhaps especially Weeks's subject matter that invites the call to change—to work past infighting, listen respectfully to opposing positions, seek out common ground, and band together to achieve social change. Grosz and Halberstam likewise voice complaints, writing in direct opposition to phallocentrism and homophobia, respectively, yet their inquiries into the very nature of postmodern representation indicate that the problems they light upon are as fascinating as they are frustrating and much more complexly embedded in the contemporary cultural experience. My own project has worked a similar transition, first critiquing points of contention dividing critics, then merely describing and analyzing the mutlivalent, cross-canceling structural features of culture, literature, film, and the critical act itself.

Grosz and Halberstam consider the inaugurating opposition in feminist and queer studies—between a phobic, repressive mainstream and the sexed, gendered, and sexual dissidents who have throughout history challenged its dictates in their lives and work. As I noted at the start of this project, I am less interested to rehearse yet again the injustices and counterstrategies that currently characterize this core opposition than to, like Weeks, consider the issues of discord and divergence within the fields of lesbian, gay, and feminist studies. As phallocentrism and homophobia remain persistent problems even within this progressive intellectual context, I have sought to delineate the varieties at work therein, as these differ importantly from the ordinary (i.e., blatant, extreme) forms characterizing the mindset and actions of the average right-wing American. Likewise have I set down the phobic adversary altogether for long stretches of this discussion, and instead attempted to mount less slanted and predetermined, more dynamic and open-ended contests (although I picture some of these as symbiotic and stylistically impressive as the choreography of Rogers and Astaire) between talented critic and enigmatic text, between persuasive, transformative analyses of a text-in-question that work their interpretive magic *only* by thoroughly undermining each other.

We might say that this entire project has been a consideration of where to draw the line—of deciding who is included within a group and its subgroups; what counts as normal and pathological gendered and sexual identity; what distinguishes inclusive from phobic literary, cinematic, or interpretive practice; when (if ever) a mark of representation is so damaging to those it targets that it cannot be rescued by interpretive appropriations, no matter how thinly or skillfully stretched. Yet line drawing is recognized by some as theoretically retrograde and analytically unproductive. Representative is George E. Haggerty and Bonnie Zimmerman's comment:

> Various readers of this book in manuscript have insisted that we outline the terms of contradiction among the essays here and that we articulate what we see as the "fault lines" in lesbian and gay studies. Neither of us feels that these fault lines are of major interest to us or to a majority of the readers of this book. Aside from broadly divergent areas of interest, this book does not represent a field in conflict. (4–5)

These writers identify a postidentity, postcategory milieu in which recognizable points of conflict, lines that divide, and ties that bind are all called into question. While I am as little inclined as are Haggerty and Zimmerman to read such points, lines, and bonds as permanently placed or singular in significance, I am equally disinclined to part with them altogether: a critical field unshaped, unbounded, and undelineated, however provisional and dynamic these landmarks may be, is as meaningless as a page lacking its written lines and its argumentative points.

This study has sought throughout to define and analyze those lines and ties necessarily maintained as well as those in need of expansion, rearrangement, or dismantling. Lines of identification and division enable a school of thought to define and develop itself, while allowing those outside the field to differentiate and appreciate its specific contributions. Forming the intersections where these various schools come together, regardless of how contentious or cacophonous the results, these dividing lines are themselves the ties that bind these groups into relationships that are certain to continue in highly dynamic mode. They enable members of the lesbian, gay, and feminist trialogue to engage in debate, face annihilation in the presence of inversely related positions advanced by other camps, and emerge from the fray not only intact but also more clearly defined, and readier therefore to engage in ever-intensifying rounds of conflict, counterpoint, and discovery.

NOTES

INTRODUCTION: OPEN BOOKS, PRIVATE LIVES

1. Considering the "convergence of sexuality and textuality" in the writing of Emily Dickinson, Thomas Foster raises a similar issue. Noting that in one letter to her beloved sister-in-law Dickinson had signed a post-script, "open me carefully," Foster argues that the phrase itself "raises the possibility of interpretive violence as sexual violence, violence against women. In other words, Dickinson ends her letter in the hope that Susan Gilbert will not take the potentially hostile position of a male reader in relation to her text" (241).

2. I define this term simply, as "a way to think" (often paired with its simple opposite, practice, "a way to act")—not as the intellectually sophisticated form of contemporary literary criticism derived from continental philoso-phies. Therefore, for myself, all criticism issuing from these fields that offers its readership repeatable methods and approaches or new ways to understand the text(s) in question belongs to the category of theory.

3. I refer here to a trailing off in titles related to "straight" feminism—discussions of women versus men, uninflected by more contemporary concerns with history, environment, ethnicity, age, etc. Pop feminism of the Katie Roiphe/Naomi Wolfe/Susan Faludi variety has in fact taken up this basic opposition, while Susan Gubar's essay "What Ails Feminist Criticism?" laments the loss of "woman" as a solid and stable category in contemporary discourse.

4. I appreciate Schlichter's critical response to earlier writing of my own and find other moments of this essay valuable as well. As I do elsewhere in this study, Schlichter critiques Daphne Patai's *Heterophobia* and moves toward the point I make here when she observes that the binary construction of some queer criticism is "supplemented by limited, often stereotypical representations of straights. As a synecdoche for straight life, the figure of the white suburban couple committed to reproduction . . . and fully in sync with power structures dominates even queer writings that intend to subvert the hetero/homo division" (549).

5. Consider for instance the equation created in the titles of works by Duberman and Levay. In addition, Goldberg's *Queering the Renaissance* is described on its back cover as "a major reassessment of the field of Renaissance studies . . . within the perspective of gay and lesbian studies."

6. Chris Cagle's work on bisexuality interestingly critiques the monosexu-alist's reliance on identifiable categories such as these. He describes bisexuality as in part eliciting "the crisis of sexual taxonomy" (242) and calls attention to the problems with categories in and of themselves. Well aware of the problems attached to an overzealous faith in solidly demarcating lines, I must still maintain these categories as provisional critical constructs, so as to interrogate the relationships among them.

CHAPTER 1   THE TRIALS OF TRIALOGUING IN LESBIAN, GAY, AND FEMINIST STUDIES

1. Jeffreys (*Anticlimax*) is bothered by almost all gay sexual habits, including cross-dressing ("gender fetishism"), cruising and casual sex ("phallo-centrism"), and interest in pornography (a la MacKinnon/ Dworkin, an "eroticization of violence"); Frye's views are close to hers.
2. See also Boone 12. While he in fact singles out Owens's essay as one of three "thoughtful commentaries" in the Smith/Jardine collection, he gives reasons for this praise only for the other two commentators, leaving his defense of Owens somewhat weak.
3. Owens accuses Irigaray of making "patently homophobic" formulations in her work and accuses Nochlin and Showalter of "Tootsie Rolling," a term denoting both the presumption that all gay men are effeminate (or transvestites) and the "outing" of male critics whether they be gay or not.
4. Queer theory's at-best reluctant embrace of the phenomenon of effem-inacy is evident in multiple writings. In his study of popular film, Brett Farmer determines effeminacy to be largely a matter of cultural percep-tion: "Because male homosexuality is widely represented in our culture as possessing strong, even constitutive ties with femininity, an active assumption of a male homosexual identity will potentially occasion marked identification with the feminine at several levels" (127). Elsewhere, the curiously ambivalent position of sociologist Martin P. Levine, at times coauthoring with and being posthumously edited by Michael S. Kimmel, deserves special mention here. Unwilling to posit various natural types of gay subjectivity, Levine argues that "neither 'butch' nor 'swish' styles are innate in gay physiology" (56) but that both are constructed from influences placed on them by straight society. Gay men have passed through "swish" and "butch" stages progressively, says Levine; in preliberation days, the swish identity was imposed on them by stereotypes they had learned from youth, while, curiously, gay liberation has led them to a more heterosexual/ist form of manhood—the macho posturings of clone culture that were also learned in childhood. While Levine later allows a quote from a subject— "Darling, beneath all this butch drag, we are all still girls" (63)—to close a discussion, he and Kimmel ultimately argue that only AIDS caused the death of clone

culture and the reemergence of the softer gay man. At different places in *Gay Macho*, Levine seems to argue for the social constructedness and underlying reality of both "swish" and "butch" modes.

5. See also Walters, whose emphasis is not on urban dwelling but who considers "well-meaning heterosexuals" (xvii) and their indeed problematic recourse to an ethic of "acceptance" (16) of gay and lesbian lifestyles.

CHAPTER 2 WHAT'S IN A NAME: SEMANTIC SLIPS AND SLIDES IN LESBIAN, GAY, AND FEMINIST STUDIES' KEY TERMS

1. In fact, Butler herself has questioned the sufficiency of these terms, specifically in the early pages of *Gender Trouble*, while here refraining from qualifying their deployment in a way that implicitly ratifies the gender = man/woman equation.

2. See also Jackson and Scott 16–17 and Stanley 32.

3. The term refers here both to system malfunction and system apprehension-through-dissection; as Butler sees it, the political genealogy of gender is that which would "deconstruct the substantive appearance into its constitutive acts and locate and account for those acts within the compulsory frame" (*Gender Trouble* 33).

4. I speak here solely in terms of societal "looksism," which rewards beautiful people (even gay and lesbian ones) with a literal and metaphorical opening of doors that are often closed to (or closed upon) those deemed less attractive, regardless of their belonging to other privileged social categories (straightness, whiteness, etc.).

5. See for instance essays by Ross, Robert K. Martin, Seltzer, and Vorlicky.

6. Butler ("Against Proper Objects" n.8), Biddy Martin ("Extraordinary Homosexuals" and "Sexualities without Genders"), and Harris and Crocker make similar moves.

7. See also de Lauretis "Sexual Indifference" 147, Livia and Hall 6, and Paul Smith 6. An interesting exception is Boone and Cadden's reference to "the category of gender ('gay') as a separate analytic tool" (5).

8. Butler is clearly aware of the challenge facing her as she opens her inquiry in *Bodies That Matter*. In the Preface to this work she concedes that bodies are in fact material and that her assertion regarding the utter constructedness of sex differences is "hardly a self-evident claim" (x). Shortly thereafter, however: "The category of 'sex' is, from the start, normative; it is what Foucault has called a 'regulatory ideal.' In this sense, then 'sex' not only functions as a norm, but is part of a regulatory practice that *produces the bodies* it governs" (1, emphasis added).

9. See also Delphy 54–55 and Fausto-Sterling 26. Jackson and Scott argue that "Just as class struggle seeks to do away with classes, so feminist struggle should aim to do away with sex differences" (17).

10. Susan Gubar has also challenged Butler's obfuscating approach (125–29). See also Charnes.

11. Halberstam's desire to clear a space for the specific focus of female masculinity—to the exclusion of male masculinity and even to the seeming companion subject of male effeminacy—causes her to make another interesting slide—from issues of gender to issues of sexuality—at important points in her argument. A centerpiece of this early discussion is her critique of sex-segregated bathrooms, where, she claims, the problem is much worse for masculine women than it is for effeminate men. The argument gives way, however, when, on the authority of a single essay by Lee Edelman, who explores a specific, historical context, Halberstam concludes that "whereas men's rest rooms tend to operate as a highly charged sexual space in which sexual interactions are both encouraged and punished, women's rest rooms tend to operate as an arena for the enforcement of gender conformity" (24). Later, " in the women's room . . . *all* gender-ambiguous females . . . are scrutinized, whereas in the men's room biological men are rarely deemed out place" (26). Yet I question so cut-and-dried a distinction, which disregards not only issues of gender in the men's room—the difficulties still faced, for instance, by effeminate boys bullied in junior high and high school restrooms—but also the issue of sexuality in the women's room: while Halberstam glances at the necessity of sex-segregated bathrooms "to protect women from male predations" (24), she offers no solution to this problem in the model of common-use facilities she calls for. For another slide from gender to "sex" (sexual activity), see her discussion 9–12.

12. In *Tendencies*, for instance, Sedgwick ruminates frequently on the issue of AIDS and on her own dealings with breast cancer, two themes that call frequently into question the fragility of the material body. See especially "White Glasses."

Chapter 3   The Critical Impasse: Inverse Relations among Lesbian, Gay, and Feminist Approaches

1. In her reading of the film *The Crying Game*, Maria Pramaggiore describes a similar dynamic among Fergus, Jody (his male adversary), and Jude (his female ally), who becomes an "increasingly cruel and crude female outsider" (284) as the bond between the men intensifies, and is eventually killed by yet another male rival (the transvestite Dil). Although the interpretive issues surrounding the textual death of Jude are not Pramaggiore's primary focus, the "either-or" relationship

between Fergus's two choices—despite Pramaggiore's emphasis on the "both-and" qualities of this bisexual scenario—is evident here.

2. I mean to lean hard on the particularity of the aspect of the gay-feminist relationship under consideration here, implying neither that most gay men dislike straight women nor that effeminate gay men are a cultural myth or "race traitors" in any way.

3. While Michael P. Brown cites several women theorists in his text and would have to acknowledge that lesbians are as subjected to metaphoric and material cultural closets (his main theme) as are gay men, he notes that lesbians will be included only in the discussion of national census statistics, while personal, urban, and international scales will be discussed in terms of their meaning for gay men alone (23). Higgs provides a lengthy disclaimer in his introductory section "Why male-centered?" (2–4), while Leap and his several male contributors make (and indeed owe) no apologies for their male-only focus: so evidently plain in the minds of these several writers is the connection between public sex and gay *male* activity that no language anywhere in the volume was evidently necessary to justify the exclusion of women.

4. Other theorists grant visitor status to the "other group" in their respective discursive neighborhoods in similar fashion. In the midst of his otherwise all-male tour of gay Christchurch, for instance, Michael P. Brown refers to "the city's most popular gay and lesbian bar" (80). In fact this bar's owner is male, and references to the clientele here and in the sauna he visits next are plainly indicated to be male. In the next paragraph, Brown points out that "Lesbian space is extremely hidden in Christchurch, much more so than gay space. Traditionally, activists informed me, it has been produced only in the private space of women's homes" (81). See also Binnie 197.

5. See also Hemmings 147 and Polchin 387. In her discussion, Hemmings is one of the few women to elide the specificity of the lesbian lifestyle in a phrase like the following: "the importance of public spaces—streets, parks, backrooms, and baths—in the formation of a contemporary gay and lesbian identity" (147). As "streets, parks, backrooms, and baths" must be acknowledged as overwhelmingly the domains of gay men, the addition of the "and lesbian" seems perfunctory and disconnected here.

6. In a geography similar to Park Slope, Vancouver's eastern neighborhoods boast a visible lesbian presence in local businesses— "[f]rom vegetable markets to Italian coffeeshops . . . to economic alternatives such as co-ops"— all of which welcome lesbian customer as an "equal and valued citizen" (40). Meanwhile, these customers come and go from the commercial settings, while what remain to define the atmosphere of the neighborhood are businesses lacking any overtly lesbian appearance or theme. Munt would credit "moment[s] of presence" for such lesbian *flâneurs* as these with "spatial reconstruction," arguing that "Lesbian identity is constructed in the temporal and linguistic mobilisation of space, and as we

move *through* space we imprint utopian and dystopian moments on urban life" (124–25). Yet Munt herself points to the tenuousness of such mobilizations with her comment, "we need our fictions of consciousness or we will disappear" (125).

7. See also Bouthillette 218–27, Elsie Jay, Quilley 286, Retter 207, and Walters 243–44. To the degree that gay men indeed tend to maintain stronger purchasing power than lesbians, "commercialization" and "revitalization" of formerly depressed communities, as referred to by Quilley here and by Polchin (387) are often buzz terms for a specifically gay presence in urban neighborhoods.

8. I extend this emphasis on *representation* to every reference to gay and lesbian urban dwellers in play here. I recognize that dichotomies between affluence and poverty, public and private sexual activities, and sexual versus cultural forms of expression speak not at all to the great, ultimately immeasurable diversities characterizing gay and lesbian populations throughout western society, yet they prevail overwhelming in the contemporary critical discourse about such groups.

9. See for instance Lo and Healy 35, Rothenberg 175, and Davis 291–92.

10. For delineation of the tradition of conflict dividing gays and lesbians over the issue of public space, see Califia 187, Quilley 282, Sommella 433, and Moyer et al. 439. Multiple theorists have noted the ultimately limited amount of public grounds on which these dilemmas can be resolved, raising the stakes regarding the outcome. See Ingram " 'Open' Space" 122 and Califia 183.

11. It is argued that certain gay men—especially lower class or homeless ones—engage in outdoor sex only because they lack adequate private housing, yet it is acknowledged just as often that much outdoor sexual activity occurs because such exposure intensifies the thrill of the encounter. Chauncey 249–50 is most persuasive on the issue of forced public exposure from a historical perspective; more recently, Clatts has investigated homeless youth hustling for cash or drugs in Greenwich Village, while Michael Brown reads a similar population in Yaletown, Vancouver. See also Ingram " 'Open' Space" 101 and 120, Tattleman "The Meaning" 394 and "Presenting" 234.

12. See Bronski *Culture Clash* 205–06; elsewhere the editors of *Queers in Space* blame the misogynist tradition of threatening women who dare to occupy public space (especially after dark) *and* the heterosexism of the feminist movement for lesbians' "sanitized sexuality" (12), while Ingram ("Marginality") applauds the radical photographic compositions of Del LaGrace Volcano, which position female models in outdoor, nighttime, sexual arrangements. Warner presents a striking reversal of this argument: "Gay journalists are repudiating the legacy of safer sex, depicting lesbians as sexless homebodies whom gay men should imitate" (163).

13. Because of this term's multiple connotations, critics differ significantly on whether "visibility" is or is not a proper goal. See Bell 82, Clarke 12, Ingram " 'Open' Space" 122, Nestle 63, Polchin 385–86, Tattleman "Presenting" 254 and "The Meaning" 403, Walters, and Wolfe 303. See Berlant (*Queen of America*) for an insightful variation on this theme.

14. Peter Coviello points to a similar catch-22 created for gay men by the AIDS crisis: "queer communities are a great deal more visible now than they were fifteen years ago, and . . . such visibility comes, at least in part, as a rather direct result of AIDS, which has in that brief time turned upon gay men in particular the full glare of any number of differently calibrated public gazes" (42).

15. Rechy's comment is part of a larger discussion as to whether sex in parks is an inherently political activity or whether it is gay men's comparatively desexualized occupations of park space that constitute real activism. Ingram insists that "furtive sexual contact in public places is often limited," then later in that paragraph describes the same park as "a highly eroticized and commodified landscape of constant sex" (" 'Open' Space" 104). Ingram and his coeditors warn against "emphasiz[ing] eroticism at the expense of domesticity" (376), as this would limit the full development of queer urban spaces, while John Grube contends both that " 'open space' . . . was not only a place for sex but also for touching base with other members of the community" (132) *and* that anonymous, silent orgy episodes were political statements in their own right (132–33).

CHAPTER 4   WHAT WE READ: LESBIAN, GAY, AND FEMINIST APPROACHES TO FICTION

1. In Judith Fetterly's still-influential formulation: "To read the canon of what is currently considered classic American literature is perforce to identify as male" (xii).

2. Discussing a related medium, Richard Dyer makes a similar observation: "I'll happily teach *The Searchers* (John Ford) as a John Wayne movie about race, but as soon as it's *Dance, Girl, Dance* (Dorothy Arzner) or *Car Wash* (Michael Schultz) I'm wanting students to worry about whether you can tell they were directed by a woman or a black person, respectively, and how, and whether it matters. . . . [I]t does make a difference who makes a film, who the authors are" (185).

3. As Rachel Blau DuPlessis comments in another context, "If I had not become a feminist, I would not have been able to write much or think anything especially interesting in any original way" (97–98). Although DuPlessis is likely reversing the point I make here—that feminism did not give her something to complain about, as it were, but gave her the means by which to voice her complaints—we must

acknowledge that this relationship, between the politics and theory of feminism and the woman's "voice," is a two-way street.

4. My arguments here are close to those of Gubar, Ch. 7, esp. 142–45.

5. This is Lillian Faderman's position, when she determines Hall to be under the unfortunate influence of "the English and German sexologists" ("What is Lesbian Literature?" 50) who did so much to pathologize lesbianism at the turn of the 20th century. In that same reading, Faderman even describes the negative influence of "the nineteenth-century French male aesthete-decadent writers, whose purpose was to 'astound the bourgeoisie' . . . through the most shocking image they could devise, namely two women being sexual together" (50). See also Faderman "Who Hid Lesbian History?" Clearly, Zola's *Nana* belongs to this targeted canon, while Castle later credits the novel for freeing up the lesbian subtext in James's *The Bostonians.*

6. Castle herself delves into this dilemma in a later chapter: "by raising her arms to 'ward off' the oncoming phantoms, Radclyffe Hall's self-loathing heroine somewhat oafishly pantomimes the repressive theatrics we've seen before in Defoe, Diderot, McKenzie, and Strachey. But it's a useless move now. . . . [W]hat ensues, despite the maundering mock religiosity of Hall's presentation, is a loopy, delirious, untrammeled consummation: a kind of sex scene with ghosts" (*Apparitional* 51).

7. Castle questions the absent lesbian in Sedgwick's erotic triangle, arguing that only a lesbianizing of the woman in question will challenge patriarchal rule. Yet her model is only partially analogous to the model she critiques; Castle accuses Sedgwick of a "nervous avoidance of the topic of lesbianism" (*Apparitional* 13), but her own triangle neglects the figure of the gay man. Using *Summer Will Show* as a test case, Castle's triangulated figures are a lesbian couple and one lover's patristic husband; the women are not figured as homosocial rivals for the man's affections—in fact they could not care less about him—but the economic aspects of Castle's model are too close to Sedgwick's own to represent a true alternative: the lesbian romance does not empower the women to control their financial situation (i.e., engage in subversive trafficking in men) but instead seriously threatens this.

8. Markedly diverging from Castle's interpretation, Robert L. Caserio reads Warner's work within a long tradition of stories of "celibate" sister-figures, who turn their traditionally defined chastity toward revolutionary praxis. Caserio's Marxist reading argues that depicting thes women engaged in lesbian relations would capitulate to the status quo as fully as would depicting them as heterosexually active (259). Warner's novel is described as an intensely political and theoretical novel that works toward "Sophia's politically correct separation from Minna's allegedly amateurish revolutionism" (268). The argument is suffused with a heterocentrist rhetoric, as Caserio constantly pictures the women as "delivering" and "giving birth to" Marxist politics and late in the article refers to "Warner's intercourse with Marx" (274).

Strikingly, Caserio makes use of Castle's own key trope, the apparitional, describing both *The Communist Manifesto* and Minna's dead
body as "haunting specters" throughout the story. Yet Caserio's argument is no holdover from an old-school misogynist critical period but
part of a recent collection titled *Engendering Men.* Meanwhile, his
brand of "feminism" moves, in a fashion I have noted many times in
this study, detrimentally away from themes of lesbianism, sexuality,
and typical definitions of subversion.

9. This emphasis in Stevens's argument juxtaposes somewhat uncomfortably with his Foucault-inspired observation that many of James's
characters "need to confess" their sexual irregularities. Just ahead in
this chapter, I will argue that gay male theory is as indebted to the
ideas of Foucault as it is involved with these questions of silence; in
Stevens's study, this double involvement leads to the paradoxical situation of "sexuality, like hysteria, [being] characterized not only by the
absence of speech but also by linguistic excess" (7; see also 147–48).

10. In a related argument, in search of his own "ambiguous conclusions"
in Austen, Robin Grove in fact contrasts more open endings (such as
that found in *Mansfield Park*) with the situational certainties promised at the end of *Northanger Abbey*, whose final phrase, "that we are
all hastening together toward perfect felicity" (qtd. in Grove 183)
reproduces the tone and even word choice evincing "sarcasm" for
Litvak: "unblemished happiness really is waiting for Henry and
Catherine, for whom, inside the world of the novel, the present claim
is no mockery but rather a statement of happy truth" (Grove 183).

11. Kipling's story "The Janeites" depicts a cadre of artillerymen whose
secret society formed from their shared affection for Austen's work
enables them to recognize an intimate alliance and cope with the horrors of World War I. Interrupting a discussion as to whether or not
Austen died childless, the verbose (and intoxicated) Macklin
announces, " 'She *did* leave lawful issue in the shape o' one son; an' 'is
name was 'Enery James' " (qtd. in Claudia Johnson "Divine" 31).

12. "Threaten" is as interestingly ambiguous a term as is "desperation."
When Lisa L. Moore argues, for instance, that in *Emma* "female
freindship is represented in the novel as the significant threat to
Emma's virtue and marriageability" (121), she may be arguing (and
in fact makes both cases persuasively) either that the novel therefore
uses this threat to challenge these ideological strongholds *or* that it
sets up female friendship as a stumbling block to the marriage plot
expressly to devalue such friendships.

13. See also Gerster 116–17, 129 and Chandler. Alice Chandler's argument is of a vintage (originally published in 1975) that in part explains
its myopia with respect to an adequate definition of "sexuality." Her
several assumptions about "the antitheses and hostilities of the sexes"
(38) in fact tend to reinstate the gender-based status quo rather than
disrupt it.

14. Moore, in her survey of critical responses to *Emma*, in fact classifies Claudia Johnson's as a feminist reading, whose focus on "heterosexual manhood" (115) depicts the novel's "gender-based censure of masculine characters" (115), to the exclusion of questions of "feminine sexuality" (115).

15. This discussion parallels some having taken place recently with respect to *The Portrait of a Lady*. Sheldon M. Novick informs us in neutral tones that "Osmond, indeed is a portrait of [James's] long-time friend, Paul Zhukovsky" (9), while he is detested by most feminist readers (e.g., Tessa Hadley, who calls him a "monster" [17]).

16. Hugh Stevens also links Olive's politics and "virginity," though this latter term is as confusing as is Fetterly's substituting "sexuality" for "fertility" above. Stevens argues that Olive belongs to "a feverish cult of virginity, a virginity preserved for political ends" (97). If for Stevens Olive is a virgin simply because she has never been sexually penetrated, he only removes her from the sphere of heterosexual activity. If, however, virginity in this argument precludes any sexual contact or organism, then for Stevens, lesbianism would detract from her political efficacy as well. Finally, Stevens does aver that Olive makes an "extremely convincing [lesbian] indeed" (99), though not because of her politically powerful (because virginal/nonpenetrative) modes of sexual expression but because of her "tragic" solitude. (See also Caserio, n.8).

CHAPTER 5   WHY WE WATCH: LESBIAN, GAY, AND FEMINIST APPROACHES TO FILM

1. Farmer provides a helpful survey of straight and lesbian feminists' charges of misogyny leveled against gay drag culture (128, 137). Also Doty has responded to similar arguments by Julie Burchill ("There's Something Queer Here" 76).

2. See for instance Bronski *Culture Clash* 99 and "Judy Garland" 205, Doty *Flaming Classics* 93, Farmer 133, Sheldon 17, and White 33.

3. Elizabeth Ellsworth's frequently cited study determined that lesbian viewers seeking "illicit pleasures" from what was ultimately a mainstream Hollywood film "ignored large sections of narrative material focusing on heterosexual romance" (54) and were able to "interpret the film's ending as a validation of lesbianism" (55). Additionally, these viewers "redefined 'main character' and 'supporting character' in order to elevate Patrice Donnelly as the film's star" and "named and eroticized illicit moments of the film's 'inadvertent lesbian verisimilitude' "(54). Interestingly, Ellsworth's article, subtitled "Feminist Spectators and *Personal Best*," refers directly to lesbian viewing practice only in the last pages, in a section persistently titled "Feminist Reviews of *Personal Best*"; throughout, "feminist" functions alternately as a term for feminists regardless of orientation and as

another name for "lesbian," when in fact her lesbian-centered research constitutes her significant contribution and receives, not surprisingly, the bulk of the attention from more recent sexuality film theorists.

4. In fact, Mayne's text, *Framed: Lesbians, Feminists, and Media Culture*, plays this game constantly, conducting cultural studies-style readings of film, television, and cultural events. Mayne's focus is on proto- or pseudo-lesbian situations in these texts or, as with her reading of *L.A. Law*, actual lesbian characters and their homophobic handling by mainstream media.

5. Clare Whatling's *Screen Dreams: Fantasizing Lesbians in Film* works along similar lines. Chapters 1 and 2 of her text focus almost exclusively on reviews of relevant theory and very little on film itself, while her third chapter's emphasis on identification and desire provides the bridge to her specifically cultural studies-style analyses of nostalgia, gossip, and Jodie Foster in the last three chapters.

6. Despite questioning Mulvey's pessimistic dichotomizing of sex roles in cinema, both Gaylyn Studlar and Steve Neale ultimately concede the dominance of the system Mulvey describes: Studlar considers it "naive to assume that the identification of female scopophilia or fetishism would open a gap for the female spectator within dominant cinema" (216), while Neale "concur[s] with [Mulvey's] basic premise that the spectatorial look in mainstream cinema is implicitly male" (263).

7. Rodowick's defense of Mulvey is just as biology-based, however: "Rather, her argument is searching to define the specificity of the female body as the locus of a repressed yet articulate being. Recognition of this body and the representations proper to it, would thus enable both the recognition of a subjectivity so far elided under patriarchy and the overthrow of the discursive and social practices that censor this subjectivity" (194).

8. See for instance Doane "Film" 425, Weiss 141, and Traub "Ambiguities" 119. In addition to these theoretical considerations of women's lesser response to visual sexual stimuli, we might glance around at contemporary culture to compare the obvious discrepancies in market share between *Playgirl* and *Playboy* magazines and between the waning fad of Chippendales performances and the always-burgeoning market for female dancers for gentleman's clubs and even restaurant chains like Hooters. Women's encounter with male sexual display often triggers a laugh response; they may buy *Playgirl*, a sex toy, or the services of a male stripper to embarrass a friend on the eve of her wedding, while the atmosphere at male strip shows often includes hilarity, romantic adulation, and a competitive sense of pride (that we can do this as well as the boys) but rarely sexual intensity.

9. Sue-Ellen Case's critique of Doane in this instance rests on shaky ground. Taking Doane to task for her very emphasis on spectatorship, Case attempts to forge a link between spectatorship, passivity, and

heterosexuality. She negatively compares Doane's "passive" cinematic spectator to "the femme" who "actively performs her masquerade" ("Towards a Butch-Femme Aesthetic" 66), thus faulting Doane for turning her attention to film and the film-viewing experience, instead of the lived social realm where actual butches and femmes subvert patriarchy. The untenable nature of this argument is apparent, as it makes impossible the necessarily passive activity (after all, one must sit and watch) of even lesbian film theorists.

10. At the outset of the essay, Riviere informs readers that the situation in which "intellectual pursuits for women were associated almost exclusively with an overtly masculine type of woman . . . has now changed" (33), indicating that intellectual women are more and more the norm, that intellectual women are ordinary women. Following elaboration of her primary case history, she turns to several briefer examples from "everyday life" (39), but each example features accomplished professional women, and Riviere insists ultimately upon their extraordinarity—the rarity of the achievements, the pathology of their psyches. Interestingly, feminists have made use of Riviere's insights for decades, while the remarkable strain of antifeminism on display in her most famous essay is rarely if ever mentioned. Primarily, limitations of historical context lead Riviere to "diagnose" intellectual women as homosexuals (with no word here as to how Riviere's own intellectual success pathologizes her psychic makeup). For Riviere, the masquerade is less a clever survival strategy than a vigorously barred closet door; this striking "prefeminist" statement only postpones the moment at which a third alternative (between traditional housewifery and pathologized sapphism) presents itself for women. Yet again, the lesbian and feminist alternatives function here in inverse relation.

11. Mulvey argues that though "her visual presence tends to work against the development of a story line, to freeze the flow of action in moments of erotic contemplation," ultimately the woman's "alien presence . . . has to be integrated into cohesion within the narrative" (62). While her status as spectacle thus challenges the narrative's progress, this challenge in fact necessitates the very movement (beyond these barriers) that constitutes narrative structure—we might say that in classical film, the woman "happens to" the man—so that recuperation of the spectacle is inherent in its very form.

12. In an endnote Mayne states that "What I am calling 'homotextual' is what Eve Kosofsky Sedgwick would describe as 'homosocial' "(*Woman* 232 n.31); why she borrows this concept without retaining Sedgwick's terminology is not clarified, but what Mayne sets up as an equation cannot really stand as one: we would have to be talking about at least two texts—homotextual relations between two or more films—to parallel Sedgwick's delineation of homosocial relations "between men." If Mayne in fact refers to film characters, these are confused with the

film itself if she designates them as "texts," and although she makes a loose connection between Sedgwick's ideas and her own by noting their shared theme of "the sexual and its erasure," this definition is only briefly elaborated upon and never introduced into the chapter itself.

13. In chapter 2, I questioned Traub among others for deploying the term "gender" where "sex" is the more productive term. Here, gender comes to us in "binary categories" and thus resembles and supports the "binary teleology that upholds a structural heterosexuality" (*Desire* 117). As per my discussion in chapter 2, I posit a wide-ranging gender spectrum of masculinities and femininities, not an entrenched dichotomy (characteristic of two sexes). Elsewhere Traub refers to "the belief that homoerotic desire depends on gender similitude" (126) and may be suggesting the image of two femmes or two butches (the way two lesbians might do their actual gender) or simply two women, in which case her reference should have been to sex similitude.

14. See for instance Russo, Weiss 53–55, and Patricia White's readings of the film throughout *Uninvited*. White specifically responds to Doane ("*Caught* and *Rebecca*"), as I am doing here, and to Tania Modleski's reading that instills, similar to Rose's oedipalization of *The Birds*, mother-daughter relationships between the two otherwise lesbianized figures, Mrs. Danvers and Rebecca, and the second Mrs. DeWinter (64–67).

15. While she has another use for this term, Ruth Goldman has urged consideration of "class" within gay/lesbian textual analyses, to advance a more effectively queer agenda both within and outside the academy (179). As valuable as suggestion this, I remain interested in the de-eroticizing effects of the class reading in this case and the persisting mutual exclusivity of the class-based (i.e., feminist) and lesbian readings of this film.

16. In Janet Meyer's oft-quoted formulation, "The qualities [women on screen] projected, of being inscrutable to the men in the films and aloof, passionate, direct, could not be missed. They are all strong, tough and yet genuinely tender. In short, though rarely permitted to hint it, they are lesbians" (qtd. in Sheldon 18). See also Britton (86–87). His critique of Meyer relates to my discussion here, though I do not share his harsh judgment of camp (88).

17. I appreciate the discussion of Becker et al. on a related subject, 28–29. Here the frequently denounced "lesbian continuum" is deployed for subversive effect.

18. Heilbrun opposes the ensnaring "erotic plot" of fiction and lived experience to the "quest plot" in various forms (49), always open to men and regaled in auto/biographies about them—and here reproduced in the image of Colette Lafonte on the rescuing white charger. Heilbrun's text is not especially vocal on the issue of lesbian relationships, but at certain points she opposes women's isolating erotic

attachments in general to liberating interactions among women, as sisters and "close women friends" (47).

19. White, acknowledging the influence of de Lauretis early in *Uninvited*, also speaks against "the tendency in straight feminist theory to defuse lesbianism by using it as a metaphor for female bonding" (xxii). Again, however, the question remains as to the political and theoretical merits of isolating moments of "female bonding" throughout popular film (as White herself will go on to do at length) and deploying these as "metaphors" for lesbianism.

20. In Mulvey's "reluctant men" we in fact find a subtle critique of the homophobia she is charged with; consider the similar import of an observation from Steve Neale's more overtly gay-affirmative discussion of "male to-be-looked-at-ness": "The (unstated) thesis behind these comments seems to be that in a heterosexual and patriarchal society, the male body cannot be marked explicitly as the erotic object of another male look: that look must be motivated in some other way, its erotic component erased" (258).

21. In a related context, Elizabeth Young mounts an impressive reading of the film's feminist elements then avers that in fact its homophobia undoes its feminist intent. Yet can Young have it both ways? As persuasive as is her feminist reading—we might even credit her interpretive skills more than the film itself—it is difficult to accept her abrupt decampment from this position when she declares in her essay's second movement that "such a celebratory reading of the film, obviously schematic, is also premature" (17). Moving through her negative analysis (of the film's homophobia), Young reaches a summation: "This reading of *The Silence of the Lambs . . .* may at this point sound entirely condemnatory" (21), yet she simply doth protest too much: the reader has hardly forgotten the sympathetic-feminist tour de force with which the analysis began. After attempting to establish her argument's condemnatory stance, Young returns to favorably assessing the film's "productive confusion" (21), though the zigzag fashion of her argumentative line only indicates yet again the near-impossibility of creating a unified text analysis from both feminist and gay male perspectives. The article is somewhat long, owing to Young's basically writing two (or perhaps three) in the space of one, and her witty accusation, that the film "cannibalizes its own food for thought," is applicable to her own reading of it.

22. See also Young 20. Writing from the feminist perspective, Adrienne Donald delights in the film's final placement of "the murderous gay dandy" Lecter—he is about to feast on the reprehensible Dr. Chiltern—as this enables "a form of subversive energy turned against a figure of administered life" (359). Meanwhile, though Donald senses the homophobic element in her argument— "Delighting in a fiendish gay killer is ultimately not that much different from hating him" (359)—she shrugs off the problem by asking, "But what more could one ask

of a film? We turn to the passing distractions of art not for a substitute for the world but for a shock that will make us recognize our desire for another world" (359).

23. Donald describes this scene as "startling, since Foster's performance, like almost all of the film, is otherwise tastefully understated. Indeed, it is bizarrely comic" (353). Wardrop observes that "the final encounter with Bill still posits Clarice very much as a victim" (97).

Works Cited

All About Eve. Dir. Joseph L. Mankiewicz. Twentieth-Century Fox, 1950.

Barale, Michèle Aina. "When Jack Blinks: Si(gh)ting Gay Desire in Ann Bannon's *Beebo Brinker.*" 1992. *The Lesbian and Gay Studies Reader,* ed. Henry Abelove, Michèle Aina Barale, David M. Halperin. New York: Routledge, 1993. 604–15.

———. "When *Lambs* and *Aliens* Meet: Girl-Faggots and Boy-Dykes Go to the Movies." *Cross-Purposes: Lesbians, Feminists, and the Limits of Alliance,* ed. Dana Heller. Bloomington: Indiana University Press, 1997. 95–106.

Bartlett, Neil. *Who Was That Man?: A Present for Mr. Oscar Wilde.* London: Serpent's Tail, 1989.

Becker, Edith, Michelle Citron, Julia Lesage, and B. Ruby Rich. "Lesbians and Film." *Out in Culture: Gay, Lesbian, and Queer Essays on Popular Culture,* ed. Corey K. Creekmur and Alexander Doty. Durham, NC: Duke University Press, 1995. 25–43.

Bell, David. "One-Handed Geographies: An Archaeology of Public Sex." *Queers in Space: Communities, Public Places, Sites of Resistance,* ed. Gordon Brett Ingram, Anne Marie Bouthillette, and Yolanda Retter. Seattle: Bay Press, 1997. 81–87.

Bell, David, and Gill Valentine. "Introduction: Orientations." *Mapping Desire: Geographies of Sexualities.* ed. David Bell and Gill Valentine. London: Routledge, 1995. 1–27.

Berger, James. *After the End: Representations of Post-Apocalypse.* Minneapolis: University of Minnesota Press, 1999.

Bergstrom, Janet. "Enunciation and Sexual Difference." *Feminism and Film Theory,* ed. Constance Penley. New York: Routledge, 1988. 159–85.

———. "Rereading the Work of Claire Johnston." *Feminism and Film Theory,* ed. Constance Penley. New York: Routledge, 1988. 80–88.

Berlant, Lauren. *The Queen of America Goes to Washington City: Essays on Sex and Citizenship.* Durham, NC: Duke University Press, 1997.

Berlant, Lauren, and Michael Warner. "Sex in Public." *Critical Inquiry* 24.2 (1998): 547–66.

Bersani, Leo. "Is the Rectum a Grave?" *AIDS: Cultural Analysis, Cultural Activism,* ed. Douglas Crimp. Cambridge, MA: MIT Press, 1988. 197–222.

Binnie, John. "Trading Places: Consumption, Sexuality, and the Production of Queer Space." *Mapping Desire: Geographies of Sexualities,* ed. David Bell and Gill Valentine. London: Routledge, 1995. 182–99.

Boone, Joseph A. "Of Me(n) and Feminism: Who(se) Is the Sex That Writes?" *Engendering Men: The Question of Male Feminist Criticism*, ed. Joseph A. Boone and Michael Cadden. New York: Routledge, 1990. 11–25.

Boone, Joseph A., and Michael Cadden, eds. "Introduction." *Engendering Men: The Question of Male Feminist Criticism*. New York: Routledge, 1990. 1–7.

Bordo, Susan. *The Male Body: A New Look at Men in Public and Private*. New York: Farrar, Straus, and Giroux. 1999.

———. "Reading the Male Body." *The Male Body: Features, Destinies, Exposures*, ed. Laurence Goldstein. Ann Arbor: University of Michigan Press, 1994. 265–306.

Bouthillette, Anne-Marie. "Queer and Gendered Housing: A Tale of Two Neighbourhoods in Vancouver." *Queers in Space: Communities, Public Places, Sites of Resistance*, ed. Gordon Brett Ingram, Anne Marie Bouthillette, and Yolanda Retter. Seattle: Bay Press, 1997. 213–32.

Bristow, Joseph. "Homophobia/Misogyny: Sexual Fears, Sexual Definitions." *Coming On Strong: Gay Politics and Culture*, ed. Simon Shepherd and Mick Wallis. London: Unwin Hyman, 1989. 54–75.

Britton, Andrew. *Katharine Hepburn: Star as Feminist*. London: Studio Vista, 1995.

Bronski, Michael. *Culture Clash: The Making of a Gay Sensibility*. Boston: South End Press, 1984.

———. "Judy Garland and Others: Notes on Idolization and Derision." *Lavender Culture*, ed. Karla Jay and Allen Young. 1978. New York: New York University Press, 1994. 201–12.

Brown, Julia Prewitt. *Jane Austen's Novels: Social Change and Literary Form*. Cambridge: Harvard University Press, 1979.

Brown, Michael P. *Closet Space: Geographies of Metaphor from the Body to the Globe*. London: Routledge, 2000.

———. "Sex, Scale, and the 'New Urban Politics': HIV Prevention Strategies from Yaletown, Vancouver." *Mapping Desire: Geographies of Sexualities*, ed. David Bell and Gill Valentine. London: Routledge, 1995. 245–63.

Butler, Judith. "Against Proper Objects." *differences: A Journal of Feminist Cultural Studies* 6.2–3 (1994): 1–26.

———. *Bodies That Matter: On the Discursive Limits of "Sex."* New York: Routledge, 1993.

———. *Gender Trouble: Feminism and the Subversion of Identity*. New York: Routledge, 1990.

Cagle, Chris. "Rough Trade: Sexual Taxonomy in Postwar America." *RePresenting BiSexualities: Subjects and Cultures of Fluid Desire*, ed. Donald E. Hall and Maria Pramaggiore. New York: New York University Press, 1996. 234–52.

Calhoun, Cheshire. "Separating Lesbian Theory from Feminist Theory." *Ethics* 104 (April 1994): 558–81.

Califia, Pat. "San Francisco: Revisiting 'The City of Desire.' " *Queers in Space: Communities, Public Places, Sites of Resistance*, ed. Gordon Brett Ingram, Anne Marie Bouthillette, and Yolanda Retter. Seattle: Bay Press, 1997. 177–96.

Case, Sue-Ellen. "The Final Frontier: A Roundtable Discussion." Moderator Tania Modleski. *Queer Frontiers: Millennial Geographies, Genders, and Generations*, ed. Joseph A. Boone, Martin Dupuis, Martin Meeker, Karen Quimby, Cindy Sarver, Debra Silverman, and Rosemary Weatherston. Madison: University of Wisconsin Press, 2000. 316–39.

———. "Towards a Butch-Femme Aesthetic." *Discourse* 11.1 (1988–89): 55–73.

Caserio, Robert L. "Celibate Sisters in Revolution: Towards Reading Sylvia Townsend Warner." *Engendering Men: The Question of Male Feminist Criticism*, ed. Joseph A. Boone and Michael Cadden. New York: Routledge, 1990. 254–74.

Castle, Terry. *The Apparitional Lesbian: Female Homosexuality and Modern Culture*. New York: Columbia University Press, 1993.

———. "Sister-Sister" (Review). *London Review of Books*, August 3, 1995, 3 +.

———. "Response." *London Review of Books*, August 24, 1995. 4.

Chambers, Ross. "Messing Around: Gayness and Loiterature in Alan Hollinghurst's *The Swimming-Pool Library*." *Textuality and Sexuality: Reading Theories and Practices*, ed. Judith Still and Michael Worton. Manchester: Manchester University Press, 1993. 207–17.

Champagne, John. "Homo Academicus." *Boys: Masculinities in Contemporary Culture*, ed. Paul Smith. Boulder: Westview Press, 1996. 49–79.

Chandler, Alice. " 'A Pair of Fine Eyes': Jane Austen's Treatment of Sex." *Modern Critical Views: Jane Austen*, ed. Harold Bloom. New York: Chelsea House, 1986. 27–42.

Charnes, Linda. "Styles That Matter: On the Discursive Limits of Ideology Critique." *Shakespeare Studies* 24 (1996): 118–47.

Chauncey, George. " 'Privacy Could Only Be Had in Public': Gay Uses of the Streets." *Stud*, ed. Joel Sanders. New York: Princeton Architectural Press, 1996. 224–52.

Clarke, Eric O. *Virtuous Vice: Homoeroticism and the Public Sphere*. Durham, NC: Duke University Press, 2000.

Clatts, Michael C. "Ethnographic Observations of Men Who Have Sex with Men in Public." *Public Space / Gay Space*, ed. William L. Leap. New York: Columbia University Press, 1999. 141–55.

Connell, R.W. *Masculinities*. Berkeley: University of California Press, 1995.

Cook, Pam. "Approaching the Work of Dorothy Arzner." *Feminism and Film Theory*, ed. Constance Penley. New York: Routledge, 1988. 46–56.

Cook, Pam, and Claire Johnston. "The Place of Woman in the Cinema of Raoul Walsh." *Feminism and Film Theory*, ed. Constance Penley. New York: Routledge, 1988. 25–35.

Cooper, Michael A. "Discipl(in)ing the Master, Mastering the Discipl(in)e: Erotonomies of Discipleship in James' Tales of Literary Life." *Engendering Men: The Question of Male Feminist Criticism*, ed. Joseph A. Boone and Michael Cadden. New York: Routledge, 1990. 66–83.

Coviello, Peter. "Apocalypse from Now On." *Queer Frontiers: Millennial Geographies, Genders, and Generations*, ed. Joseph A. Boone, Martin Dupuis, Martin Meeker, Karen Quimby, Cindy Sarver, Debra Silverman, and Rosemary Weatherston. Madison: University of Wisconsin Press, 2000. 39–63.

Cowie, Elizabeth. "The Popular Film as Progressive Text—A Discussion of *Coma*—Parts 1 and 2." *Feminism and Film Theory*, ed. Constance Penley. New York: Routledge, 1988. 104–40.

Creekmur, Corey K., and Alexander Doty. "Introduction." *Out in Culture: Gay, Lesbian and Queer Essays on Popular Culture*, ed. Corey K. Creekmur and Alexander Doty. Durham, NC: Duke University Press, 1995. 1–11.

Crimp, Douglas. "Right On, Girlfriend!" *Fear of a Queer Planet: Queer Politics and Social Theory*, ed. Michael Warner. Minneapolis: Minnesota University Press, 1993. 300–20.

Davis, Tim. "The Diversity of Queer Politics and the Redefinition of Sexual Identity and Community in Urban Spaces." *Mapping Desire: Geographies of Sexualities*, ed. David Bell and Gill Valentine. London: Routledge, 1995. 284–303.

D'Emilio, John. *Sexual Politics, Sexual Communities: The Making of a Homosexual Minority in the United States, 1940–1970*. Chicago: University of Chicago Press, 1983.

de Lauretis, Teresa. *Alice Doesn't: Feminism, Semiotics, Film*. Bloomington: Indiana University Press, 1984.

———. *The Practice of Love: Lesbian Sexuality and Perverse Desire*. Bloomington: Indiana University Press, 1994.

———. "Sexual Indifference and Lesbian Representation." 1988. *The Lesbian and Gay Studies Reader*, ed. Henry Abelove, Michèle Aina Barale, David M. Halperin. New York: Routledge, 1993. 141–58.

———. *Technologies of Gender: Essays on Theory, Film, and Fiction*. Bloomington: Indiana University Press, 1987.

Delphy, Christine. "Rethinking Sex and Gender." *Gender: A Sociological Reader*, ed. Stevi Jackson and Sue Scott. London: Routledge, 2002. 51–59.

Doane, Mary Ann. "*Caught* and *Rebecca*: The Inscription of Femininity as Absence." *Feminism and Film Theory*, ed. Constance Penley. New York: Routledge, 1988. 196–215.

———. "Film and the Masquerade: Theorizing the Female Spectator." *Feminism and Film*, ed. E. Ann Kaplan. Oxford: Oxford University Press, 2000. 418–36.

———. "Remembering Women: Psychical and Historical Constructions in Film Theory." *Psychoanalysis and Cinema*, ed. E. Ann Kaplan. New York: Routledge, 1990. 46–63.

———. "Woman's Stake: Filming the Female Body." *Feminism and Film Theory*, ed. Constance Penley. New York: Routledge, 1988. 216–28.

Donald, Adrienne. "Working for Oneself: Labor and Love in *The Silence of the Lambs*." *Michigan Quarterly Review* 31 (1992): 346–61.

Doty, Alexander. *Flaming Classics: Queering the Film Canon*. New York: Routledge, 2000.

———. "There's Something Queer Here." *Out in Culture: Gay, Lesbian, and Queer Essays on Popular Culture*, ed. Corey K. Creekmur and Alexander Doty. Durham, NC: Duke University Press, 1995. 71–90.

Duberman, Martin, ed. *A Queer World: The Center for Lesbian and Gay Studies Reader*. New York: New York University Press, c.1996.

DuPlessis, Rachel Blau. "Reader, I Married Me: A Polygynous Memoir." *Changing Subjects: The Making of Feminist Literary Criticism*, ed. Gayle Green and Coppélia Kahn. London: Routledge, 1993. 97–111.

Dyer, Richard. "Believing in Fairies: The Author and the Homosexual." *Inside/Out: Gay Theories, Lesbian Theories*, ed. Diana Fuss. New York: Routledge, 1991. 185–201.

Edelman, Lee. "At Risk in the Sublime: The Politics of Gender and Theory." *Gender and Theory: Dialogues on Feminist Criticism*, ed. Linda Kauffman. New York: Basil Blackwell, Inc., 1989. 213–24.

———. *Homographesis: Essays in Gay Literary and Cultural Theory*. New York: Routledge, 1994.

———. "*Rear Window*'s Glasshole." *Out Takes: Essays on Queer Theory and Film*, ed. Ellis Hanson. Durham, NC: Duke University Press, 1999. 72–96.

———. "Tearooms and Sympathy, or, the Epistemology of the Water Closet." *The Lesbian and Gay Studies Reader*, ed. Henry Abelove, Michèle Aina Barale, and David M. Halperin. New York: Routledge, 1993. 553–74.

Edwards, Tim. *Erotics & Politics: Gay Male Sexuality, Masculinity, and Feminism*. New York and London: Routledge, 1994.

Ellmann, Richard. *Henry James and Homo-Erotic Desire*, ed. John R. Bradley. London: MacMillan Press, 1999. 25–44.

Ellsworth, Elizabeth. "Illicit Pleasures: Feminist Spectators and *Personal Best*." *Wide Angle* 8.2 (1986): 45–56.

Elwood, Sarah. "Lesbian Living Spaces: Multiple Meanings of Home." *From Nowhere to Everywhere: Lesbian Geographies*, ed. Gill Valentine. Binghamton: Haworth Press, 2000. 11–27.

Faderman, Lillian. "What Is Lesbian Literature?: Forming a Historical Canon." *Professions of Desire: Lesbian and Gay Studies in Literature*, ed. George E. Haggerty and Bonnie Zimmerman. New York: MLA, 1995. 49–59.

———. "Who Hid Lesbian History?" *Lesbian Studies: Present and Future*, ed. Margaret Cruikshank. Old Westbury, NY: The Feminist Press, 1982. 115–21.

Farmer, Brett. *Spectacular Passions: Cinema, Fantasy, and Gay Male Spectatorships*. Durham, NC: Duke University Press, 2000.

Fausto-Sterling, Anne. *Sexing the Body: Gender Politics and the Construction of Sexuality*. New York: Basic Books, 2000.

Ferguson, Moira. "*Mansfield Park*: Slavery, Colonialism, and Gender." *Critical Essays on Jane Austen*, ed. Laura Mooneyham White. New York: G.K. Hall, 1998. 103–21.

Fetterly, Judith. *The Resisting Reader: A Feminist Approach to American Fiction*. Bloomington: Indiana University Press, 1978.

Flynn, Elizabeth A., and Patrocinio P. Schweickart. "Introduction." *Gender and Reading: Essays on Readers, Texts, and Contexts*, ed. Elizabeth A. Flynn and Patrocinio P. Schweickart. Baltimore and London: Johns Hopkins University Press, 1986. ix–xxix.

Foertsch, Jacqueline. *Enemies Within: The Cold War and the AIDS Crisis in Literature, Film, and Culture*. Champaign: University of Illinois Press, 2001.

———. "In Theory of Not in Practice: Straight Feminism's Lesbian Experience." *Straight with a Twist: Queer Theory and the Subject of Heterosexuality*, ed. Calvin Thomas. Urbana: University of Illinois Press, 2000. 45–59.

Foster, Thomas. "Homelessness at Home: Placing Emily Dickinson in (Women's) History." *Engendering Men: The Question of Male Feminist Criticism*, ed. Joseph A. Boone and Michael Cadden. New York: Routledge, 1990. 239–53.

Foucault, Michel. *The History of Sexuality* Vol. 1. Trans. Robert Hurley. New York: Vintage/Random, 1990.

———. "What Is an Author?" 1979. *The Foucault Reader*, ed. Paul Rabinow. New York: Pantheon Books, 1984.

Foxhall, Lin. "Pandora Unbound: A Feminist Critique of Foucault's *History of Sexuality*." *Rethinking Sexuality: Foucault and Classical Antiquity*, ed. David H.J. Larmour, Paul Allen Miller, and Charles Platter. Princeton: Princeton University Press, 1998. 122–37.

Fraiman, Susan. "Jane Austen and Edward Said: Gender, Culture, and Imperialism." *Janeites: Austen's Disciples and Devotees*, ed. Deirdre Lynch. Princeton: Princeton University Press, 2000. 206–23.

Fuss, Diana. *Essentially Speaking: Feminism, Nature, and Difference*. New York: Routledge, 1989.

———. "Monsters of Perversion: Jeffrey Dahmer and *The Silence of the Lambs*." *Media Spectacles*, ed. Marjorie Garber, Jann Matlock, and Rebecca L. Walkowitz. New York: Routledge, 1993. 181–205.

Frye, Marilyn. *The Politics of Reality: Essays in Feminist Theory*. Trumansburg, NY: The Crossing Press, 1983.

Garber, Marjorie. "Spare Parts: The Surgical Construction of Gender." 1989. *The Lesbian and Gay Studies Reader*, ed. Henry Abelove, Michèle Aina Barale, and David M. Halperin. New York: Routledge, 1993. 321–36.

Gerster, Carole. "Rereading Jane Austen: Dialogic Feminism in *Northanger Abbey*." *A Companion to Jane Austen Studies*, ed. Laura Cooner Lambdin and Robert Thomas Lambdin. Westport, CT: Greenwood Press, 2000. 115–30.

Gever, Martha. "Response, Writers on the *Lamb*: Sorting out the Sexual Politics of a Controversial Film." *Village Voice*, March 5, 1991. 49 +.

Gilbert, Sandra, and Susan Gubar. "Shut Up in Prose: Gender and Genre in Austen's Juvenilia." *Modern Critical Views: Jane Austen*, ed. Harold Bloom. New York: Chelsea House, 1986. 69–86.

Goldberg, Michael, ed. *Queering the Renaissance*. Durham, NC: Duke University Press, 1994.

Goldman, Ruth. "Who Is That *Queer* Queer?: Exploring Norms around Sexuality, Race, and Class in Queer Theory." *Queer Studies: A Lesbian, Gay, Bisexual, and Transgender Anthology*, ed. Brett Beemyn and Mickey Eliason. New York: New York University Press, 1996. 169–82.

Gough, Jamie. "Theories of Sexual Identity and the Masculinization of the Gay Man." *Coming On Strong: Gay Politics and Culture*, ed. Simon Shepherd and Mick Wallis. London: Unwin Hyman, 1989. 119–36.

Grosz, Elizabeth. *Space, Time, and Perversion: Essays on the Politics of Bodies*. New York: Routledge, 1995.

———. *Volatile Bodies: Toward a Corporeal Feminism*. Bloomington: Indiana University Press, 1994.

Grove, Robin. "Austen's Ambiguous Endings." *Modern Critical Views: Jane Austen*, ed. Harold Bloom. New York: Chelsea House, 1986. 179–90.

Grube, John. " 'No More Shit': The Struggle for Democratic Gay Space in Toronto." *Queers in Space: Communities, Public Places, Sites of Resistance*, ed. Gordon Brett Ingram, Anne Marie Bouthillette, and Yolanda Retter. Seattle: Bay Press, 1997. 127–46.

Gubar, Susan. *Critical Condition: Feminism at the Turn of the Century*. New York: Columbia University Press, 2000. 113–34.

Hadley, Tessa. *Henry James and the Imagination of Pleasure*. Cambridge: Cambridge University Press, 2002.

Haggerty, George E., and Bonnie Zimmerman. *Professions of Desire: Lesbian and Gay Studies in Literature*. New York: MLA, 1995.

Halberstam, Judith. *Female Masculinity*. Durham, NC: Duke University Press, 1998.

———. "Skinflick: Posthuman Gender in Jonathan Demme's *The Silence of the Lambs*." *Camera Obscura* 27 (1991): 37–54.

Halperin, David. "Is There a History of Sexuality?" 1989. *The Lesbian and Gay Studies Reader*, ed. Henry Abelove, Michèle Aina Barale, and David M. Halperin. New York: Routledge, 1993. 416–31.

Hanson, Ellis. "Introduction: Out Takes." *Out Takes: Essays on Queer Theory and Film*, ed. Ellis Hanson. Durham, NC: Duke University Press, 1999. 1–19.

Harris, Laura, and Elizabeth Crocker, eds. *Femme: Feminists, Lesbians, and Bad Girls*. New York: Routledge, 1997.

Heilbrun, Carolyn G. *Writing a Woman's Life*. New York: W.W. Norton & Company, 1988.

Hemmings, Clare. "From Landmarks to Spaces: Mapping the Territory of a Bisexual Genealogy." *Queers in Space: Communities, Public Places, Sites of Resistance*, ed. Gordon Brett Ingram, Anne Marie Bouthillette, and Yolanda Retter. Seattle: Bay Press, 1997. 147–62.

Hollinghurst, Alan. *The Swimming-Pool Library*. New York: Vintage International/Random House, 1989.

Hoogland, Renée C. *Lesbian Configurations.* New York: Columbia University Press, 1997.

Ingram, Gordon Brett. "Marginality and the Landscapes of Erotic Alien(n)ations." *Queers in Space: Communities, Public Places, Sites of Resistance,* ed. Gordon Brett Ingram, Anne Marie Bouthillette, and Yolanda Retter. Seattle: Bay Press, 1997. 27–52.

———. " 'Open' Space as Strategic Queer Sites." *Queers in Space: Communities, Public Places, Sites of Resistance,* ed. Gordon Brett Ingram, Anne Marie Bouthillette, and Yolanda Retter. Seattle: Bay Press, 1997. 95–125.

Ingram, Gordon Brett, Anne Marie Bouthillette, and Yolanda Retter, eds. *Queers in Space: Communities, Public Places, Sites of Resistance.* Seattle: Bay Press, 1997.

Jackson, Stevi, and Sue Scott. "Introduction." *Gender: A Sociological Reader,* ed. Stevi Jackson and Sue Scott. London: Routledge, 2002. 1–26.

Jay, Elsie. "Domestic Dykes: The Politics of 'In-difference.' " *Queers in Space: Communities, Public Places, Sites of Resistance,* ed. Gordon Brett Ingram, Anne Marie Bouthillette, and Yolanda Retter. Seattle: Bay Press, 1997. 163–68.

Jay, Karla. "Ties that Bind: Friendship Between Lesbians and Gay Men." *The Harvard Gay and Lesbian Review* 4.1 (1997): 9–12.

Jeffreys, Sheila. *Anticlimax: A Feminist Perspective on the Sexual Revolution.* Washington Square, NY: New York University Press, 1990.

———. "The Essential Lesbian." *All The Rage: Reasserting Radical Lesbian Feminism,* ed. Lynne Harne and Elaine Miller. New York: Teachers College Press, 1996. 90–113.

Johnson, Barbara. "Lesbian Spectacles: Readings *Sula, Passing, Thelma and Louise,* and *The Accused.*" *Media Spectacles,* ed. Marjorie Garber, Jann Matlock, and Rebecca L. Walkowitz. New York: Routledge, 1993. 160–66.

Johnson, Claudia L. "The Divine Miss Jane: Jane Austen, Janeites, and the Discipline of Novel Studies." *Janeites: Austen's Disciples and Devotees,* ed. Deirdre Lynch. Princeton: Princeton University Press, 2000. 25–44.

———. " 'Not at All What a Man Should Be!': Remaking English Manhood in *Emma.*" *Critical Essays on Jane Austen,* ed. Laura Mooneyham White. New York: G.K. Hall, 1998. 146–59.

Johnston, Claire. "Dorothy Arzner: Critical Strategies." *Feminism and Film Theory,* ed. Constance Penley. New York: Routledge, 1988. 36–45.

Johnston, Lynda and Gill Valentine. "Wherever I Lay My Girlfriend, That's My Home: The Performance and Surveillance of Lesbian Identities in Domestic Environments." *Mapping Desire: Geographies of Sexualities,* ed. David Bell and Gill Valentine. London: Routledge, 1995. 99–113.

Kahane, Claire. *Passions of the Voice: Hysteria, Narrative, and the Figure of the Speaking Woman, 1850–1915.* Baltimore: Johns Hopkins University Press, 1995.

Kaplan, E. Ann. "The Case of the Missing Mother: Maternal Issues in Vidor's *Stella Dallas.*" *Feminism and Film,* ed. E. Ann Kaplan. Oxford: Oxford University Press, 2000. 466–78.

————. "Motherhood and Representation: From Postwar Freudian Figurations to Postmodernism." *Psychoanalysis and Cinema*, ed. E. Ann Kaplan. New York: Routledge, 1990. 128–42.

Kennard, Jean. "Ourself behind Ourself: A Theory for Lesbian Readers." *Gender and Reading: Essays on Readers, Texts, and Contexts*, ed. Elizabeth A. Flynn and Patrocinio P. Schweickart. Baltimore and London: Johns Hopkins University Press, 1986. 63–80.

Kessler, Susanne J. "Defining and Producing Genitals." *Gender: A Sociological Reader*, ed. Stevi Jackson and Sue Scott. London: Routledge, 2002. 447–56.

Klawans, Stuart. "Films." *The Nation* (February 25, 1991): 246–47.

Koestenbaum, Wayne. "Wilde's Hard Labor and the Birth of Gay Reading." *Engendering Men: The Question of Male Feminist Criticism*, ed. Joseph A. Boone and Michael Cadden. New York: Routledge, 1990. 176–89.

Laqueur, Thomas. *Making Sex: Body and Gender from the Greeks to Freud*. Cambridge, MA: Harvard University Press, 1990.

LaValley, Al. "The Great Escape." *Out in Culture: Gay, Lesbian, and Queer Essays on Popular Culture*, ed. Corey K. Creekmur and Alexander Doty. Durham, NC: Duke University Press, 1995. 60–70.

Leap, William L., ed. *Public Sex / Gay Space*. New York: Columbia University Press, 1999.

Levay, Simon. *Queer Science: The Use and Abuse of Research into Homosexuality*. Cambridge, MA: MIT Press, 1996.

Levine, Martin P. *Gay Macho: The Life and Death of the Homosexual Clone*, ed. and int. Michael S. Kimmel. New York: New York University Press, 1998.

Lewis, Reina, and Katrina Rolley. "Ad(dressing) the Dyke: Lesbian Looks and Lesbian Looking." *Outlooks: Lesbian and Gay Sexualities and Visual Cultures*, ed. Peter Horne and Reina Lewis. London: Routledge, 1996. 178–90.

Litvak, Joseph. *Caught in the Act: Theatricality in the Nineteenth-Century English Novel*. Berkeley: University of California Press, 1992.

————. *Strange Gourmets: Sophistication, Theory, and the Novel*. Durham, NC: Duke University Press, 1997.

Lo, Jenny, and Theresa Healy. "Flagrantly Flaunting It?: Contesting Perceptions of Locational Identity among Urban Vancouver Lesbians." *From Nowhere to Everywhere: Lesbian Geographies*, ed. Gill Valentine. Binghamton: Haworth Press, 2000. 29–44.

Looser, Devoney. "Reading Jane Austen and Rewriting 'Herstory.' " *Critical Essays on Jane Austen*, ed. Laura Mooneyham White. New York: G.K. Hall, 1998. 34–66.

Lynch, Deirdre. "Introduction: Sharing with Our Neighbors." *Janeites: Austen's Disciples and Devotees*, ed. Deirdre Lynch. Princeton: Princeton University Press, 2000. 3–24.

Martin, Biddy. "Extraordinary Homosexuals and the Fear of Being Ordinary." *differences: A Journal of Feminist Cultural Studies* 6.2–3 (1994): 100–25.

———. "Lesbian Identity and Autobiographical Difference(s)." 1988. *The Lesbian and Gay Studies Reader*, ed. Henry Abelove, Michèle Aina Barale, and David M. Halperin. New York: Routledge, 1993. 274–93.

———. "Sexualities without Genders and Other Queer Utopias." *Diacritics* 24.2–3 (1994): 104–21.

Martin, Robert K. "Hester Prynne, *C'est Moi*: Nathaniel Hawthorne and the Anxieties of Gender." *Engendering Men: The Question of Male Feminist Criticism*, ed. Joseph A. Boone and Michael Cadden. New York: Routledge, 1990. 122–39.

Mayne, Judith: *Framed: Lesbians, Feminists, and Media Culture*. Minneapolis: University of Minnesota Press, 2000.

———. *Woman at the Keyhole: Feminism and Women's Cinema*. Bloomington: Indiana University Press, 1990.

Miller, D.A. "Austen's Attitude." *Yale Journal of Criticism* 9 (1995): 1–5.

———. *Jane Austen, or: The Secret of Style*. Princeton: Princeton University Press, 2003.

———. "The Late Jane Austen." *Critical Essays on Jane Austen*, ed. Laura Mooneyham White. New York: G.K. Hall, 1998. 223–40.

———. *The Novel and the Police*. Berkeley: University of California Press, 1988.

———. "Sontag's Urbanity." 1989. *The Lesbian and Gay Studies Reader*, ed. Henry Abelove, Michèle Aina Barale, and David M. Halperin. New York: Routledge, 1993. 212–20.

———. "Visual Pleasure in 1959." *Out Takes: Essays on Queer Theory and Film*, ed. Ellis Hanson. Durham, NC: Duke University Press, 1999. 97–125.

Moon, Michael. "Sexuality and Visual Terrorism." *The Wings of the Dove. Criticism* 28.4 (1986): 427–43.

Moon, Michael, and Eve Kosofsky Sedgwick. 1991. "Divinity: A Dossier, a Performance Piece, a Little-Understood Emotion." *Tendencies*. Durham, NC: Duke University Press, 1993.

Moore, Lisa L. *Dangerous Intimacies: Toward a Sapphic History of the British Novel*. Durham, NC: Duke University Press, 1997.

Moyer, Carrie, and Dyke Action Machine! "Do You Love the Dyke in Your Face?" *Queers in Space: Communities, Public Places, Sites of Resistance*, ed. Gordon Brett Ingram, Anne Marie Bouthillette, and Yolanda Retter. Seattle: Bay Press, 1997. 439–46.

Mulvey, Laura. "Visual Pleasure and Narrative Cinema." *Feminism and Film Theory*, ed. Constance Penley. New York: Routledge, 1988. 57–68.

Munt, Sally. "The Lesbian *Flâneur*." *Mapping Desire: Geographies of Sexualities*, ed. David Bell and Gill Valentine. London: Routledge, 1995. 114–25.

Munt, Sally, ed. "Introduction." *New Lesbian Criticism: Literary and Cultural Readings*. New York: Columbia University Press, 1992. xi–xxii.

Neale, Steve. "Masculinity as Spectacle: Reflections on Men and Mainstream Cinema." *Feminism and Film*, ed. E. Ann Kaplan. Oxford: Oxford University Press, 2000. 253–64.

Nestle, Joan. "Restriction and Reclamation: Lesbian Bars and Beaches of the 1950s." *Queers in Space: Communities, Public Places, Sites of Resistance*, ed.

Gordon Brett Ingram, Anne Marie Bouthillette, and Yolanda Retter. Seattle: Bay Press, 1997. 61–68.

Novick, Sheldon M. "Introduction." *Henry James and Homo-Erotic Desire*, ed. John R. Bradley. London: MacMillan Press, 1999. 1–24.

Orwell, George. *1984*. 1949. Rpt., New York: Signet/New American Library, 1981.

Owens, Craig. "Outlaws: Gay Men in Feminism." *Men in Feminism*, ed. Alice Jardine and Paul Smith. New York: Methuen, 1987. 219–32.

Patai, Daphne. *Heterophobia: Sexual Harassment and the Future of Feminism*. Lanham, MD: Rowan and Littlefield, 1998.

Patton, Cindy. "Tremble, Hetero Swine." *Fear of a Queer Planet: Queer Politics and Social Theory*, ed. Michael Warner. 1993. Minneapolis: University of Minnesota Press, 1995. 143–77.

Penley, Constance. "Introduction—The Lady Doesn't Vanish: Feminism and Film Theory." *Feminism and Film Theory*, ed. Constance Penley. New York: Routledge, 1988. 1–24.

Polchin, James. "Having Something to Wear: The Landscape of Identity on Christopher Street." *Queers in Space: Communities, Public Places, Sites of Resistance*, ed. Gordon Brett Ingram, Anne Marie Bouthillette, and Yolanda Retter. Seattle: Bay Press, 1997. 381–90.

Poovey, Mary. *The Proper Lady and the Woman Writer: Ideology as Style in the Works of Mary Wollstoncraft, Mary Shelley, and Jane Austen*. Chicago: University of Chicago Press, 1984.

Pramaggiore, Maria. "Straddling the Screen: Bisexual Spectatorship and Contemporary Narrative Film." *RePresenting BiSexualities: Subjects and Cultures of Fluid Desire*, ed. Donald E. Hall and Maria Pramaggiore. New York: New York University Press, 1996. 272–97.

Quilley, Stephen. "Constructing Manchester's 'New Urban Village': Gay Space in the Entrepreneurial City." *Queers in Space: Communities, Public Places, Sites of Resistance*, ed. Gordon Brett Ingram, Anne Marie Bouthillette, and Yolanda Retter. Seattle: Bay Press, 1997. 275–92.

Rechy, John. "The Final Frontier: A Roundtable Discussion." Moderator Tania Modleski. *Queer Frontiers: Millennial Geographies, Genders, and Generations*, ed. Joseph A. Boone, Martin Dupuis, Martin Meeker, Karen Quimby, Cindy Sarver, Debra Silverman, and Rosemary Weatherston. Madison: University of Wisconsin Press, 2000. 316–39.

Retter, Yolanda. "Lesbian Activism in Los Angeles, 1970–1979." *Queer Frontiers: Millennial Geographies, Genders, and Generations*, ed. Joseph A. Boone, Martin Dupuis, Martin Meeker, Karen Quimby, Cindy Sarver, Debra Silverman, and Rosemary Weatherston. Madison: University of Wisconsin Press, 2000. 196–221.

Rich, Adrienne. "Compulsory Heterosexuality and Lesbian Existence." *The Lesbian and Gay Studies Reader*, ed. Henry Abelove, Michèle Aina Barale, and David M. Halperin. New York: Routledge, 1993. 227–54.

Rich, B. Ruby. *Chick Flicks: Theories and Memories of the Feminist Film Movement.* Durham, NC: Duke University Press, 1998.

———. "Never a Victim: Jodie Foster, a New Kind of Female Hero." *Women and Film: A Sight and Sound Reader*, ed. Pam Cook and Philip Dodd. Philadelphia: Temple University Press, 1993. 50–61.

———. "Response, Writers on the *Lamb*: Sorting out the Sexual Politics of a Controversial Film." *Village Voice* 5 March, 1991. 49.

Richlin, Amy. "Foucault's *History of Sexuality*: A Useful Theory for Women?" *Rethinking Sexuality: Foucault and Classical Antiquity*, ed. David H.J. Larmour, Paul Allen Miller, and Charles Platter. Princeton: Princeton University Press, 1998. 138–70.

Riviere, Joan. "Womanliness as Masquerade." *Formations of Fantasy*, ed. Victor Burgin, James Donald, and Cora Kaplan. London: Methuen, 1986. 35–44.

Rodowick, David N. "The Difficulty of Difference." *Feminism and Film*, ed. E. Ann Kaplan. Oxford: Oxford University Press, 2000. 181–202.

Rofes, Eric. "The Ick Factor: Flesh, Fluids, and Cross-Gender Revulsion." *Opposite Sex: Gay Men on Lesbians, Lesbians on Gay Men*, ed. Sara Miles and Eric Rofes. New York: New York University Press, 1998. 44–65.

Rose, Jacqueline. "Paranoia and the Film System." *Feminism and Film Theory*, ed. Constance Penley. New York: Routledge, 1988. 141–58.

Ross, Andrew. "Cowboys, Cadillacs, and Cosmonauts: Families, Film, Genres, and Technocultures." *Engendering Men: The Question of Male Feminist Criticism*, ed. Joseph A. Boone and Michael Cadden. New York: Routledge, 1990. 87–101.

Rothenberg, Tamar. " 'And She Told Two Friends': Lesbians Creating Urban Social Space." *Mapping Desire: Geographies of Sexualities*, ed. David Bell and Gill Valentine. London: Routledge, 1995. 165–81.

Rubin, Gayle. "Thinking Sex: Notes for a Radical Theory of the Politics of Sexuality." 1984. *The Lesbian and Gay Studies Reader*, ed. Henry Abelove, Michèle Aina Barale, and David M. Halperin. New York: Routledge, 1993. 3–44.

———. "The Traffic in Women: Notes on the 'Political Economy' of Sex." *Towards an Anthropology of Women*, ed. Rayna R. Reiter. New York: Monthly Review Press, 1975. 157–210.

Russo, Vito. *The Celluloid Closet: Homosexuality and the Movies*, revised ed. New York: Harper and Row, 1987.

Schlichter, Annette. "Queer at Last?: Straight Intellectuals and the Desire for Transgression." *GLQ* 10.4 (2004): 543–64.

Schopp, Andrew. "The Practice and Politics of 'Freeing the Look': Jonathan Demme's *The Silence of the Lambs*." *Camera Obscura* 53 (2003): 125–50.

Sedgwick, Eve Kosofsky. "The Beast in the Closet: James and the Writing of Homosexual Panic." *Sex, Politics, and Science in the Nineteenth-Century Novel*, ed. Ruth Bernard Yeazell. Baltimore: Johns Hopkins University Press, 1985. 148–86.

———. *Between Men: English Literature and Male Homosocial Desire.* 1985. New York: Columbia University Press, 1992.

———. *Epistemology of the Closet*. Berkeley: University of California Press, 1990.

———. *Tendencies*. Durham, NC: Duke University Press, 1993.

Seidman, Steven. "Identity Politics in a 'Postmodern' Gay Culture: Some Historical and Conceptual Notes." *Fear of a Queer Planet: Queer Politics and Social Theory*, ed. Michael Warner. 1993. Minneapolis: University of Minnesota Press, 1995. 105–42.

Seltzer, Mark. "The Love-Master." *Engendering Men: The Question of Male Feminist Criticism*, ed. Joseph A. Boone and Michael Cadden. New York: Routledge, 1990. 140–58.

Sheldon, Caroline. "Lesbians and Film: Some Thoughts." *Gays and Film*. 1978, ed. Richard Dyer. London: British Film Institute, 1980. 5–26.

Sibalis, Michael D. "Paris." *Queer Sites: Gay Urban Histories Since 1600*, ed. David Higgs. London: Routledge, 1999. 10–37.

The Silence of the Lambs. Dir. Jonathan Demme. Orion/Strongheart-Demme, 1991.

Silverman, Kaja. "Historical Trauma and Male Subjectivity." *Psychoanalysis and Cinema*, ed. E. Ann Kaplan. New York: Routledge, 1990. 110–27.

———. *Male Subjectivity at the Margins*. New York: Routledge, 1992.

———. "Too Early/Too Late: Subjectivity and the Primal Scene in Henry James." *Novel* 21 (Winter/Spring 1988). 147–73.

Smith, Johanna M. "The Oppositional Reader and *Pride and Prejudice*." *A Companion to Jane Austen Studies*, ed. Laura Cooner Lambdin and Robert Thomas Lambdin. Westport, CT: Greenwood Press, 2000. 27–40.

Smith, Paul. "Introduction." *Boys: Masculinities in Contemporary Culture*, ed. Paul Smith. Boulder: Westview Press, 1996. 1–7.

Sommella, Laraine. "This Is about People Dying: The Tactics of Early ACT Up and Lesbian Avengers in New York City" (Interview with Maxine Wolfe). *Queers in Space: Communities, Public Places, Sites of Resistance*, ed. Gordon Brett Ingram, Anne Marie Bouthillette, and Yolanda Retter. Seattle: Bay Press, 1997. 407–37.

Stacey, Jackie. "Desperately Seeking Difference." *Feminism and Film*, ed. E. Ann Kaplan. Oxford: Oxford University Press, 2000. 450–65.

———. "Feminine Fascinations: Forms of Identification in Star-Audience Relations." *Feminist Film Theory: A Reader*, ed. Sue Thornham. Edinburgh: Edinburgh University Press, 1999. 196–209.

Staiger, Janet. "Taboos and Totems: Cultural Meanings of *The Silence of the Lambs*." *Film Theory Goes to the Movies*, ed. Jim Collins, Hilary Radner, and Ava Preacher Collins. New York: Routledge, 1993. 142–54.

Stanley, Liz. "Should 'Sex' Really be 'Gender'—or 'Gender' Really be 'Sex'?" *Gender: A Sociological Reader*, ed. Stevi Jackson and Sue Scott. London: Routledge, 2002. 31–41.

Stein, Marc. *City of Sisterly and Brotherly Loves: Gay and Lesbian Philadelphia, 1945–1972*. Chicago: University of Chicago Press, 2000.

Stevens, Hugh. *Henry James and Sexuality.* Cambridge: Cambridge, University Press 1998.

Straayer, Chris. "The Hypothetical Lesbian Heroine in Narrative Feature Film." *Out in Culture: Gay, Lesbian, and Queer Essays on Popular Culture,* ed. Corey K. Creekmur and Alexander Doty. Durham, NC: Duke University Press, 1995. 44–59.

Studlar, Gaylyn. "Masochism and the Perverse Pleasures of the Cinema." *Feminism and Film,* ed. E. Ann Kaplan. Oxford: Oxford University Press, 2000. 203–25.

Suter, Jacquelyn. "Feminine Discourse in *Christopher Strong.*" *Feminism and Film Theory,* ed. Constance Penley. New York: Routledge, 1988. 89–103.

Tattleman, Ira. "The Meaning at the Wall: Tracing the Gay Bathhouse." *Queers in Space: Communities, Public Places, Sites of Resistance,* ed. Gordon Brett Ingram, Anne Marie Bouthillette, and Yolanda Retter. Seattle: Bay Press, 1997. 391–406.

———. "Presenting a Queer (Bath)House." *Queer Frontiers: Millennial Geographies, Genders, and Generations,* ed. Joseph A. Boone, Martin Dupuis, Martin Meeker, Karen Quimby, Cindy Sarver, Debra Silverman, and Rosemary Weatherston. Madison: University of Wisconsin Press, 2000. 222–58.

Taubin, Amy. "Response, Writers on the *Lamb*: Sorting out the Sexual Politics of a Controversial Film." *Village Voice* (1991): 56.

Tharp, Julie. "The Transvestite as Monster." *Journal of Popular Film and Television* 19.3 (1991): 106–13.

Tillmann-Healy, Lisa M. *Between Gay and Straight: Understanding Friendship across Sexual Orientation.* Walnut Creek: Altamira P/Rowan and Littlefield, 2001.

Traub, Valerie. "The Ambiguities of 'Lesbian' Viewing Pleasure: The (Dis)articulations of *Black Widow.*" *Out in Culture: Gay, Lesbian, and Queer Essays on Popular Culture,* ed. Corey K. Creekmur and Alexander Doty. Durham, NC: Duke University Press, 1995. 115–36.

———. *Desire and Anxiety: Circulations of Sexuality in Shakespearean Drama.* New York: Routledge, 1992.

Tuite, Clara. "Decadent Austen Entails: Forster, James, Firbank, and the 'Queer Taste' of *Sanditon* (comp. 1817, publ. 1925)." *Janeites: Austen's Disciples and Devotees,* ed. Deirdre Lynch. Princeton: Princeton University Press, 2000. 115–39.

Tyler, Carole-Anne. "Desiring Machines?: Queer Re-visions of Feminist Film Theory." *Coming Out of Feminism?* ed. Mandy Merck, Naomi Segal, and Elizabeth Wright. Oxford: Blackwell Publishers, 1998. 123–53.

Van Leer, David. "A World of Female Friendship: *The Bostonians.*" *Henry James and Homo-Erotic Desire,* ed. John R. Bradley. London: MacMillan Press, 1999. 93–110.

Vorlicky, Robert. "(In)Visible Alliances: Conflicting 'Chronicles' of Feminism." *Engendering Men: The Question of Male Feminist Criticism,* ed.

Joseph A. Boone and Michael Cadden. New York: Routledge, 1990. 275–90.

Walters, Suzanna Danuta. *All the Rage: The Story of Gay Visibility in America*. Chicago: University of Chicago Press, 2001.

Wardrop, Stephanie. "They Don't Have a Name for It Yet: Patriarchy, Gender, and Meat-Eating in Jonathan Demme's *The Silence of the Lambs*." *LIT* 5 (1994): 95–105.

Warner, Michael, ed. *Fear of a Queer Planet: Queer Politics and Social Theory*. Minneapolis: University of Minnesota Press, 1993.

———. *The Trouble with Normal: Sex, Politics, and the Ethics of Queer Life*. Cambridge: Harvard University Press, 1999.

Waugh, Thomas. *The Fruit Machine: Twenty Years of Writing on Queer Cinema*. Durham, NC: Duke University Press, 2000.

Weeks, Jeffrey. *Sexuality and Its Discontents: Meanings, Myths, and Modern Sexualities*. London: Routledge and Kegan Paul, 1985.

Weiss, Andrea: *Vampires and Violets: Lesbians in Film*. New York: Penguin Books, 1992.

Whatling, Clare. *Screen Dreams: Fantasising Lesbians in Film*. Manchester: Manchester University Press, 1997.

White, Patricia. *Uninvited: Classical Hollywood Cinema and Lesbian Representability*. Bloomington: Indiana University Press, 1999.

Williams, Linda. " 'Something Else Besides a Mother': *Stella Dallas* and the Maternal Melodrama." *Feminism and Film*, ed. E. Ann Kaplan. Oxford: Oxford University Press, 2000. 479–504.

Wittig, Monique. "One Is Not Born a Woman." 1992. *The Lesbian and Gay Studies Reader*, ed. Henry Abelove, Michèle Aina Barale, and David M. Halperin. New York: Routledge, 1993.

Wood, Robin. "The Murderous Gays: Hitchcock's Homophobia." *Out in Culture: Gay, Lesbian, and Queer Essays on Popular Culture*, ed. Corey K. Creekmur and Alexander Doty. Durham, NC: Duke University Press, 1995. 197–215.

Wolfe, Maxine. "Invisible Women in Invisible Places: The Production of Social Space in Lesbian Bars." *Queers in Space: Communities, Public Places, Sites of Resistance*, ed. Gordon Brett Ingram, Anne Marie Bouthillette, and Yolanda Retter. Seattle: Bay Press, 1997. 301–24.

Young, Elizabeth. "*The Silence of the Lambs* and the Flaying of Feminist Theory." *Camera Obscura* 27 (1991): 5–35.

Zita, Jacquelyn N. *Body Talk: Reflections on Sex and Gender*. New York: Columbia University Press, 1998.

INDEX